TOMMY'S WAR

TOMMY'S WAR

The Western Front in Soldiers' Words
and Photographs

Richard van Emden

B L O O M S B U R Y

LONDON · NEW DELHI · NEW YORK · SYDNEY

First published in Great Britain 2014

Copyright © 2014 by Richard van Emden

The moral right of the author has been asserted

No part of this book may be used or reproduced in any manner whatsoever
without written permission from the publishers except in the case of
brief quotations embedded in critical articles or reviews

Every reasonable effort has been made to trace copyright holders of material reproduced
in this book, but if any have been inadvertently overlooked the publishers would be glad to
hear from them. For legal purposes the acknowledgements, sources and picture credits
on pages 368–70 constitute an extension of the copyright page

Bloomsbury Publishing plc
50 Bedford Square
London
WC1B 3DP

www.bloomsbury.com

Bloomsbury is a trademark of Bloomsbury Publishing plc

Bloomsbury Publishing, London, New Delhi, New York and Sydney

A CIP catalogue record for this book is available from the British Library

ISBN 978 1 4088 4436 6

10 9 8 7 6 5 4 3 2 1

Designed and typeset by Libanus Press Ltd, Marlborough
Printed and bound in China by C&C Offset Printing Co. Ltd

*Half-title page: An officer of the King's Own Scottish Borderers relaxes
during training in Scotland.
Frontispiece: The undying spirit of comradeship.
Overleaf: The 2nd Dragoon Guards (Queen's Bays) in Ploegsteert Wood.*

To Dominic Field

CONTENTS

Introduction

> Most of the time the infantry soldier is a navvy with the
> chance of being killed. During his four or six days in
> the trenches, he may have many things to complain
> about, but being idle is not one of them.
>
> An anonymous Scotsman, 1915

———

The Great War is so much more than the sum of its military engagements: it is an endlessly gripping story of 'another world' that kept a generation of young men and women in its thrall for more than four long years. Perhaps too often the story has been told through its campaigns and battles from August 1914 until the Armistice in November 1918. In contrast, this book creates a new, more immediate and personal narrative of the war, focusing on the individual soldier's physical, mental and emotional experience.

Tommy's War is the culmination of more than twenty-five years' research into the lives of our soldiers who served a hundred years ago on the Western Front, and it draws exclusively on the soldiers' experience in their own words and images, written and taken at the time.

Letters and diaries have an immediacy, a sense of personal urgency, about them, especially when they are scribbled down during or directly after the incident being described. 'I write this [letter] by the light of a candle stuck at the bottom of an empty tumbler,' wrote Lieutenant Eliot Crawshay-Williams, 110th Battery, Royal Field Artillery, as he sailed to France in June 1915. 'The electric light of the troopship has been cut off at the main since we left port, and obscure forms blunder and collide in the corridors and stumble down the staircases.'

Other stories, of necessity, are written a while afterwards. Private Thomas Lyon was blown into the air and buried by a shell explosion, dug

Britain's brightest and best: Maurice Browne (left), Coldstream Guards, killed September 1915, and Richard Stokes, MC and Bar, Royal Field Artillery, Captain of Downside School, later Labour Party MP and Lord Privy Seal. Nephew of Sir Wilfred Stokes, the inventor of the Stokes mortar.

out and evacuated from the line. His extraordinarily vivid account must have been written at least two or three weeks later and probably more, but not much more. 'We had just reached the corner of the traverse when earth and heaven seemed to come together and to become one vast tongue of leaping flame; I felt myself falling through space and was conscious of a shattering roar.'

In all cases, I have used only stories written by serving soldiers on or after 4 August 1914 and on or before 28 June 1919, the day that the Versailles Peace Treaty was signed. There is one caveat here: in a very small number of cases it is not absolutely clear whether a veteran, with a view to having his story published immediately post-war, has used his detailed diary and letters and, before publication, expanded on what he wrote at the time.

The scores of diaries and memoirs I have drawn on include unpublished sources, but also many that were published during the war years as well as a number of books published 'In Memoriam', either during or shortly after the war, in which letters from fallen officers were published by grieving families in an effort to pay tribute to their sons' service and to leave a legacy for family and friends. These books offer the reader much that is often lost in memoirs produced many years later, not only their immediacy but a deeper insight: it is possible, for example, to appreciate the mood swings or variations in the temperament of a soldier. This subtlety is often lost in the smoothing out of emotions when a man reflects on his war from the comfort of the sitting-room chair. Ten years later he might write that he was exhilarated or depressed during an incident, but there is a qualitative difference between telling the reader that was how he felt, and the reader discerning this in the writing. There is also the problem of hindsight: reflecting on his experiences from the peaceful setting of his home, with the knowledge of victory won, a soldier's perception of his experiences might be influenced by his later life. He might be buffeted, too, by national events since the war: the Depression, the rise of Nazism and indeed the concomitant British anti-war movement or relatively recently, in the 1960s, the generally unfair maligning of the High Command. More parochially, a man might easily remember only what he wanted to remember, with the horror or the disaster not necessarily forgotten but put away in the back of the writer's mind as too emotionally disturbing to be revisited. Of course, these events might not have influenced his recollections at all, but the possibility cannot be discounted.

I have always been a little wary of soldiers' diaries and letters that were published during the war. Without close examination, I assumed – erroneously as it has turned out – that publishers would be keen to fall into step with the prevailing orthodoxy of the time for, logically, that would be commercially sensible. If the mood of the country was vehemently patriotic and against all things German, publishers would be likely to choose material which pandered to the buying public's instincts. If this were so, publications would tend not to challenge the reader either with the full horror of war or with the consequences of indecision or poor communication that would inevitably cost the lives of the men in the British front line.

In fact, these books are often astonishingly candid. There is a popular misconception that men traditionally spared their families back home the grim details of war, but that is not the case. When the suffering and the sense of loss were at the forefront of soldiers' minds, they perhaps found solace in writing down their thoughts and their emotions; if tactical defeat resulted from inefficiency, this was not excised.

All officers and other ranks were obliged under King's Regulation 453 to submit before publication any book or article based on war service to the army's appropriate authorities. However, owing to wartime conditions, the army proposed that any such publication could be sent direct to the Censor's Department at the War Office for clearance. There was considerable disquiet when it became apparent that some officers were bypassing all censorship and offering their memoirs directly to publishers. Captain William Watson, who had been commissioned from the ranks in 1915, was one such example. His memoirs, *Adventures of a Despatch Rider* (1916), written during convalescence in England, came to the notice of the army. In a memo dated 24 April from a home-based staff officer, it was noted that 'Permission under King's Regulation 453 has not been obtained in the case of the publication mentioned. In present circumstances it has been decided that books of this nature purporting to give experiences of the present war cannot be published. The fact that they are published without permission causes much discontent amongst those who have applied for and been refused official sanction for publication.' The War Office had previously cleared a small number of books but had become perturbed by the rush to print and the fear that sensitive information might be disclosed to the enemy. By 1916, the desire to reassert some control was in evidence and refusals to allow publication were commonplace. The army authorities were proposing to take unspecified action against Watson, although whatever that action was did not appear to damage his military career. He later transferred to the Tank Corps, winning the Distinguished Conduct Medal in 1917. What is remarkable is that the censor passed such honest accounts and that they were published at all.

In addition, there is a fiction that there was a decade's silence after the Armistice until the 'great' memoirs of the war appeared, such as Robert Graves' *Goodbye to All That* and Siegfried Sassoon's trilogy, *The Complete Memoirs of George Sherston*. While these men were gifted with remarkable literary skill, it does not follow that the memoirs that came out during the war or shortly afterwards had no qualities to recommend them: they were often vivid, moving and well-informed.

The Great War lasted 1,559 days. On the Western Front, approximately a third of that time was taken up with British and Empire troops either directly attacking enemy positions or fighting tooth and nail to defend their own. However, any one battalion was likely to have been involved in such offensive or defensive action for a total of between twenty-five and thirty-five days only, or around 5 per cent of all occasions in which contact was made with the enemy during a general offensive. In other words, a soldier might have been engaged in battle for rather less than 2 per cent of the entire duration of the war. As Private Robert Sturges wrote in 1917:

> Everyone has read stirring descriptions of the British soldier in attack … but, I think, the reading of such thrilling events is liable to produce a wrong impression in the mind of the reader. He is inclined to imagine that attacks, charges and desperate hand-to-hand encounters are the daily experience of every soldier, and he forgets to think, or at best only forms a vague idea, of the life of the average British soldier as it was during the past eighteen months, and still is along the greater part of the line.

'Fighting is only a small part of war even in the firing line,' wrote one anonymous Scotsman in 1915.

Most of the time the infantry soldier is a navvy with the chance of being killed. During his four or six days in the trenches, he may have many things to complain about, but being idle is not one of them. The amount of hard labour required in winter to keep trenches passable, let alone habitable, is beyond the comprehension of anyone who has not actually occupied them. And when a unit is relieved, the corresponding period in billets, after the first day, is simply a repetition of fatigues, sometimes thinly disguised as 'working-parties'. The physical discomfort of the life is tremendous.

And what better way, for soldiers telling their own story, to illustrate that version of the truth than with the photographs they themselves took, showing us directly, one hundred years later, what mattered to them. Not that every soldier was armed with a camera, far from it; the possession of cameras was largely, but not exclusively, the preserve of officers. By the spring of 1915, the army made possession of a camera illegal and the numbers kept, in defiance of this order, were much reduced. Nevertheless, enough soldiers serving overseas held on to their cameras to ensure that pictures were taken on probably every day of the conflict.

Over the last ten years, I have built up a collection of two thousand privately taken photographs of the Great War. These images give a different view of the conflict from that offered by the small number of official war photographers who were permitted (only from 1916 onwards) to go to the Western Front and take images for propaganda purposes as well as for the historical record.

As this book is the soldiers' own story, it is my intention to keep out of the narrative as far as possible, other than to give, where required, a brief overview of the progress of the war. The strategic position, to the soldier at the time, was of almost no interest whatsoever, other than as a guide to whether the war was being won or lost and when, eventually, he might go home. My job has been to guide the narrative, to link stories where necessary or to make additional points that may be of interest and, wherever possible, to link the images with the stories.

The last veterans of the war died some five years ago, but the soldiers and airmen who fought in that great conflict still speak to us through the pages of this book in a fresh and engaging way. This testimony is their legacy.

The VPK camera

I got leave from the Colonel to go up into the town [of Boulogne] to buy a Kodak but all the 'Vest Pocket Kodaks' were sold out though I tried five shops.

20 October 1914, Lieutenant Thomas McKenny Stewart,
1/28th London Regiment (Artists' Rifles)

Amongst the tens of thousands of British soldiers embarking for France was a small but not insignificant number, overwhelmingly officers, who, in packing their equipment, took a camera with them as any like-minded civilian might do on holiday; it was, after all, the first truly international conflict any of these professional soldiers had been involved in, and a small, compact camera would document their exploits. In many ways, a camera was the perfect additional wartime accessory in that, like rifle or revolver, it had a cartridge that was loaded, aimed and shot. Furthermore, at the start of the war at least, the army did not prohibit its servicemen from taking private cameras overseas.

Such cameras were to capture startling images of life at the front, made possible by rapid developments in photographic technology. In particular, lighter cameras, faster shutter speeds, improved exposure times and superior lenses lessened the need for, among other things, cumbersome tripods.

At the end of the nineteenth century, photography had become a popular public pastime, if not quite for the masses then for a sizeable minority. The marketing in 1907 of the development tank, for example, permitted this stage to take place in daylight, in an ordinary front room. As a dark room was no longer necessary for developing film, 'many people,' wrote one journalist in February 1909, 'have been tempted to take up photography who would otherwise never have done so ... It is now possible to do photographic work without ever having to pass a moment in the dim red light of the ruby lamp; and that not makeshift but the best photography.'

Two unknown officers: the man on the right is holding a Vest Pocket Kodak.

Photographers did not have to be masters of a difficult craft, but were ordinary men and women, empowered to go out and take their own photographs at any time, anywhere. Between 1895 and 1914, Kodak's annual profits grew from £49,000 to £2.4 million. *Kodak News* was first published in 1895 and a touring exhibition soon followed to great acclaim and huge public interest. In 1912 and 1913, the *Daily Mail* in association with Kodak offered a prize of £1,000 (twenty times the average annual working-class wage) for the best summer holiday snapshots taken on a Kodak camera: the competition was open to even the cheapest Box Brownies, sold for as little as five shillings. 'The beginner with a Kodak has just as good a chance as an expert', an advertisement boasted.

After Kodak introduced the first roll film in 1888, the number of amateur photographers grew steadily, and when inexpensive folding pocket 'kodaks' were produced in 1899, with postcard-size prints, a revolution in amateur photography was guaranteed. In 1912 the small Vest Pocket Kodak (VPK), with its 127mm film, was manufactured, producing smaller 1⅝ by 2½ inch images, so that by the time war broke out soldiers of any rank could take a camera with them, if they could afford it. The camera's compact shape, its retractable bellows lens and its durable all-metal construction made it ideal for the tunic or greatcoat pocket. Kodak was not shy when it came to advertising its VPK as the perfect camera for the front: 'the Soldier's Camera' they called it and while the cost (thirty shillings) was a lot for other ranks to pay, it was not entirely prohibitive to the committed enthusiast.

Kodak was an American company, but Houghtons Ltd, a British competitor, had its range of retractable cameras, too, one of which was the 'Ensignette'. In marketing its products to the soldier, the company naturally focused on its camera's suitability for front-line life, especially its durability and flexibility. But it also cleverly picked up on the significance and, indeed, the historical importance of the images that were already being taken at the front. To give such a camera to a soldier, it argued persuasively, would be to ensure that a loved one did not miss out on recording such a hugely significant event as a European war. In February 1915, Houghtons ran an advertisement in the *Amateur Photographer and Photographic News*:

> Judging from the number of cameras known to have been taken to
> the front by officers – and, no doubt, by many privates – a vast number

of unique records and some most valuable material must rapidly be accumulating. Much will be of great historical interest and scientific value, while the incidental interest of a good deal of the rest will be remarkable. Perhaps you have a soldier friend going to France. New drafts are going continually, and an 'Ensignette', which can be stowed away in a tunic pocket or strapped to a belt, is the one and only camera that is really strong, easy to load, and useful under all circumstances.

Britain's newspaper industry was also aware of the commercial opportunities afforded by private war photography. They were no more interested in the 'historical value' or the 'unique record' of these soldier-shot images than Houghtons. The company wanted to sell cameras and newspaper editors were single-minded in their desire to increase their circulation; and it stood to reason that Fleet Street would want to get hold of the best possible images.

Just as camera technology had moved on in the immediate years before the Great War, so had newspaper production, most notably the introduction of half-tone printing that simplified images into a series of closely packed dots, making the publication of pictures cheap and simple. For daily or weekly newspapers that relied heavily on the visual image, such as the *Daily Mirror*, *The Sphere* and the *Illustrated London News*, this advance fundamentally altered news delivery. In 1904, a year after its launch, the *Daily Mirror* introduced half-tone printing and was therefore, a decade later, more than capable of publishing, to public interest and clamour, photographs taken at the front.

As if the market were not congested enough in 1914, these established newspapers were joined in the general scrum by new titles launched specifically to report the war. One of the most notable was *The War Illustrated*, a weekly paper launched with considerable fanfare. The first edition, published the week ending 22 August 1914, told the buying public exactly what it could expect.

The War Illustrated, while being a weekly news-picture review of the great happenings that are making these our days for ever memorable in the world's history, also possesses the value of a permanent record ... The best resources of modern journalism are at its command – the camera of the war photographer, the pencil of the trained war artist, the pen of the skilled writer, will fill its pages week by week with an unrivalled budget of illustrations and letterpress.

This newspaper was not just reporting the war, it was offering readers the chance to buy into the idea of newspapers being both a historical record and a worthy souvenir.

Circulation of *The War Illustrated* quickly grew to 750,000. But while the finances to publish were firmly in place, the anticipated access to news and photographs was not. No accompanying press or military photographers landed with the British Expeditionary Force in France, and it had not occurred to anyone in the War Office that they should do so. Consequently, the press was starved of images of British soldiers overseas during the first months of the war. After the public hype, *The War Illustrated*, like the dailies, relied heavily not on images of its own soldiers, but rather of French and German troops supplied by international press agencies. For weeks all images of British soldiers overseas were restricted to the French port of Boulogne. Otherwise, pictures were of activities at home, either of troops about to embark for France or of the wounded arriving back in England. 'Action' shots were necessarily hand-drawn caricatures of Tommy valour. *The War Illustrated* had very few images of soldiers at 'the front' until issue 14, dated 21 November 1914, in which it ran a half-page picture of soldiers retreating under fire and with it an interesting and rather apologetic caption explaining the paucity hitherto of such photographic scoops:

> From the pictorial point of view, modern warfare lacks much which the battlefields of the past provided. Soldiers today are fighting enemies on the Continent whom they never see, and in London not a few of the wounded brought home to recuperate lament that they have received their injuries without ever getting a glimpse of those who inflicted them.
>
> For this reason the great mass of photographs which reach us from the front do not show actual hostilities in progress, but the above [the picture opposite, right] is vividly interesting, having been taken by a British officer at the moment when a shell was passing over a high road during the Battle of the Aisne. The alarm of the men and horses is depicted in their attitudes, and the whole scene conveys to us a remarkable impression of the reality of modern warfare.

The key words were 'taken by a British officer'. If newspapers were going to tell the story of 'our boys abroad' then it would be down to those 'boys' to supply the photographs. This first privately taken image to appear in *The War Illustrated* – it appeared in other newspapers, too – was taken by Lieutenant Robert Money, serving with the 1st Cameronians. The image is interesting first and foremost for its unposed and gritty realism, but secondly for the artificial addition to the print of a puff of black smoke on a flat grey sky – an exploding shell – presumably in order to make the scene more intelligible to readers. The photograph was taken on 8 September during the BEF's readvance to the Marne after the famous Retreat from Mons. In other words, it had taken more than two months for this first 'action' image to reach the newspapers. Lieutenant Money took a camera with him to France and sent the films home to Glasgow to be developed. A number of the images he took in 1914 found their way into newsprint, including editions of *The Sphere*.

The press, desperate for 'front-line' images, began to offer cash inducements to serving soldiers to submit their best images for publication, although none of the obliging officers was referred to by name. Another picture taken by Money of Lancers resting under trees was published in *The War Illustrated* in January 1915. This time the picture was captioned as 'a photograph exclusive', with the attribution 'by one of our special photographers with the Expeditionary Force'. The amounts of money on offer to serving soldiers were extraordinary. The *Daily Sketch*, which claimed a daily circulation in excess of one million copies, had a 'prize picture scheme' into which it poured £10,000 for the best photographs

Below left: the original picture taken by Lieutenant Robert Money.

Below right: the image doctored to add to the drama of a shellburst, as it appeared in The War Illustrated.

taken at the front. In July 1915 it featured what it called 'the finest picture of the war', an 'in action' photograph taken, it was claimed, during the Second Battle of Ypres. It purported to show hastily entrenched British soldiers about to open fire on advancing Germans, a group of whom could be seen in the distance. 'So remarkably vivid is the snapshot that some readers have thought it impossible,' the paper claimed. 'We reproduce it absolutely untouched', which suggested, of course, that other images were tampered with. Theirs was also a tacit acknowledgement that, as most readers had found, few images were genuinely groundbreaking. The newspaper paid £600 for the scoop.

The *Daily Mirror* was also in pursuit of soldiers' photographs. In February 1915 it ran a series of advertisements promising to pay soldiers 'large sums of money' for the best snapshots and on 25 February ran a headline 'War snapshots that will win £1,000: amateurs' chance' (worth around £80,000 today). This sum, the newspaper stressed, was 'the largest ever offered for a news picture in the history of illustrated journalism for the most interesting snapshot of a war happening'. The promotion ran to the end of July and those who contributed were offered free film development and, as the army looked ever more darkly on such activities, anonymity.

In the competitive market of newspaper publishing, such a bullish approach by one newspaper was bound to be challenged by its competitors. Within days of the *Daily Mirror* offer, other newspapers offered ever greater cash prizes for pictures. The *Amateur Photographer and Photographic News* even offered its readers suggestions as how to best to take pictures without getting into trouble. In an article captioned 'Photography at the front: Some practical notes from one who has been there', a correspondent using the pseudonym 'Medico' offered a few cautious suggestions: 'Don't flourish your camera about in the face of generals ... don't take pictures that could possibly be of the smallest assistance to the enemy; you might be captured ... Don't ever photograph the horrible, you will find war quite horrible enough, without perpetuating the seamy side of it.' Otherwise it was apparently open season.

In reality, privately taken pictures that appeared in the press did not generally command such large payment. Headline figures of £1,000 grabbed attention, but no editor was going to pay that sum, or anything like it, for good but hardly exceptional images. Second Lieutenant Herbert Preston served overseas with 120th Battery, Royal Field Artillery. The photographs he took were sent to his wife who offered them to the press under the pseudonym 'Maxwell'. In all, she is believed to have sold between seventy and eighty photographs to various larger and smaller newspapers. Surviving account sheets and bills of sale indicate her husband received between seven and eleven shillings for each picture, and that in a relatively short space of time, around a month or more, he was paid a total of £28, doubling a second lieutenant's monthly pay: nice but hardly a fortune. Bills show, for example, that the *Daily Mirror* paid ten shillings and sixpence for one photograph of a dog, a trench terrier; the *Daily News* a similar amount for a picture of the Manchester Regiment in camp. Interestingly, among the paperwork there is a letter from the Topical Press Agency dated 7 July 1915, which appears to suggest that the Agency is collecting publishing fees on behalf of 'Mrs Maxwell'. She had supplied a photograph entitled 'Respirator Drill at [the] Front' to the *Mirror* for their exclusive use, but the image had subsequently appeared in *The Illustrated War News*. 'Shall we collect fee for same?' they asked her.

Second Lieutenant Preston had embarked for France in April 1915, taking his camera. He was injured in an accident later that year and returned to Britain, before being passed fit for service once more. He returned to the front and, on 19 August 1917, he died of enteric fever. As was usual, the effects of a deceased officer, his uniform and personal belongings, were returned to his family. The inventory listed items such as a leather case, three pipes and a pocket knife. It also included one 'Kodak camera in case with sling' and two 'rolls film'.

What connected all these financial inducements was the almost ubiquitous reference to 'snapshots'. The newspapers were not interested in posed images or photographs taken well behind the lines, in comfort and security. Snapshots, by their very nature, were taken on the hoof; they had a vibrancy and immediacy of their own and might have been taken in a moment of great danger. These pictures were uncensored and reflected the immediate preoccupations of the soldier at war.

In the absence of official photographs, the military authorities had unconsciously encouraged a feeding frenzy. The army and politicians were slow to see the advantages of using press power to circulate government-inspired propaganda to further the nation's cause. The rising influence of newspapers, and of newspaper barons such as Lord Northcliffe and Lord Rothermere, remained under-appreciated, and the involvement of military correspondents at the front was eyed with suspicion and deemed a risk to security. Only in 1915, after mounting pressure, did Lord Kitchener, the Secretary of State for War, reluctantly allow a small number of newspaper reporters to take up residence on the Western Front, which in reality meant General Headquarters. Here they could be easily controlled and heavily censored. It would be a further year before the first official war photographer, Ernest Brooks, went to the Western Front. His pictures, superb though they are, were not uncensored, passing through two filters: first the army overseas and secondly the press bureau at home. Only one more official photographer, John Warwick Brooke, was sent to the Western Front in 1916, and by the end of the war there were only sixteen British war photographers across all fronts. By contrast, there were twice as many French official photographers and three times as many German.

In order to keep soldiers in touch with home, newspapers were sent out to the Western Front either as continental editions or in parcels from loved ones. Either way, they gave the men in the trenches the opportunity to examine how journalists and newspaper editors appreciated the war in word, image and illustration. Most soldiers were unimpressed by what they saw.

It was easy for an experienced soldier to scoff at artists' impressions of fighting, but the photographs were often dull or downright misleading, the editor's caption being used to pep up an otherwise dull story as told by a picture. For men overseas, it became clear that some images were faked or used deliberately to hoodwink readers as to where and even when they were taken. Gunner Cecil Longley, serving with the Royal Field Artillery, wrote home on 17 May 1915, describing in scathing terms the work of some of the young journalists on the Western Front, kept miles from the fighting line but who were still able to write 'journalistic blather' about events at the front. Older journalists, in Longley's view, were wilier and even more dishonest.

I see the latest gag of the older journalists is to write long articles under their photographs and have themselves described as 'Mr. W., the greatest military authority and critic.' Or 'Mr. F., whose knowledge of naval matters is unsurpassed.' Probably you'd find that Mr. F. couldn't tell you the difference between a picket boat and an officer's cutter, and Mr. W. would confound a surcingle-pad with a trail-spade gear, or imagine a drag-rope was the same as a throat-lash. Probably their knowledge of strategy and tactics – which they so finely criticize — would be as exhaustive as their technical knowledge.

I myself have seen a photo – lyingly alleged to be 'somewhere in France with our gallant gunners' – obviously taken on Salisbury Plain at any rate months before the war, as the harness on the horses is such as has not been used during the war, but was discarded, I believe, in autumn, 1913.

Second Lieutenant Alexander Gillespie, serving with the 2nd Argyll and Sutherland Highlanders, was no less suspicious of the pictorial evidence before his eyes. On 12 May 1915 he wrote home:

I have just been looking at a full-page photo in an illustrated weekly with the stirring title, 'How three encountered fifty and prevailed,' and a footnote describing their gallant deeds in detail. The dauntless three belong to this regiment, but we were a little puzzled, because we have never been at La Bassée, where their exploit took place. A closer inspection showed that the trees were in full leaf, and that the men were wearing spats and hose-tops, which we have long since abandoned for general use. Finally, someone recognised the sergeant as our shoemaker sergeant, and his companions as two men from our second line transport. They are usually at least three miles from the trenches, and the whole story is a lie from beginning to end, without a shadow of truth in it. It makes one distrust all newspapers more than ever, to catch them out like that.

Most pictures were genuine, albeit rather lacklustre. Then, that first Christmas, some more pictures began to circulate. All were taken by serving soldiers and these were anything but dull, indeed they caused a sensation. Pictures of British and German soldiers meeting in no-man's-land on apparently friendly terms appeared in the national press and undoubtedly unsettled the army's senior command. Much effort had been expended in demonising the enemy: horror stories of atrocities had fuelled enlistment in 1914. At odds with this portrait of the enemy were pictures of men

Overleaf: 'A friendly chat with the enemy', according to the contemporary caption. British and German troops mingle on Christmas Day, 1914.

smiling and at ease with each other; of men who looked remarkably similar but for the cut of the uniform they wore. These images were hardly conducive to the maintenance of the fighting spirit at home or abroad but British newspapers loved them. One image showing a number of British and German soldiers standing together featured in the *Daily Sketch*, which described it as 'one of the most remarkable photographs ever taken of this war'. For once this was not journalistic hyperbole.

The BEF's Commander-in-Chief, Sir John French, was alarmed at the appearance of soldiers' own photographs in the press before subversive images of the Christmas Truce grabbed the headlines. French had issued a ban on soldiers' contact with the press on 22 December. General Routine Order 464 was his attempt to stop this contact. 'It has been brought to notice that drawings, photographs, and letters are being sent to the Press. This practice is forbidden. The taking of photographs is not permitted.'

Not everyone serving in the trenches would have been aware of this order by Christmas Day. Sergeant Christopher Pilkington, a professional photographer in civilian life, was seconded from the Artists' Rifles to the 2nd Scots Guards in order to photograph the battalion's exploits. According to his diary dated 5 January, he was vaguely aware of regulations banning cameras, but believed these had not yet been introduced. Furthermore a General Routine Order was a 'fix' for the Western Front only, and would not have been read to officers and men about to embark for overseas service. They remained ignorant of the new rules.

There was a general and ongoing fear over security that naturally troubled the army, and so the apparent dithering over a ban seems puzzling. In particular, there was heightened anxiety over the presence of spies behind the line in the winter of 1914 and the spring of 1915, and a general ban on cameras on top of an existing prohibition on the keeping of diaries would scotch two activities that spies were likely to be involved in: photography and the taking of notes. The 46th North Midland Divisional War Diary noted in April 1915 that most of the stories concerning spies 'did not as a rule hold water'. Nevertheless, there had been 'some unpleasantness caused by the arrest of innocent people on charges of "acting in a suspicious manner"'. It seems entirely possible that innocent use of a camera might have been misconstrued as suspicious activity.

The first move to ban cameras comprehensively occurred on 16 March 1915. A War Office Instruction declared: 'The taking of photographs is not permitted and the sending of films through the post is prohibited. Any officers or soldiers (or other persons subject to military law) found in possession of a camera will be placed in arrest, and the case reported to the General Headquarters as to disposal.'

On 27 March, Second Lieutenant Gillespie wrote: 'all cameras have to be sent home now, so I'm afraid I shall get no more photos', adding ruefully, 'If they would only trust you to take nothing which could do any harm, you might get a lot of interesting things.' In the 1/8th Sherwood Foresters, one of the battalions in the 46th North Midland Division, the duty of confiscating cameras fell to one of its officers, Captain Robert Hodgkinson. 'He acted [temporarily] as Censor,' wrote another officer, Captain William Wheetman. 'In this capacity, he was obliged, to our great annoyance, to carry out the order to relieve us of our cameras, which were sent home.' Their great annoyance was due in no small part to the fact that the unit had only just arrived in France, and no one had had the opportunity to snap any souvenir photographs.

Curiously, the ban appears to have been temporarily lifted, at least according to officers serving in the 6th Division. On 30 March, Gillespie wrote again: 'Just after they [the cameras] had all gone off [home] came a counter-order, to say that they might be kept, to the great annoyance of everyone who had packed and posted his camera.' Denis Barnett, serving in the 2nd Leinsters, in the same division as Gillespie, was also aware of the change of policy. 'We've just heard that the order about cameras is washed out,' he wrote on 1 April, 'so can I have mine back, please?'

Alexander Gillespie suspected that this was just a temporary reprieve. On 5 April he had written home hoping that his camera would arrive back quickly 'so that I can take some photos before they change the rule again'. By 13 April he had his camera once more. 'I shall try to get some photos with it before I have to send it home … but I don't expect to get any very startling pictures, for I have no experience with these small films, and there is nothing very exciting to snap just here at present.'

Another army-wide instruction, finally banning cameras once and for all, appeared on 19 April 1915 in War Office Instruction 173:

Brigadier General William McClintock (on the right), commanding 145th Infantry Brigade, poses for a photograph at least a month after the ban on private cameras.

> General Routine Order No. 464 issued by the F.M.C.[ommander]-in-C[hief], the British Army in the Field, prohibits the taking of photographs and the sending of drawings and photographs to the press; and by an Order issued on the 16th March, photographic cameras are not allowed to be in possession of officers, N.C.O.s or men, while serving with the British Army in the Field. Instructions should be issued by G.O.s C.-in-C to all serving under their command that on no account are cameras to be taken when any unit or reinforcing draft proceeds overseas.

The additional ban on sending photographs to the press allayed some publicly expressed anxieties that soldiers, in search of a great picture and an even better press pay cheque, would concentrate more on loading, aiming and shooting their camera than their weapons.

Reluctantly, most officers gave up their cameras. 'Isn't it sickening about the camera?' Denis Barnett wrote on 20 April. 'He's got to go, though I don't want to lose him.' Gillespie, too, was annoyed although it took him another week to effect a parting. On 21 April he wrote:

> I took some photos – one along the railway line toward the German trenches – which I hope will come out, for I just held it up on the parapet above my head, and snapped without putting my head up to see the view-finder. It's a very neat little camera.

Thankfully for posterity, an unquantifiable number of officers disobeyed the order. Lieutenant Alec Johnston was serving with the 1st Shropshire Regiment. He wrote regularly for *Punch* magazine and, after his death in action in April 1916, his musings were published in 1917 in a book entitled *At the Front*. In one interesting passage he referred to the use of cameras and how officers in one unnamed battalion got round the restrictions:

> Not long ago it seemed good to the état majeur that no officer should be in possession of the means of supplying the pictorial daily with pictorial war. Every company in every battalion duly rendered a certificate that it was without cameras. Now there was a certain battalion much given to photographic studies. And when the day came that the certificate should be signed and rendered, the commander of A Company bethought him of his old-time friendship with the commander of B Company; and in token of his sincere esteem sent to him as a gift the three cameras which his officers had no further use for. This done, he forwarded his certificate. B Company, though delighted at the gift and the spirit in which it was offered, had already four cameras in possession of its officers. Moreover, the time for B Company to render its certificate was at hand. And seeing that there was much friendship subsisting between B and C Companies the OC B Company remembered that the OC C Company was a keen photographer, and one likely to welcome a gift of seven cameras. Having despatched them, he signed and certified for B Company. C Company, whose gratitude cannot easily be described, was nevertheless in an obvious predicament. So, when C Company certified, D Company was in possession of thirteen cameras; and finding that A Company had now no cameras at all rendered unto it the very large stock with which it was reluctantly obliged to part, and unto the CO a certificate that D Company was cameraless; and the CO certified in accordance with company notifications.
>
> That evening company commanders dined together, and latest advices advise that the wicked battalion still spends its spare time in photographing approaching shells, devastated churches and Tommy at his ablutions.

The army would not have found Johnston's musings in the least bit funny. Security was key and in the weeks leading up to the first joint Allied offensive of the war in September 1915, orders were reissued making it clear that there would be serious consequences for anyone caught with a camera. On 9 September, two weeks before the offensive, First Army reissued the warnings given in March of immediate arrest for anyone caught with a camera. 'The rule is very strict now …' wrote Gillespie.

Gillespie was clearly anxious. Since the ban, he had ceased taking pictures but he had not ceased asking his family for prints from his existing negatives. 'Send out several prints of any that are good for all the men are sure to want to send them home; they are promising them in their letters already,' he had written at the end of April. By August, he was much more circumspect. 'When you send out photos, send them in an ordinary parcel, otherwise the censor might think I had been taking photos these last three months, which, of course, I have not done, and it would take a lot of correspondence to explain that they were old prints.'

With the ban came a commensurate drop in the number of privately taken photographs that appeared in the press, though a number still appeared in print; quite when some were taken, before or after the ban, remains open to debate. Private Frederick Fyfe's images are a notable exception. While serving in the 1/10th King's Liverpool Regiment, Fyfe took a number of photographs, including three of the battalion in action on 16 June in fighting near Bellewaarde, in the Ypres Salient. Fyfe was a twenty-five-year-old former newspaper photographer for the *Daily Sketch*. His graphic images, taken while he was lying down, wounded in the legs, appeared in, among other publications, *The War Illustrated*, issue 47, dated 10 July 1915. Fyfe had taken a considerable risk. Despite the publicity the pictures received, no action was taken against him and Fyfe was subsequently commissioned, winning a Military Cross in 1916.

Private Frederick Fyfe, 1/10th King's Liverpool Regiment, took these pictures while wounded in the legs during fighting at Bellewaarde at around 6 a.m., 16 June 1915. Nine officers and 142 men were killed in the attack.

What were the consequences of being caught with a camera? Those caught would in all likelihood be charged under Section 40, the army's catch-all offence of 'Conduct to the prejudice of good order and military discipline', a deliberately vague charge that dealt with all crimes not covered by existing military law such as that governing drunkenness, desertion or theft. One surviving case concerned Private Cyril Cook, a London civil servant serving with the 15th County of London Regiment. He was caught in possession of a camera on 28 February 1916 and charged under Section 40. Section 40 had two echelons: those crimes not of a serious nature and those of a more serious nature. For other ranks, this could mean a maximum punishment of twenty-eight days' detention for crimes for the lower tariff and up to 112 days' detention for the higher tariff. For commissioned ranks the consequences of conviction could be more serious, with an officer facing the humiliation of being cashiered from the army. Nevertheless, the non-specific nature of crimes dealt with under Section 40 gave those prosecuting miscreants considerable latitude when it came to handing down a punishment.

For two weeks, Cook was held in confinement while he awaited a Field General Court Martial, convened on 13 March. He had been accused of disobeying General Routine Order 1137 of 11 September 1915 in that 'he was in possession of a camera'. He was found guilty although his sentence appears reasonably light. He was awarded twenty-eight days' Field Punishment No. 2, returning to his unit without, presumably, his camera. Officers were also threatened with Court Martial. Captain Harry Trounce, serving with the Royal Engineers, left for France on the last day of 1915. He recalled:

> At the first officers' parade, at Rouen after I arrived in France, we were all informed by the camp adjutant that cameras were forbidden and that any man who had a camera in his possession after twenty-four hours would be court-martialled. I had one – a small vest-pocket-kodak – but after this order decided to send it back to a friend in England. Some six months later I was fortunate enough to secure a small kodak in one of the villages behind the lines and managed to get the few pictures …

Interestingly, not only did he use this camera but he gave some prints to the publishers of his memoirs that showed him standing in his steel helmet in the trenches. The book, *Fighting the Boche Underground*, was published a month before the Armistice, in October 1918.

It seems likely that most officers who kept their cameras were under the impression that as long as they did not 'flourish' them under the noses of generals, then their own commanding officer would turn a blind eye. Being discreet was key and within the battalion an officer was among friends. This does not mean that all officers were the same. Regular officers who were used to obeying the letter of the law and who, naturally, had one eye on continuing their post-war careers in the army, were far less likely to keep their cameras after the ban than, for example, territorial officers. These part-time soldiers were more civilians than soldiers and were among pre-war friends who were not as bothered as regular officers certainly were, about adherence to strict military discipline. Finally, those officers belonging to Kitchener's New Army were, in the main, less able to rely on the cosiness of such pre-war friendships and were therefore a little more circumspect when it came to keeping cameras than territorial officers. The number of surviving albums reflects these quite distinct differences in the officer corps.

A surprisingly large number of albums survive, although it is impossible to know how many have been lost. In the 1960s and 1970s, albums and other Great War memorabilia were not seen as being of any great value, and large numbers of such artefacts were thrown away and probably ended up in landfill sites. A dustman working in Sussex in the early 1970s recalled finding gallantry medals, brooches made from shrapnel and a Turkish flag captured at Gallipoli among the 'waste' thrown away. He also recovered photograph albums including images of the London Scottish serving on the Aisne in 1914, two of which appear in this book.

Over the last ten years I have acquired nearly fifty such albums. Some feature photographs taken almost exclusively behind the lines, as far back as the base camps of Boulogne and Rouen. Pictures taken at such distance from the fighting may have been considered of minimal intelligence value to the enemy and unlikely in any case to fall into their hands. That could be the view of a commanding officer who trusted his immediate subordinates to restrict themselves to images of friends and billets. Other albums include as many shots in the trenches as behind them. John Polgreen started taking pictures in France *as* the ban came into force. He was a private serving with the 1/28th London Regiment but was commissioned into the 9th Rifle Brigade in September 1915. For the next year, until he was wounded during the Battle of the Somme, he took photographs in and out of the trenches and of almost every officer in the battalion, including the adjutant and the CO, Lieutenant Colonel Morris. Polgreen clearly felt uninhibited when it came to taking photographs and a number of his images appear in this book. Lieutenant Richard Hawkins of the 11th Royal Fusiliers also took pictures throughout his time on the Somme. Would these men have risked being cashiered had they not believed that their commanding officers were happy to look the other way?

Should the need arise, commanding officers could always claim that they did not know that pictures were being taken within their unit, and so could hope to avoid censure. The Commanding Officer of the 17th Highland Light Infantry, a service battalion, had no such convenient exit strategy. When his battalion was sent overseas in late November 1915, cameras accompanied the unit, including one belonging to Private David Hourston. He was a keen amateur photographer and he took pictures of the battalion throughout training in Britain and subsequently in France. Within weeks, his pictures of front-line life were appearing in *The Outpost*, the regimental magazine printed and published back home in Glasgow. It was a blatant violation of military law and yet the CO was seemingly unconcerned and there was no attempt by the regiment to hide their contributor's name. David Hourston was later commissioned and was killed in August 1918.

Interestingly, the ban on cameras did not appear to stop their advertisement in *The Outpost*, aimed at both other ranks and officers. Among the numerous advertisements for military outfitters, opticians and tobacconists are those from photographers. In the February 1916 issue, three advertisements were from Glasgow dealers. Robert Ballantine of Vincent Street offered to sell 'Cameras for Military Use', as well as offering the 'best class work' in developing, printing and enlarging. In West Nile Street, W. M. Blackadder appealed directly to soldiers in camp who had cameras but no facilities for developing and printing. Such soldiers, he said, 'cannot do better than send their work to me'. W. W. Scott and Co. of

Sauchiehall Street were offering to sell 'For Active Service' the 'Soldier's Camera', in this case the No. 1 and No. 2 Ensignette, a foldaway camera that would fit 'any Pocket'.

Other ranks were far less likely to be given the latitude allowed to officers by COs, and far fewer albums exist of photographs taken by these men. Of those that survive, not all prove that the soldier concerned actually took them. Private James Cripps' small collection of photographs taken in the trenches while serving with the 8th Rifle Brigade were prints given to him by Captain Leslie Woodroffe, to whom James Cripps was batman in 1915. Other ranks who kept cameras hid them, and took them out only when they felt confident to do so, as did Lance Corporal William Smallcombe, serving with the 12th Gloucestershire Regiment, who took pictures at Arras and on the Somme in 1916. Private Sidney Banyard, who served as a signaller with 215 Siege Battery, Royal Garrison Artillery, was, according to his daughter, well aware of the fact that possession of a camera was strictly forbidden. He went to France in January 1917 and hid his camera throughout his service, taking it out when no one, other than his close comrades, was looking.

Banyard's images are rare, not purely because they belonged to a private, but because of their date. It is noticeable that, as the war became increasingly dehumanised, so enthusiasm for photography waned. It was as if the excitement and curiosity that was a feature of many early privately taken images had gone as the war became an open-ended and hard-fought bloody slog to the finish. The non-availability of film stock may also have exacerbated this decline, so that privately taken images of 1917 and 1918 are much rarer than those of 1914, 1915 and even 1916.

So how do pictures taken by soldiers themselves differ from those taken by official photographers? Overlaps between professional and amateur exponents of the same medium were inevitable, but there are crucial differences. First, and the most obvious, is the relaxed attitude of close friends when photographed by a comrade. The official photographer was unlikely to get precisely the same natural response to the invasiveness of the camera. Second, in many albums those photographed are identified, names given to men who might or might not go on to survive the war. It gives invaluable identity to those who fought, identity that was all but absent from official photographs in which a wider 'story' was the objective, not the individuals behind it. Third, private photographs were by their very nature depictions of the war as the private soldier saw it: partial, personal and unfettered, an image not influenced by the demands of a paid profession or the requirements of propaganda. Fourth, and finally, soldiers' photographs cover the war at a time when there were no official photographers present on the battlefield: the only pictorial record we have of the famous Christmas Truce of 1914 is that taken on soldiers' private cameras. These soldiers of the Great War were holding today's camera phones, less ubiquitous, certainly, but common enough until they were banned, and used them to record a broad spectrum of incidents and experience that a mere handful of professional photographers could not hope to emulate.

Looking out of a dugout entrance at a man, possibly an Australian, on a field telephone. There is a spur-of-the-moment informality about this picture that is normally absent in official images.

An official photograph. Note the slightly posed attitude. Each man is holding an unlit cigarette, probably given by the official photographer to gain their cooperation.

Overleaf: Bayonet practice.

1914

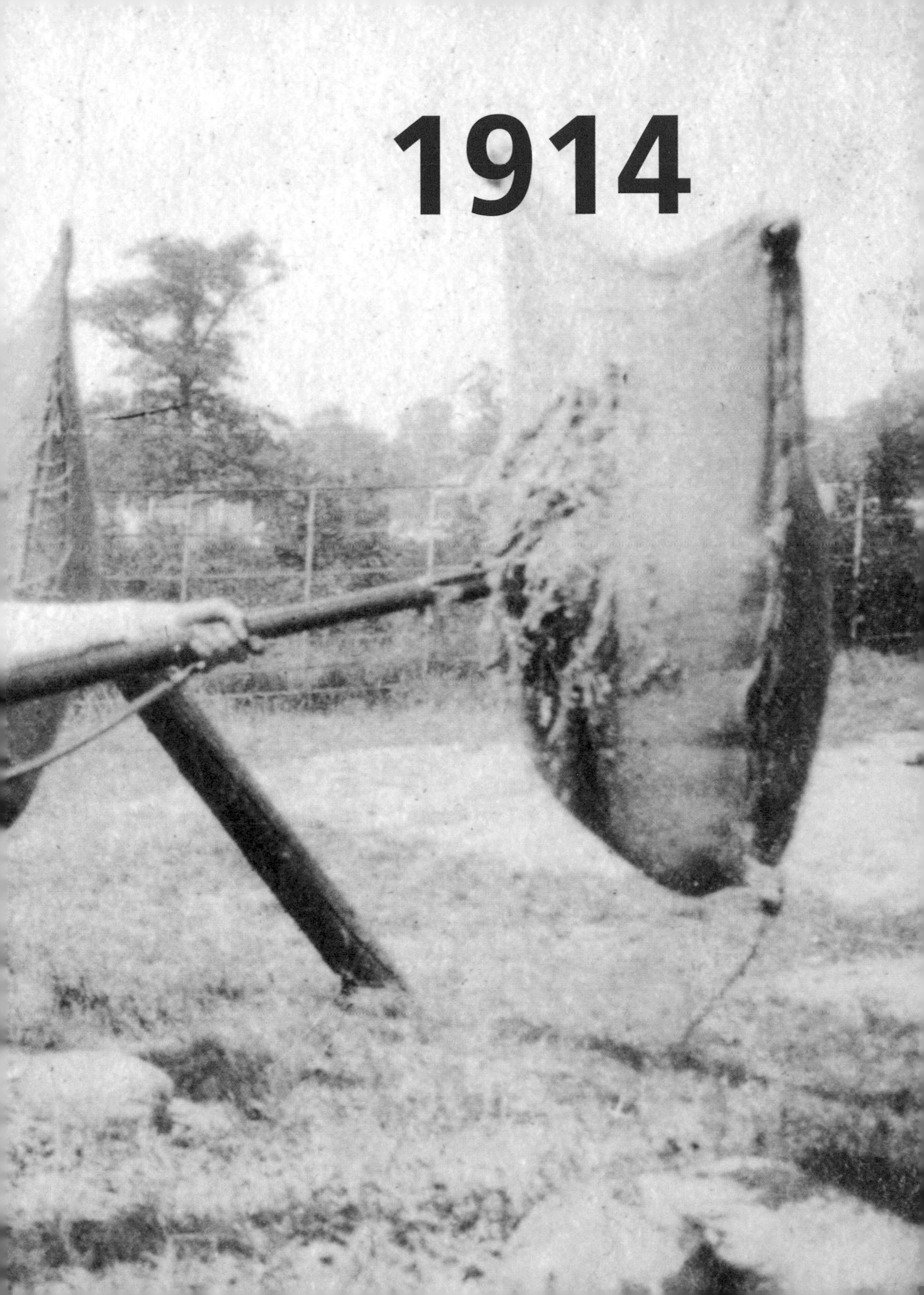

I rather like this dirty nomad life, trekking every day, always fresh scenes and fresh faces, no luggage, no washing or shaving or changing of clothes, and up every morning at the latest by four.

Lieutenant Colonel Philip Howell, 4th (Queen's Own) Hussars

———————

'Report yourself to OC 1st Battalion at ___ [The Curragh] immediately. Group.' So the time had come. Of course I guessed what was going to be in the wire before I opened it, but somehow the pink telegraph envelope, and that little word 'Group' at the end of the message, shook me out of an exciting daydream into reality. For years we had been brought up on the word 'Group', which was to come at the end of the order for mobilisation. Now it was being flashed over wires all over the country. Our training was to bear fruit. The happy, careless – some people say, rather useless – life of the army officer in peacetime was over. The country had gone to war.

Captain Arthur Mills, 1st Duke of Cornwall's Light Infantry

I went up to my rooms in London to collect a few things. My landlady was breathless with helping me pack, aghast at the national crisis, and rather shocked at my levity. Levity – yes, I suppose I was flippant. What else could one be when suddenly told one was going to war with Germany? I was rather enjoying the packing and everything up to a point, but as I ransacked drawers I came on a bundle of letters with some absurd comic postcards. The letters had a faint scent of violet about them. They had to be sealed up and left behind, with directions for their disposal if I didn't come back. And there was a photograph to be taken from the mantelpiece and put in a pocket-book, a photograph which had been in many places with me. Well, now it must go on its travels again. I got an aching in the back of my throat and hurried to my club for a drink.

A brief period of rest is taken by officers and men of the 11th Hussars during the Retreat from Mons, 2 September 1914.

From the club, I went to the station. There was a big crowd on the platform of the boat train [for Ireland]. Many women had come to see their menfolk off, and some to travel with them as far as they could … At the camp I reported myself to the adjutant. There was little in his manner to show that he was getting a regiment ready to go to war, except that he showed an indisposition to talk, and seemed trying to keep his mind clear of everything except for the sequence of things which had to be done. After reporting to the adjutant I went across to the mess. The mess was in a state of packing. Cases, boxes and litter of all descriptions blocked the corridors; each officer's room was like the interior of a furniture removal van, and the mess waiters were busy packing away all the regimental silver and pictures. The only things which stood out clearly from the jumble were the field-service kits of the different officers. These were for the most part all neatly rolled up in brown or green valises ready to be thrown on the transport wagon at an instant's notice. Now and again an officer would come to a pair of scales outside the mess, weigh his kit, and then start frantically to undo it, pull out a pair of boots or a blanket, and roll it up again. It took some nice adjustment to get all that was wanted into the 35 lb. [just over 15 kilos] allowed.

The following morning we heard a band and cheering, and looking out of the window saw some three hundred men marching up from the station. All the regiment turned out to greet the new arrivals – they were fine men in the prime of life, and swung along evidently well used to pack and rifle. They were the old soldiers of the regiment – reservists who had been called back to the colours on mobilisation from civil life. They had been down to the depot, thrown off their civilian clothes and taken up their rifles once more. They had most of them served under many of the officers who were still with the regiment. It put heart into all, and strengthened the general feeling of confidence that we should see the thing through, to see so many old faces coming back to march with the regiment once more.

For a night or two before the regiment embarked we dined in mess thirty-strong. I used to wonder, as we sat round the table, looking at the faces of my brother officers, what fate held in store for them, how many would come back, how others would die. It was going to be 'a hell of a war'.

The 2nd Scots Guards pack their kit before leaving the Tower of London for France.

All were agreed on that. There was no feeling of going off for a day's hunting about anyone. Men made their wills quietly, packed their belongings, and wrote letters of goodbye to their friends.

The British Expeditionary Force (BEF) was efficiently readying itself for deployment to France and keen to go. However, the Liberal government, led by Prime Minister Herbert Asquith, did not reflect this sense of urgency. Despite the outbreak of war, senior politicians remained strangely lackadaisical as to the ramifications of its prosecution, and naive as to its consequences. 'Business as usual' was proclaimed in the belief that home security and stability were of pre-eminent importance at a time of national crisis; the problem was that this fostered an attitude of complacency that inveigled its way into the mindset of Westminster politicians. 'Carrying on pretty much as before' was not a sustainable option but actively pursued for many months until a crisis on the Western Front rudely woke the government to the harsh realities of conflict. Not that the rank and file of serving soldiers cared about or were even conscious of any such carelessness.

Sergeant Bradlaugh Sanderson, 2nd King's Royal Rifle Corps

5 August: The scene remarkable. Met chums of early soldiering days. Within two hours was equipped and ready, 4,000 King's Royal Rifles, 4,000 Rifle Brigade [reservists] to be dealt with. My old colour sergeant wants me to stay and go with the 6th Battalion, but I wish to go with the 2nd so I'm shoved into the first draft of 300 proceeding to Blackdown. It's quite a remarkable system at the Mobilisation Store. You give in a ticket, and at once you are taken to a pigeon hole where your name and number are pasted above. There is a brand new outfit, to size in every detail, no trouble whatsoever. Feels nice to be in regimentals once more.

Private Frederick Bolwell, 1st Loyal North Lancashire Regiment

I downed tools; and, although a married man with two children, I was only too pleased to be able to leave a more or less monotonous existence for something more exciting and adventurous. Being an old soldier, war was of course more or less ingrained into my nature, and during those few days before the final declaration I was at fever heat and longing to be away … I had rather a long journey before me, having to go from a town on the South Coast, where I then resided, to a town in Lancashire, that being the depot of my regiment. During the journey to London I had a conversation with a clergyman, and of course the topic was war. We agreed that it could not last for any length of time, and I remember telling him that I was going to try and get a soft job, and that I expected to have a nice holiday.

Captain Cecil Street, a regular officer in the Royal Garrison Artillery, did not have quite the faith in the reservists that either Captain Mills had professed or the reservists had seen in one another. Not every man was a hardened old soldier from the Boer War.

The Mobilisation Store at a big depot was a very interesting sight, with a certain space allotted to each reservist attached to the depot, and in it his uniform, kit, and equipment, most carefully labelled and numbered, ready for instant issue. It was the pride of the quartermaster's heart, and woe betide the unfortunate man who inadvertently displaced the smallest item, or who unwittingly marred the immaculate cleanliness of the floor by so much as a microscopic particle of mud!

This, then, was the condition of the depots on the outbreak of war, and this the deliberate procedure that governed the training of recruits. Time was of no importance compared with the attainment of efficiency ... The normal floating population of this depot, excluding, that is, the permanent staff of officers, NCOs, clerks, and so on, was about seventy. And upon the ears of this happy little family, as upon the rest of an astonished nation, sounded the clarion call. One word, brought by an ordinary telegraph boy in the familiar orange envelope, the one vital word 'mobilise', and peace became in an instant the most strenuous preparation for war.

The first organisation to feel the shock was, of course, the Mobilisation Store. Many hundred reservists had been warned by telegram to rejoin, and in a few hours these men began to troop in from every corner of the British Isles. Accommodation had to be found for them, barrack-rooms improvised out of dining rooms and sheds, tents pitched upon the hitherto inviolate cricket ground, even for a while upon the barrack square itself. Night and day the deluge continued, the weary staff toiled incessantly at the monotonous task of marshalling a disorderly rabble into squads and companies, telling them off to their quarters, inventing ways and means of cooking their food and serving it in as civilised a method as possible. It almost seemed as though human endurance had reached its limit, when the greatest blow of all fell, the order for the permanent staff to rejoin their batteries immediately.

Imagine the plight of the Commanding Officer! Bereft of all his trusted assistants, face to face with a horde of men, more than half of whom had in the years since their discharge forgotten the first duty of a soldier, the art of looking after themselves, and trying to discover amongst their ranks the few NCOs who were capable of shepherding and of instructing the rest. The difficulty was accentuated by the fact that some eight years before the

Captain Cecil Street, 23rd Siege Battery, Royal Garrison Artillery outbreak of war the terms of service had been three years with the colours and nine with the reserve, consequently a large proportion of the mobilised reservists were men who had only had three years' service originally, and, at the moment of this calling up, had completely forgotten the lessons of discipline that this short term had taught them. The chaos existing at this stage can better be imagined than described.

But worse was to follow. No sooner had the pressure upon the improvised staff been relieved by the drafting of the more efficient of the mobilised reservists to service units, than the scheme for the formation of the New Armies came into operation, and a fresh flood descended upon the depot.

The pressure on the army was intense and not only in its husbandry of humans. It was still largely unmechanised and the requirement for horses, from cavalry chargers to heavy draught horses, was acute. In 1914 many officers were required to ride a horse, and every gun, wagon or limber would require a team of horses. The army had 25,000 serving horses and mules but this number expanded rapidly, for on the outbreak of war the government immediately ordered a further 140,000 to be requisitioned from farmers and landowners, from urban businesses and from heavy industry. Some 40,000 horses and mules would immediately embark with the BEF for France.

Captain Cecil Brownlow, Royal Field Artillery

On mobilisation, the [artillery] batteries were expanded with drafts of men and horses to war strength, but the ammunition columns had to be formed in entirety. Officers and reservists from all parts of the kingdom, impressed horses of every description, unused wagons and brand new harness, were collected, dumped together, and told to form themselves into a unit to be ready in a few days to march to war.

At first it seemed a hopeless task. When I arrived, the column consisted of the vehicles lined in rows in a sloping field, of a few disconsolate men, and of a taciturn quartermaster sergeant who sat gloomily in the mobilisation shed.

During the next few days the captain, the second subaltern and the remainder of the men and horses arrived, the latter in batches and at odd moments, often in the middle of the night.

Then work at high pressure began. The men [reservists] were organised and instructed. Their minds were turned from the ways of civil life to the ways of the army. Daily orders were issued and a hundred details attended to. The impressed horses, some straight from grass, some from butchers' and bakers' carts, some from livery stables, some from private stables, were carefully sorted into teams and allotted to the various subsections. The hard yellow harness was stamped, punched, fitted, dubbined and soaped. Hundreds of articles were checked and issued – buckets, nosebags, picketing ropes, head ropes, harness, blankets, tools of all descriptions, rifles, ground sheets and technical instruments.

The men, accommodation being short, had to sleep in odd sheds and tents, and in consequence caught colds and grumbled. The horses, tied to picketing ropes which ran from vehicle to vehicle, gave vent to their displeasure at not being in their accustomed stables by kicking and squealing, and when fed in strange nosebags threw their heads indignantly in the air so that the corn was spilled and wasted.

At the end of the week the whole column went out for the first time in marching order. Across the way a battery was quietly filing out to manoeuvre, but we started amid shouts and revilings and the crack of whips. One team in six jibbed, and three teams bolted across the plain and disappeared from view. The bakers' horses pulled themselves to pieces, the grass-fed horses sweated, sat back in the breeching and refused to move, and the aristocrats from private stables kicked with indignation.

The captain galloped back and forth blowing his whistle and threatening all and sundry, the sergeant major uttered curses in a harsh voice, the sergeants shouted in unison, and the drivers worked hard with whip and spur. But the next day we had improved, and the day after we were better still, until about 14 August we felt we had accomplished the impossible and were at last ready for the field.

6 August to 11 August: Time occupied in training and route marching. Colonel says he has never seen such a well set-up battalion. General Hutton and the King inspected us today. Was quite impressive. We were told that we had no reputation to make, but one to keep. Issued out with ball ammunition, this means business. We are off tomorrow.

Sergeant Bradlaugh Sanderson, 2nd King's Royal Rifle Corps

Ten days after the order to mobilise, four infantry divisions and one cavalry division of the British Expeditionary Force were ready to set sail for the French ports of Le Havre and Boulogne. All pre-war preparations for such a deployment had been worked out meticulously and in their execution the army had proved itself ready. The one thing that was at odds with normal peacetime routine was the absence of family or friends to see the men off at the ports, closed to the public for reasons of security.

Second Lieutenant Arnold Gyde, 2nd South Staffordshire Regiment

No cheers, no handkerchiefs, no bands. Nothing that even suggested the time-honoured scene of soldiers leaving home to fight the Empire's battles. Parade was at midnight. Except for the lighted windows of the barracks, and the rush of hurrying feet, all was dark and quiet. It was more like ordinary night operations than the dramatic departure of a unit of the First British Expeditionary Force to France. As the battalion swung into the road, I could not help thinking that this was indeed a queer send-off. A few sergeants' wives, standing at the corner of the parade ground, were saying goodbye to their friends as they passed. 'Goodbye, Bill'; 'Good luck, Sam!' Not a hint of emotion in their voices. One might have thought that husbands and fathers went away to risk their lives in war every day of the week. And if the men were at all moved at leaving what had served for their home, they hid it remarkably well.

Captain Cecil Brownlow, Royal Field Artillery

Early next morning, before the sun had risen, I was mounted on my charger, making my way to the field where the column lay. A white mist clung to the ground and a delicious freshness tinged the air. When I arrived I found the section ready and waiting, and, having carefully inspected the loaded wagons, the steady horses and silent accoutred men, I shouted a command, the drivers' whips moved together, the horses leant forward to the breast-collar, and the long line moved across the grassy plain to the straight white road which led to the supreme adventure.

On approaching the station, I trotted ahead and received instructions from the regimental transport officer as to the entrainment. The men were divided into two parties, the one loaded the vehicles on to open trucks, and the other boxed the horses. After an hour and a half's hard work everything was aboard except one refractory young cob, whom neither coaxings nor blows could urge into the cattle truck. The matter was getting desperate, when the farrier and a burly shoeing smith each passed a thick arm about the horse's quarters, gripped hands, and, with an immense heave, lifted the startled animal off its feet, and shot it into the truck.

After the men were aboard, and after a last inspection of the horses, who, packed close together, stood gazing inquiringly about them with great brown eyes, I entered my compartment, and in a few minutes the prosaic little station and the bare downs were slipping rapidly away. Sitting in that railway carriage I watched the English country in the full bloom of summer, sweeping past the windows, now deep pasture land, now an old manor house with shaven lawn and dark cedar tree, now a quaint and mellow village clustering about a grey church tower, and I found it hard to believe that the shadow of war had indeed fallen upon our land.

Towards noon we arrived at Southampton, passed through a mass of sidings and warehouses, and eventually pulled up in an open shed, at the

The 11th Hussars arrive at the port of Le Havre, 16 August 1914. The arrival of the British Expeditionary Force (BEF) was greeted with wild enthusiasm by civilians.

far end of which was the quay and the slab sides of a transport. Hardly had the train stopped than an excited officer with 'Embarkation Staff' on an armband appeared from nowhere, and in a disagreeable voice said, 'Hurry up, please, and get your unit out. I can't have the train waiting here all day.' Indignantly, I pointed out that we had not arrived ten seconds, and that we had no orders where the men and horses were to go.

'Oh, get them in that part of the shed, I'll have your vehicles unloaded with a gang of dockhands.' In a pleasanter voice he added, 'I'm worked off my feet', and then he vanished as he had come. Within half an hour the train was empty and had departed. The men and horses were collected in one part of the great shed, while the vehicles, heavy with ammunition, had been run by dockhands to the quayside, and were being whisked into the air and dropped into the bowels of the great ship. Two horse brows, great gangways of wood, were hoisted, one forward and one aft, against the ship's side, and up these the horses were sent, to be packed into rough wooden stalls which had been prepared on the various decks. At fixed intervals of time other troop trains arrived, and poured forth their living burdens, until the whole quay was congested with a mass of men, horses and vehicles. All through the day and far into the night the work of loading continued amid the shouts of men, the stamp of horses, and the hiss and rattle of winches and electric cranes.

Second Lieutenant Arnold Gyde, 2nd South Staffordshire Regiment

The Colonel stood by the gangway talking to an embarkation officer. Everything was in perfect readiness, and I was soon able to secure a berth. There was plenty of excitement on deck while the horses of the regimental transport were being shipped into the hold. To induce 'Light Draught,' 'Heavy Draught' horses and 'Officers' Chargers' – in all some sixty animals – to trust themselves to be lowered into a dark and evil-smelling cavern, was no easy matter. Some shied from the gangway, neighing; others walked peaceably on to it, and, with a 'this far and no farther' expression in every line of their bodies, took up a firm stand, and had to be pushed into the hold with the combined weight of many men. Several of the transport section narrowly escaped death and mutilation at the hands, or rather hoofs, of the Officers' Chargers. Meanwhile, a sentry, with fixed bayonet, was observed watching some lascars, who were engaged in getting the transport on board. It appeared that the wretched fellows, thinking that they were to be taken to France and forced to fight the Germans, had deserted to a man on the previous night, and had had to be routed out of their hiding places in Southampton. Not that such a small thing as that could upset for one moment the steady progress of the embarkation of the army. It was like a huge, slowly moving machine; there was a hint of the inexorable in its exactitude. Nothing had been forgotten – not even eggs for the officers' breakfast in the captain's cabin.

No sooner had we left our moorings than we ran down a lighter, killing one man on her and knocking a big hole in her side. None of us below had the slightest idea of what was happening; all we heard was an awful noise, with the lowering of the anchor. We all declared that we had been either mined or torpedoed; but after a while things quietened down, and we all tried to obtain a little sleep.

Private Frederick Bolwell, 1st Loyal North Lancashire Regiment

There had been issued to us on starting seven-pound tins of jam with our other rations. One was placed near the spot I had made for myself to sleep in. It was one of the darkest parts of the hold; and, being tired, I was soon fast asleep. On awakening next morning, to my horror I found myself covered from head to foot in jam, a sorry plight indeed, as we were not allowed to carry more kit than what we stood up in. However, after fighting for a few drops of cold tea, which had to satisfy me for a breakfast, and an hour in the sun and wind on deck, I had become perfectly dry, but my clothes were as stiff as a board. All I could do was to cheerfully declare that at any rate my armour was perhaps more bullet-proof than before.

My servant woke me with a heavy hand on my shoulder and a 'Time to get up, sir; party with an 'ose workin' this way'. I found myself stiff and sore lying in an alleyway, while about me were other prostrate officers yawning and stretching and cursing at the hardness of the deck. Hearing the ominous swish of water I got up hurriedly and went to the upper deck, where around was an unbroken circle of calm waters with never a sign of another vessel. Thus alone, strangely alone, in perfect weather we crossed the Channel as if we were on a pleasure cruise … Uneventfully the day passed, until about four o'clock amid a murmur of excitement we saw the coast of France,

Captain Cecil Brownlow, Royal Field Artillery

A Frenchman warmly greets a surprised Tommy after the BEF's arrival in France.

which gradually grew more and more distinct until we could distinguish the houses of Havre climbing up the cliffs and the great white building of the Casino. In the offing were anchored transport after transport heaving to the swell.

We waited some time for the tide and a pilot, and then as the sun was setting we glided through a lock into the vast docks of Havre … Two tugs towed us across the water to our berth, where on the wharfside was a knot of French Territorial soldiers, bearded, middle-aged men dressed in little kepis, long dark blue coats looped back at the knees and red baggy trousers. They looked curiously at the sunburnt faces of the Tommies crammed along the ship's side, who in turn looked curiously at them. Suddenly a voice shouted:

''Ave a cig, mate.'

And a packet of Woodbines curved in the air and fell at the foot of one of the Frenchmen, who stooped and picked it up, saying, 'Merci, Monsieur.'

Lieutenant Aubrey Herbert, 1st Irish Guards

As we came in, the French soldiers tumbled out of their barracks and came to cheer us. Our men had never seen foreign uniforms before, and roared with laughter at their colours. Stephen Burton of the Coldstream Guards rebuked his men. He said: 'These French troops are our allies; they are going to fight with us against the Germans.' Whereupon one man said: 'Poor chaps, they deserve to be encouraged', and took off his cap and waved it and shouted 'Vive l'Empereur!' He was a bit behind the times.

Captain Cecil Brownlow, Royal Field Artillery

The means of unloading were inadequate, for the French cranes were unable to lift the ammunition wagons and guns, so that all the vehicles had to be laboriously unshipped by winches and derricks on the ship itself. Besides this misfortune there was only one horse brow, and that was not in position until darkness had set in.

By the blue white light of sizzling arc lamps we toiled. The turmoil and confusion of the embarkation were repeated and augmented. Hour after hour passed and ever the noise of shouts, of commands, of stamping horses, and of rattling winches resounded along the wharfside, and ever men hurried up and down the gangways or heaved at vehicles on the quay.

In the small hours of the morning, while the busy uproar still continued, I felt my eyes grow heavy with sleep and my whole body ache with sheer fatigue. I knew if I sat down an instant I should fall asleep, so I kept mechanically at work, feeling as if I were in a nightmare and that the scene about me was but the vision of a distorted mind. However, by seven o'clock next morning the disembarkation was complete, and we filed out of the docks, tired and unshaven, with our buttons dull and the steel work of the harness rusty from the sea air. Our orders were to go to a rest camp on some high ground above the town of Havre, so we rumbled through the tortuous cobbled streets, decorated with French and English flags.

This was one of the first, if not the very first, landing of British troops in France, and to the French it was a novelty, calling for a tremendous display of open-armed welcome. Children rushed from the houses, and fell upon the men crying for 'souvenirs'. Ladies pursued them with basins full of wine and what they were pleased to call beer. Men were literally carried from the ranks, under the eyes of their officers, and borne in triumph into houses and inns. What with the heat of the day and the heaviness of the equipment and the after-effects of the noisome deck, the men could scarcely be blamed for availing themselves of such hospitality, though to drink intoxicants on the march is suicidal. Men 'fell out', first by ones and twos, then by whole half-dozens and dozens. I was scarcely strong enough to stagger up the long hills at the back of the town, let alone worry about my men. The Colonel was aghast, and very furious. He couldn't understand it. (He was riding.)

Second Lieutenant Arnold Gyde, 2nd South Staffordshire Regiment

It was now quite dark, and, for what seemed whole nights, we sat wearily waiting while the horses were taken off the transport. We made one vain dash for our quarters, but found only an enormous warehouse, strangely lit, full of clattering wagons and restive horses. We watched with wonder a battery clank out into the night, and then returned sleepily to the

Corporal William Watson, 5th Signal Company, Royal Engineers

wharf-side. Very late we found where we were to sleep, a gigantic series of wool warehouses. The warehouses were full of wool and the wool was full of fleas. We were very miserable, and a little bread and wine we managed to get hold of hardly cheered us at all. I feared the fleas, and spread a waterproof sheet on the bare stones outside. I thought I should not get a wink of sleep on such a Jacobean resting-place, but, as a matter of fact, I slept like a top, and woke in the morning without even an ache. But those who had risked the wool …!

We breakfasted off the strong, sweet tea that I have grown to like so much, and some bread, butter, and chocolate we bought off a smiling old woman at the warehouse gates. Later in the morning we were allowed into the town. First, a couple of us went into a café to have a drink, and when we came out we found our motorcycles garlanded with flowers. Everywhere we went we were the gods of a very proper worship, though the shopkeepers in their admiration did not forget to charge. We spent a long, lazy day in lounging through the town, eating a lot of little meals and in visiting the public baths – the last bath I was to have, if I had only known it, for a month.

The BEF did not rush from the Channel ports but began moving by easy stages through northern France in the general direction of Belgium. All the way, the men were welcomed and in larger towns such as Arras, the Mayor and other civic dignitaries turned out with bouquets of flowers while French soldiers formed guards of honour. Chocolates and sweets were handed out liberally to the British soldiers by cheering civilians. No one was thinking too much about when and in what numbers they would eventually meet the Germans.

Second Lieutenant Arnold Gyde, 2nd South Staffordshire Regiment

The battalion found itself at length in the theatre of operations. Peace reigned for the next five days, the last taste of careless days that so many of those poor fellows were to have. A route march generally occupied the mornings, and a musketry parade the evenings. Meanwhile, the men were rapidly accustoming themselves to the new conditions. The officers occupied themselves with polishing up their French, and getting a hold upon the reservists who had joined the battalion on mobilisation. The

French did everything in their power to make the battalion at home. Cider was given to the men in buckets. The officers were treated like the best friends of the families with whom they were billeted. The fatted calf was not spared, and this in a land where there were not too many fatted calves.

One night after the evening meal, the men of the company gave a little concert outside the mill. The flower-scented twilight was fragrantly beautiful, and the millstream gurgled a lullaby accompaniment as it swept past the trailing grass. Nor was there any lack of talent. One reservist, a miner since he had left the army, roared out several songs concerning the feminine element at the seaside, or voicing an inquiry as to a gentleman's companion on the previous night. Then, with an entire lack of appropriateness, another got up and recited 'The Wreck of the Titanic' in a most touching and dramatic manner.

On the morning of the eighteenth we bade goodbye to Esquerries, and continued in a three-days' rush up-country to Mons. The first day we covered something like sixteen miles, and came to rest in the usual farm buildings. Before we set off the next day, any man who thought that he would not be able to perform the task before us was required to give in his name to the Officer Commanding Companies. I believe we had two sent back, one with a troublesome leg through a break, and the other returned by the brigadier on account of his very low stature. He did not think that he would be able to accomplish any forced marches we might have to undergo. That day we did a matter of twenty miles.

Private Frederick Bolwell, 1st Loyal North Lancashire Regiment

On the third day out we passed through Maubeuge. We had only covered some seven miles when a halt was called and we lay on the right of the road for six hours. While there we were told that a force of about 30,000 Germans was on our front, and the cavalry had gone out on a reconnaissance.

At five o'clock they marched us into billets, but we had not been settled more than an hour and a half when a staff officer came galloping up with orders to move at once. About four miles from Maubeuge we could hear a distant boom of a gun, and all lines of communication had been cut. A halt was called in the centre of Maubeuge for one hour, and we were told that no man was to eat his 'iron ration', i.e. emergency ration, or drink any of the water which he carried in his water bottle, as we were expecting to go into action and probably should not get the supplies up for four days.

Second Lieutenant
Arnold Gyde, 2nd
South Staffordshire
Regiment

Even in the height of summer there is always a feeling of ghostliness about nocturnal parades. The darkness was intense. As might be expected, the men had not by any means recovered from the heat and exertion of the previous day, and were not in the best of tempers. I was so tired that I had to lie down on the cold road at each hourly halt of ten minutes, and, with my cap for a pillow, sleep soundly for at least eight of those minutes. Then whistles were sounded ahead, the men would rise wearily, and shuffle on their equipment with the single effort that is the hallmark of a well-trained soldier ... A few miles further, a halt for breakfast was ordered, as it was about eight o'clock. The Colonel called for Company Commanders, and while they were away Sir John French, followed by Sir Archibald Murray and a few members of the General Staff, passed by in motors. Among the hundred and one pictures that I will always carry in my mind of the opening stages of the campaign, this one stands out most vividly.

The sun was shining, but it was still cool. On the right of the road was a thick forest of young firs; on the left, a row of essentially suburban villas was being built, curiously out of place in that agricultural district. The men were sitting on the banks of the road, or clustered round the 'Cookers', drawing their breakfast rations of bread and cold bacon. Then the major came back. There was an expression on his face that showed he was well aware of the dramatic part he was about to play. Imagine him standing by the wayside, surrounded by his officers, two sergeant majors, and some half-dozen senior sergeants, all with pencils ready poised to write his orders in their field service notebooks. There was a pause of several seconds. The major seemed to be at a loss quite how to begin. 'There's a lot that I needn't mention, but this is what concerns this company,' he said with a jerk. 'When we reach' (here he mentioned a name which I have long since forgotten) 'we have to deploy to the left, and search the village of Harmigne to drive the enemy from it, and take up a position ...'

Officers were frowning over their notebooks as if afraid they had not heard correctly. The enemy here, in the western corner of Belgium? The major's orders petered out. They saluted, and returned to their platoons, feeling puzzled and a little shaken.

Early in the morning of Sunday, 23 August, I awoke to find myself lying on the floor of the brewery office, with the captain and the junior subaltern on either side. The morning was misty, and in the yard the men, with mess tins in their hands, were crowding round the steaming camp kettles in which the cooks were making tea. The owner of the brewery – a short and astonishingly stout Belgian – was walking anxiously about, trying to please the British and also trying to find out if they were damaging his property.

Leaving the column formed up in a large orchard, the captain and I rode on through the suburb of Mesvin, where the people were looking with curiosity out of their doors and windows, and reached the Artillery Brigade Headquarters at the northern end of the village. Here, in a clean, tiled room of a Belgian cottage, the Colonel explained the situation and issued orders to his battery commanders.

Captain Cecil Brownlow, Royal Field Artillery

The 4th Royal Fusiliers resting in the main square at Mons, 22 August. Shortly afterwards they marched to the canal bank at Nimy to take up positions.

The conference being over, the batteries moved off to selected positions from which they could support the infantry. The drab lines of men and horses and guns wound across the meadowland with a clink of curb and stirrup and a flash of steel, disappearing into the wooded heights of Bois la Haut. Farther to the north, but out of sight, the infantry crouched in their shelter trenches, dug in the soft loam soil of fields and orchards, now clothed in the luxuriance of jaded summer. Already the Middlesex had seen the field-grey forms of the enemy emerging from the houses and woods of Maisières. Already rifles had cracked and machine guns stuttered, and already the first dead stiffened and paled in the grassland which borders the canal.

Cavalry patrols sent out on 22 August had picked up irrefutable evidence that the Germans were approaching the BEF in large and in all likelihood over-whelming numbers. Defensive positions were taken at Mons, using as protection the canal that looped around the northern edge of the town. On the morning of 23 August, German infantry made an assault on the British positions, supported by artillery and machine guns. Accurate rifle fire, aided by the width of the canal, kept the enemy at bay for a few hours, but as the day wore on the Germans began skilfully to probe the flanks of the opposing infantry and by the late afternoon a decision was taken to withdraw the British troops from the canal, and then from Mons. The BEF had suffered around 1,600 casualties, the Germans more, but not significantly so. This was a tiny number set against the casualties suffered in the far greater battles being fought between the French and Germans to the east, and by comparison the Battle of Mons was little more than a brief, albeit intense, skirmish. As the British withdrew, the Germans followed, and what began as a tactical withdrawal rapidly developed into a headlong retreat. Mixed up with these men were the civilians who had welcomed the British infantry just the day before. On 26 August, a desperate rearguard action was fought by II Corps at Le Cateau. It was a brave attempt to halt temporarily the Germans' close pursuit of the BEF and bought precious little time for the British troops.

The Brigade Major of Artillery appeared, and told us we were to retire; accordingly we went back along the street of Mesvin, up which we had advanced in the morning, when each window and door had framed smiling faces of men, women and children, who now cowered for shelter in cellars beneath the ground …

About eight o'clock we were joined by a battery of the brigade, who, like ourselves, were without orders and without any knowledge of what was happening. After a hurried consultation between the two captains – the major of the battery had been killed – it was decided to send out search parties to locate Brigade Headquarters, and in consequence I found myself stumbling and groping through the obscurity of an exceedingly dark night. For an hour or more I wandered fruitlessly about the strange country. Once I ran into an unknown battery, where an electric torch was flashed suddenly in my face, and a voice demanded harshly who I was. Once I was stopped at the point of a bayonet by a picket on a road. Occasionally I met straying groups of men who had lost themselves in the retirement, and were now trying to rejoin their units. One of these small batches – a dozen men or so of the 4th Middlesex – I stopped and interrogated. Directly I spoke to them they came crowding round me and formed a circle of sombre

Captain Cecil Brownlow, Royal Field Artillery

Opening salvos: an 18-pounder field gun at the moment of firing.

figures and faces luminous in the darkness, saying that they were lost, relating their terrible experiences and asking what they should do.

Sergeant
Bradlaugh
Sanderson,
2nd King's Royal
Rifle Corps

24 August: About 4 a.m., the captain came and we withdrew in a hurry. We were in danger of being cut off. The cavalry division came to our assistance, and effectively helped our withdrawal. The village was being heavily bombarded. Why are we going south-west? It looks like retiring. Towards 9 a.m. we are doing a rearguard action. The 2nd Division is fighting to retake Binche where the Germans are in force. Then we go back gradually and take up a strong position at a big chateau, and fortify it.

The house is just as the people have left it. Geese and pedigree livestock in the yards. I went through the house, and everything was in apple-pie order, even to trinkets on the dressing table. The Huns are getting near. We have to withdraw back up a spur, where it appears to me that we march up and down the road, first in one position then another. Looks as if we are marching around ourselves for fun.

In the afternoon we are in for it. The Germans have been driven out of a big house and what a sight! Everything upside down. Am sure our chaps won't do that when we get into Germany. I pity anybody doing that. Bottles of wine all over, cupboards and antique ornaments broken, and looted, beds broken, and pictures torn down.

Suddenly we are withdrawn, and go back. Everybody seems to be digging trenches. Shells begin to fly, and things are lively. Rifle fire on our front. We get something to eat, bully and biscuits and hot tea, then we all fall in and march, not forward, but back into the night. Cross the railway, get into a village and batter down a door because the owner won't answer or [has] left. The owner turns up somewhat scared, but we quickly put him at ease. He was even giving up his bed to someone too ignorant to appreciate it. Anyhow I insisted on him having it back, and we cooked some bacon and slept on the floor.

Private Edward
Roe, 1st East
Lancashire
Regiment

The too young, old and infirm are fleeing before the ruthless invader towards the large inland towns with as much of their personal possessions as they can conveniently carry on wheels in box barrows. They have no horses; they tell me Mother Republic requisitioned all their horses.

Here is a young mother wheeling a barrow containing a six-month-old babe, a coffee pot, a bundle of bedding and a few little odds and ends. The grey-haired father and mother follow, struggling bravely on. What's this? A woman has fainted over a box barrow. There are two children in the barrow. She seems in delicate health. We bring her to, place her on a limber and take it in turns to wheel the barrow. An old woman of seventy is struggling along with the aid of a stick, crying and talking to herself. We 'dump' her on the back of the wagon. Scores are carrying bundles. Of course the further they go the heavier the bundles get. The bundles are thrown away in order that they can keep up with the panic-stricken crowd … We have got to clear the refugees off the roads or we would never make any progress. It's cruel; nevertheless it is a military necessity. The unfortunate people stick to their homes to the very last. It is only natural. In fact, some refuse to leave them, with the result that they are caught in the maelstrom and confusion of a retiring army and naturally get wedged in between rearguards of the retiring army and advanced guards of the pursuing army.

We pushed on in front of the infantry as fast as we could, but our best pace was no quicker than a walk, as the track became heavy and sandy and the horses were exhausted. Occasionally a team, sweating and panting, would stop dead and could only be got along by hooking in outriders and putting men to heave at the wheels. Every now and then one would look to the north-west across the rolling fields in the expectation of seeing signs of the enemy, but the whole landscape was still and void.

Captain Cecil Brownlow, Royal Field Artillery

At length we reached the old fort of Le Quesnoy, and got on to the broad, straight high road where a number of motor lorries were drawn up, from which white-bandaged wounded were being hurriedly unloaded and laid in a pitiable row along the dusty roadside. RAMC orderlies, directed by a doctor, carried them to a hospital train which was waiting on a railway track hard by. Pieces of bandages and blood-soaked gauze and filthy rags of khaki cloth littered the road and a faint smell of iodoform [a disinfectant] hung in the air …

I reached Caudry about 4.30 p.m. [25 August], where I found the ammunition column and the rest of the Artillery Brigade. The village was swarming with troops moving into billets, and more troops were still marching in. Those of the inhabitants who had not fled watched the British Tommies with interest, and the shops were doing a roaring trade in matches, chocolate, cigarettes and tinned food of all sorts. Our billets for the night were in a brickyard to the east of the village, the wagons and horses were placed in a field nearby, which, in the unceasing downpour, became a lake of sticky mud. Liquid mud covered men, horses, harness and vehicles, adding to the general misery and shortening every one's temper. The captain expressed himself very clearly to me; I had a few words with the sergeant major, the sergeant major had many words with the sergeants, the sergeants yelled ferociously at the drivers, the drivers vented themselves on the horses and the horses broke the picketing ropes and slipped their head-collars.

Corporal William Watson, 5th Signal Company, Royal Engineers

Late in the afternoon we passed through Le Cateau, a bright little town, and came to the village of Reumont, where we were billeted in a large barn. We were all very confident that evening. We heard that we were holding a finely entrenched position, and the General made a speech – I did not hear it – in which he told us that there had been a great Russian success, and that in the battle of the morrow a victory for us would smash the Germans once and for all. But our captain was more pessimistic. He thought we should suffer a great disaster.

It was a cold misty morning when we awoke, but later the day was fine enough … I spent an hour or so watching through glasses the dim movement of dull bodies of troops and shrapnel bursting vaguely on the horizon. In front of us the road dipped sharply and rose again over the brow of a hill about two miles away. On this brow, stretching right and left of the road, there was a line of poplars. On the slope of the hill nearer to us there were two or three field batteries in action. To the right of us a brigade of artillery was limbered up ready to go anywhere. In the left, at the bottom of the dip [a battery] was in action, partially covered by some sparse bushes. A few ambulance wagons and some miscellaneous first-line transport were drawn up along the side of the road at the bottom of the dip. To the NW we could see for about four miles over low, rolling fields. We could see nothing to the right, as our view was blocked by a cottage and some trees and hedges. On the roof of the cottage a wooden platform had been made. On it stood the General [Smith-Dorrien] and his chief of staff and our captain. Four telephone operators worked for their lives in pits breast-high, two on each side of the road. The signal clerk sat at a table behind the cottage, while round him, or near him, were the motorcyclists and cyclists.

We had wires out to all the brigades, and along them the news would come and orders would go: 'The ___ are holding their position satisfactorily.' 'Our flank is being turned. Should be very grateful for another battalion.' We are under very heavy shellfire ... I can still see those poplars almost hidden in the smoke of shrapnel. I can still hear the festive crash of the Heavies [Heavy Artillery] as they fired slowly, scientifically, and well. From 9 to 12.30 we remained there kicking our heels, feverishly calm, cracking the absurdest jokes. Then the word went round that on our left things were going very badly. Two battalions were hurried across, and then, of course, the attack developed even more fiercely on our right. Wounded began to come through – none groaning, but just men with their eyes clenched and great crimson bandages.

An order was sent to the transport to clear back off the road. There was a momentary panic. The wagons came through at the gallop and with them some frightened foot-sloggers, hanging on and running for dear life. Wounded men from the firing line told us that the shrapnel was unbearable in the trenches.

A man came galloping up wildly from the Heavies. They had run out of fuses. Already we had sent urgent messages to the ammunition lorries, but the road was blocked and they could not get up to us ... It was now about two o'clock, and every moment the news that we heard grew worse and worse, while the wounded poured past us in a continuous stream. I gave my water bottle to one man who was moaning for water. A horse came galloping along. Across the saddle bow was a man with a bloody scrap of trouser instead of a leg, while the rider, who had been badly wounded in the arm, was swaying from side to side.

A quarter of an hour before, the brigade on our right front had gone into action on the crest of the hill. Now they streamed back at the trot, all telling the tale – how, before they could even unlimber, shells had come crashing into them. The column was a lingering tragedy. There were teams

with only a limber and without a gun. There were bits of teams and teams with only a couple of drivers. The faces of the men were awful. I smiled at one or two, but they shook their heads and turned away.

After the fight of Le Cateau, the retreat continued without pause. The exhaustion of the men retreating was counter-balanced by the exhaustion of the men in pursuit.

We arrived at Le Fere 1 a.m., 28 August, after marching and fighting and digging, forty-six miles with two hours' sleep. A lot fell out, but the stragglers keep coming in on gun limbers. It seems a black nightmare. As the remnants march on to a bare field someone with a lantern says 'What regiment is that?' Evidently there's a wag still left, for he at once answered 'The Flying Corps, what do you think?' That raised a laugh, which bucked the boys up, but discipline was lost when we got in. They tried to form up as something resembling a company, but it was a failure, as nearly everybody was asleep.

Sergeant Bradlaugh Sanderson, 2nd King's Royal Rifle Corps

Well, we awoke at daybreak, hardly able to realise that we weren't marching. I went scouting, and got two eggs and some milk from a house nearby. After breakfast I tinkered up my feet, and finished up this attempt at a diary. Then one of my chaps gets some vegetables, and we have a dinner in fine table d'hôte style. Our happiness is short-lived. Cannon sound again. We are ordered to parade at 6 p.m. We march on far into the night. I hear the French have let them through and all sorts of rumours. The next day or so we are awfully harassed.

29 August: Since leaving Le Fere it's been simply wretched. Same old rigmarole, marching and fighting, and snatching food at short breaks. It's marvellous how we stick it. Have some lovely corns, and my boots I have cut in lots of places. In a word we're fed up. Why can't they let us scrap them, and chance it?

Opposite: Cavalry beginning the fighting retreat from Mons to the gates of Paris and beyond; between 200 and 300 miles were covered in less than two weeks.

One consolation, Sir D. Haig is in command, and I suppose our staff officers know what they are doing. Sir J. French isn't a mug. I hear the Germans are trying to overwhelm us. The Bays had a beautiful charge the other day, but A Battery got cut up a bit. They saved the guns, though.

Private Frederick
Bolwell, 1st Loyal
North Lancashire
Regiment

This running away from the enemy could not be stood at any price, and the constant cry was: 'Why don't we stand and fight them? What are we afraid of? If you bring us here to fight, let's fight otherwise put us all on a boat and dump us down in England.'

On several occasions we passed food supplies left on the roadside for the Germans: whole cheeses, tins of mustard, one of which I carried for four days, but, on getting nothing to eat with it, I threw it away. Various bulletins were issued during that retirement, I suppose to cheer up the troops. One I remember contained the report of a German who had been taken prisoner, and who had upon him a diary, which according to the bulletin declared that the German army was starving. Another, a very strong rumour, went the rounds, to the effect that we were doing a strategic retirement for the purpose of drawing the main body of the German army into France, whilst the Russians came in on the east. Two days after that, a report was out that the Russians were marching on Berlin, and were within a few days' march of the capital itself. Imagine our feelings, our delight. Remember, we were absolutely cut off from all outside news. What were we to think?

Lance Corporal
Arthur Cook, 1st
Somerset Light
Infantry

30 August: This retirement would almost seem to be beyond the possibilities of a human being, yet it is being accomplished by the British Tommy, in one of the most severe trials he has been asked to accomplish. Some of us try to keep in our disciplined formation, but it is hopeless, there are no signs of any section of fours, we are getting along in one rabble, all our peace-time training on how to march has gone by the board. Officers and senior rank are trying to set an example by sticking to their troops, but there is no 'get up in line that man' or 'left, left, left, right, left'.

31 August: On our midday halts for a meal during the retreat from Mons, the quartermaster would have everything ready for us including barrels of beer (French). Nothing was arranged for those who did not drink intoxicants. I was one of those. I stuck it out for several days, in spite of the size of my thirst on those long tiring marches in the heat of the day. I sat and watched the boys as they filed up with their mess tins to get their beer issue, soon they would be back with a mess tin full of frothy beer and drink it all in front of me, smacking their lips and pulling my leg. This

day was especially hot and my resistance began to weaken; when the order came to fall in with your mess tins I was there like a shot in that queue, returning with my tin full and running over. I sat down and thought to myself – Well, here goes, if I get intoxicated the boys will help me along. Down it all went honey sweet and I too smacked my lips, and to my astonishment I was able to walk a straight line, in fact I felt no ill effects, and from that day onwards I was always in the beer queue.

Early prisoners of the campaign: Scottish and Belgian troops are taken away into captivity by German guards.

Staff officers would stop at crossroads to direct scattered units to their proper divisions. The transport hurried on ahead so that the roads might be clear for infantry. The ASC [Army Service Corps] left piles of bread and biscuit and bully beef at each crossroad. Every man would take what he could carry, and hurry on again. Blind instinct led them towards Paris; some without caps, some with stockinged nightcaps on their heads; their rifles and ammunition and water bottles their only kit. Packs had long since been discarded, or safety would never have been reached. The Guards alone retained their full marching equipment and paid the penalty of the strict

Captain Robert Dolbey, Medical Officer Attd 2nd King's Own Scottish Borderers law of discipline. Guardsmen might fall out by the roadside or drop dead from exhaustion, but their packs would still be in place. This absolute discipline might strain a damaged heart beyond its breaking point, but the stern rules of peace training were inexorable. A Guardsman never loses anything; he has always got his entrenching tool, his emergency ration is never broached. But even the most broken man would cling to his rifle and ammunition. That he never discarded. Duty dragged us on in front. This kept all men going who would otherwise have followed the dictates of faint heart and sore feet …

None but a Regular Army could have done it; and after the war we shall worship the gods of spit and polish and barrack square again. If ever a war has shown the value of discipline and training, it is this.

Lance Corporal Arthur Cook, 1st Somerset Light Infantry

3 September: That was twelve hours' continual marching and the heat and dust were cruel, almost unbearable. We are feeling the effects of all this marching but our platoon officer, Lieutenant Pretyman, is smiling. He found a stray horse and he goes along in front of us stretched out on the horse's back fast asleep. We expect to see him fall off any moment but he doesn't. Today's march was roughly about twenty-five miles, over roads thick with dust. We look like a lot of millers, our clothes, face and hands are covered with a thick coating of dust, our mouths are horribly parched and full of dust, none of our relations would recognise us now; everybody has a beard and with no washing facilities we look a sight of horrors. Our numbers are gradually declining with men falling out every day. Being so near to Paris we expected to see some kind of defence line set up, it looks as if the French are going to surrender the capital without a fight.

News of the Retreat from Mons and the plight of the British Expeditionary Force initiated a second great surge of recruitment back in Britain. Lord Kitchener, the new Secretary of State for War, had been quick to call for the formation of a New Army on the outbreak of hostilities. He foresaw that the war would last much longer than a few months and that an army established through voluntary enlistment would be required on the Western Front. His call to the British public to volunteer was met with an immediate response. In August the first wave of recruits, mainly single young men, the unemployed, or those whose jobs were repetitive or menial, poured into recruitment offices.

Our duty at the recruiting depots was a very amusing one. We here came in contact with the first hopefuls of Kitchener's New Army. The first call to arms generally brings in a very motley crowd. The best of the recruits do not turn up during the first few days, as these have generally some domestic or business matters to arrange. It was the 'First Footers' we got in these days at Aldershot.

Lieutenant Arthur Martin, Royal Army Medical Corps

Another medical officer and myself took over one depot. We arrived at 8.30 a.m. Standing in a straggling two-deep line before the depot door were about three hundred men of the most variegated texture – some lean, some fat, some smart, some unkempt, but all looking very cheerful and hopeful. A smart RAMC sergeant is waiting at the door with a list of their names. It is our duty to examine physically this first batch of three hundred, to see if they are fit enough to train to fight Germans. Ten men are marched into the depot. Each doctor takes five at a time. At the word of command they strip and the doctor begins. He casts a professional eye rapidly over the nude recruit. A general look like this to a trained eye conveys a lot. The chest is examined, tongue, mouth, and teeth looked at. The usual sites for rupture are examined. About three questions are asked: 'Any previous illness?' 'Age?' 'Previous occupation?' A mark is placed against the name, the nude Briton is told to clothe himself, and the examination is over. It is done at express speed, and although the examination is not very thorough it is sufficient to enable an experienced man to detect most physical defects. If a man passed, he was put down for foreign service. Some had slight defects and were put down for home defence.

Some had glaring defects and were turned down altogether. We had all sorts of derelicts turn up. One weary-looking veteran, unwashed and with straw sticking in his hair, indicative of a bed in a haystack the previous night, was blind in one eye and very lame. A draper's assistant from a London shop had a twisted spine, an old soldier had syphilitic ulcers on the legs, some had bad hearts from excessive smoking, some bad kidneys from excessive drinking, some young men were really

Overleaf: Men at an unknown barracks undertake a tough regime of physical exercise, or Swedish Drill, as it was called.

sexagenarians from hard living, and so on. They were old men before their time. The occupations of our recruits were as diverse as their shapes and constitutions – a runaway sailor, a Cockney coster, a draper's assistant, a sea cook, a medical student, a broken-down parson, an obvious gaolbird, and a Sunday school teacher.

We had orders not to be too strict with our physical examination.

Among the long lines of willing recruits was a sprinkling of foreign nationals, men who were under no obligation whatsoever to enlist but who were either caught up with the emotion of the moment or treasured some idea of loyalty born of British ancestry. James Norman Hall was one of a number of Americans who felt that, as the 'worthy descendant of stalwart warriors', including a Civil War-serving grandfather, he really should enlist.

Private James Hall, 9th Royal Fusiliers (City of London Regiment)

It was on 18 August that the mob spirit gained its mastery over me. After three weeks of solitary tramping in the mountains of North Wales, I walked suddenly into news of the Great War, and went at once to London, with a longing for home which seemed strong enough to carry me through the week of idleness until my boat should sail. But, in a spirit of adventure, I suppose, I tempted myself with the possibility of assuming the increasingly popular alias, Atkins. On two successive mornings I joined the long line of prospective recruits before the offices at Great Scotland Yard, withdrawing each time, after moving a convenient distance towards the desk of the recruiting sergeant. Disregarding the proven fatality of third times, I joined it on another morning, dangerously near to the head of the procession.

'Now, then, you! Step along!'

There is something compelling about a military command, given by a military officer accustomed to being obeyed. While the doctors were thumping me, measuring me, and making an inventory of 'physical peculiarities, if any', I tried to analyse my unhesitating, almost instinctive reaction to that stern, confident 'Step along!' Was it an act of weakness, a want of character, evidenced by my inability to say no?

I was frank with the recruiting officers. I admitted, rather boasted, of my American citizenship, but expressed my entire willingness to serve in the British Army … The announcement was received with some surprise. A brief conference was held, during which there was much vigorous shaking of heads. While I awaited the decision I thought of the steamship ticket in my pocket. I remembered that my boat was to sail on Friday. I thought of my plans for the future and anticipated the joy of an early homecoming. Set against this was the prospect of an indefinite period of soldiering among strangers. 'Three years or the duration of the war' were the terms of the enlistment contract. I had visions of bloody engagements, of feverish nights in hospital, of endless years in a home for disabled soldiers. The conference was over, and the recruiting officer returned to his desk, smiling broadly.

'We'll take you, my lad, if you want to join. You'll just say you are an Englishman, won't you, as a matter of formality?' Here was an avenue of escape, beckoning me like an alluring country road winding over the hills of home. I refused it with the same instinctive swiftness of decision that had brought me to the medical inspection room. And a few moments later, I took 'the King's shilling', and promised, upon my oath as a loyal British subject, to bear true allegiance to the Union Jack …

The barracks and parade ground show plenty of space for the men, but accommodation was rarely salubrious: the army was woefully overstretched when trying to cope with 1.1 million volunteers in 1914.

The first influx of men was followed weeks later by the second. Now married men also began enlisting in greater numbers. They had sought to safeguard their family's welfare and waited until the government published all-important separation allowances before offering themselves to the army. Frederick Keeling was twenty-eight and married with one child. He enlisted in the first week of September.

Corporal Frederick
Keeling, 6th Duke
of Cornwall's Light
Infantry

As one of a party originally numbering three, I made a preliminary visit to the Scotland Yard Recruiting Station before actually being sworn in. Each of us was about six feet high, and we were at first pressed by the recruiting officer to enlist in the Guards. 'That's the place for fine young fellows like you,' he said. We were flattered, but deterred by imaginary visions of ceremonial drill. As we were all moved by a terror of horses, the cavalry was out of the question. I had a weakness for artillery, but a musician in the party objected to being deafened. We therefore decided by a method of exclusion on the infantry. 'Well, then,' said the recruiting officer, 'why not try a county light infantry regiment? You'll like it better than a regiment recruited from London or a big town.' We hit more or less by accident on the [Duke of Cornwall's] Light Infantry, and four days later returned to Scotland Yard at 8.45 a.m. for the purpose of being sworn in.

In connection with the preliminaries to this process, some of us protested against the official system of religious classification. 'What religion?' said the inquiry clerk. 'No religion,' I replied firmly. 'Come, come, you must have some religion,' he urged. 'Well, atheist, if you like,' I said. 'That isn't a religion,' he said. I didn't want to clog the machine, so I said, 'Well, you can call me a bit of a Unitarian, if you like.' (After all, anyone can be 'a bit of a Unitarian.') 'Well, I'll write in "Unitarian" specially to oblige you,' he said, 'but that isn't really in the list either.' As we don't attend church parade till we get our uniforms, I have not yet discovered what provision the army makes for Unitarians. To avoid trouble I have decided in the last resort to go with the Presbyterians. After being sworn in and receiving our first day's pay, we were sent off to the regimental depot, a train journey of some seven hours.

While many men flocked to Kitchener's Army, others who had served as pre-war Territorials naturally remained with the units they had served in part-time and the good friends they had made. One Territorial battalion, the 28th London Regiment, was known as the Artists' Rifles. This had been formed in 1859 as Rifle Volunteers and encompassed professional musicians, artists and actors among other creative professionals. As time passed, recruitment to this unit had become increasingly elitist, so that recommendation by serving members was the restrictive route in for anyone wishing to join. The Artists' Rifles was largely composed of public school boys and university graduates and during the Great War acted as a feeder battalion for the Officer Cadet Battalions set up in Britain and France. Two-thirds of all the men who joined the Artists' Rifles were commissioned. One was John Polgreen whose private photographs taken in France appear in this book. Another was Geoffrey Fildes, son of Sir Samuel Luke Fildes, the celebrated English painter and Royal Academician.

'… and [I] will observe and obey all orders of His Majesty, his Heirs and Successors, and of the Generals and Officers set over me. So help me God.'

Private Geoffrey Fildes, 2/28th London Regiment (Artists' Rifles)

The officer's voice ceased, and with it our repetition, leaving our group awaiting the next formality. For an instant his glance swept our ranks, then: 'Kiss the Book.'

One by one we did so, as it came to each in turn. Thus we became recruits in the Territorials. So quickly had one event followed another through the last half-hour that I could hardly realise the momentous change that had come into my life. The medical examination, the filling in and signing of attestation papers, and, lastly, this ceremony of being sworn in, impressed a civilian mind by their unfamiliarity and gravity.

'Party – 'Shun!'

A sergeant, instructed by another officer who had preserved hitherto an air of detachment, called our squad of raw recruits to attention, thereby banishing individual thoughts.

'Parade nine o'clock, Russell Square, tomorrow morning; wear anything you like. On the command "Dismiss", turn smartly to your right and dismiss.'

'How does one do that?' I wondered.

'Party – Dis-miss!'

We turned as ordered, horribly uncertain whether to salute or not. For a moment we stood there wavering, then, our civilian habits overcoming our doubts, we fell out …

Proceeding homewards, one could not help feeling that henceforth everything was changed. So great did the change in my own lot seem, that I fancied something of it must be visible to every passer-by. For oneself, during the last month, the world had turned upside down, and the incident just finished seemed to complete the final overthrow. As I made my way toward the 'Tube', it seemed incredible that the surrounding world could continue in just the same leisurely fashion as before. Surely so great a crisis should leave some token of its presence, some fresh landmarks on the scene?

But along the streets, little or nothing in the outward appearance of things served to indicate the great catastrophe which had visited us. True, the crowds had a sprinkling of khaki, but nothing more that suggested the new epoch. Buses, taxicabs and pedestrians wore just the same aspect of unconcerned preoccupation as ever.

Private James Hall, 9th Royal Fusiliers (City of London Regiment)

'A mob' is genuinely descriptive of the array of would-be soldiers which crowded the long parade-ground at Hounslow Barracks during that memorable last week in August. We herded together like so many sheep. We had lost our individuality, and it was to be months before we regained it in a new aspect, a collective individuality of which we became increasingly proud. We squeak-squawked across the barrack square in boots which felt large enough for an entire family of feet. Our khaki service dress uniforms were strange and uncomfortable. Our hands hung limply along the seams of our pocketless trousers.

We must have been unpromising material from the military point of view. That was evidently the opinion of my own platoon sergeant. I remember, word for word, his address of welcome, one of soldier-like brevity and pointedness, delivered while we stood awkwardly at attention on the barrack square.

'Lissen 'ere, you men! I've never saw such a raw, roun'-shouldered batch o' rookies in fifteen years' service. Yer pasty-faced an' yer thin-chested. Gawd 'elp 'Is Majesty if it ever lays with you to save 'im! 'Owever, we're 'ere to do wot we can with wot we got. Now, then, upon the command, "Form Fours", I wanna see the even numbers tyke a pace to the rear with the left foot, an' one to the right with the right foot. Like so: "One-one-two!" Platoon! Form Fours! Oh! Orful! Orful! As y' were! As y' were!'

If there was doubt in the minds of any of us as to our rawness, it was quickly dispelled by our platoon sergeants, regulars of long standing, who had been left in England to assist in whipping the new armies into shape.

Naturally, they were disgruntled at this, and we offered them such splendid opportunities for working off overcharges of spleen. We had come to Hounslow, believing that, within a few weeks' time, we should be fighting in France, side by side with the men of the first British Expeditionary Force. Lord Kitchener had said that six months of training, at the least, was essential. This statement we regarded as intentionally misleading. Lord Kitchener was too shrewd a soldier to announce his plans; but England needed men badly, immediately. After a week of training, we should be proficient in the use of our rifles. In addition to this, all that was needed was the ability to form fours and march, in column of route, to the station where we should entrain for Folkestone or Southampton, and France.

Outdoor life was both pleasant and invigorating during the late summer months.

As soon as the battalion was up to strength, we were given a day of preliminary drill before proceeding to our future training area in Essex. It was a disillusioning experience. Equally disappointing was the undignified display of our little skill, at Charing Cross Station, where we performed before a large and amused London audience. For my own part, I could scarcely wait until we were safely hidden within the train.

There's so much about this New Army I'd like to tell you that I shall never get it finished. You'd probably like to hear about the men. Well, they're not the 'flower of English manhood' or, if they are, I pity the weeds. But the regular officers think them better than ordinary recruits, and they really are showing considerable keenness. A full eight hours a day on parade is double the ordinary recruits' course, and they are living of course in much less comfortable ways than if they were in barracks. But there is only a small percentage of the men who are not throwing themselves really hard into the work.

In my own platoon, three thoroughly bad men and three rather bad instantly disclosed themselves even to the eagle eye of a junior subaltern.

Second Lieutenant Arthur Heath, 6th Royal West Kent Regiment

But even of these one is not really slack so much as imbecile. Not so imbecile as another man who was in the company for a little time, but then discharged as 'unlikely to become an efficient soldier'. He had only got in by accident. He was a mad organ-grinder, and, according to his own account, had been kidnapped and enlisted by press-gang methods. Anyway he has now been weeded out, and if I might only weed out about five more I think something might be done. It would be a great advantage in some ways of course to be serving in one of these Public School Corps. But the men here are more the ordinary recruiting class, and it's a newer and more interesting experience to have to deal with them. They are not – with a few exceptions – unemployables, but they are not 'gentlemen'. They remind me more of some of the Oxford village labourers than of any other class, though they have a touch of London smartness to help them. One or two are comparatively swells, but I shouldn't think that many of them have earned more than thirty shillings a week. The difficulty is chiefly with the NCOs. In my platoon one section stands out above the rest simply because it has been run by a lance corporal who is an elementary schoolmaster by profession. His military experience is antiquated; but he certainly has arranged to train his men in every way. The contrast between him and the miserable old idiot who has medals and years of service behind him is the most striking proof I've yet seen of the advantages of education.

Private Geoffrey Fildes, 2/28th London Regiment (Artists' Rifles)

Many of the parade grounds of different units were to be found in the strangest localities. Russell Square, Hyde Park, Regent's Park, even Holland Park, were soon trampled bare by the mobs of London recruits. Organisation certainly did exist, discipline flourished most astonishingly, but the appearance of these battalions beggars description. Except in the case of three or four non-commissioned officers lent them by reserve depots, uniforms and equipment were entirely lacking. An old leather belt or a forage cap, dating from volunteer days, gave an air of conspicuous distinction to its proud wearer. Caps, bowlers, straw hats, almost every variety of headgear, undulated in serpentine fashion as one's gaze travelled down these long columns of men. Every tailor, storeman or pawnbroker must have contributed to the clothing of these battalions when on parade. These hordes of lusty men, whistling on the march the newly discovered air of the 'Marseillaise', or the popular 'Tipperary', swinging along with measured step, would have been laughable, had they not been sublime. Average Londoners are not prone to demonstration, but the passage of a battalion of 'Kitchener's' men, as they were popularly called, was in those days greeted with uncovered heads. Recognition of their spirit was general everywhere, and familiarity with it had not yet dulled the first instincts of spectators. I never saw more than three officers in one of these battalions until October. Their discipline, taught by those few they could boast of, was maintained by the men themselves.

Although mine was a London regiment, we had men in the ranks from all parts of the United Kingdom. There were north countrymen, a few Welsh, Scotch and Irish, men from the Midlands and from the south of England. But for the most part we were Cockneys, born within the sound of Bow Bells. I had planned to follow the friendly advice of the recruiting sergeant. 'Talk like 'em,' he had said. Therefore, I struggled bravely with the peculiarities of the Cockney twang, recklessly dropped aitches when I should have kept them, and prefixed them indiscriminately before every convenient aspirate. But all my efforts were useless. The imposition was apparent to my fellow Tommies immediately. I had only to begin speaking, within the hearing of a genuine Cockney, when he would say, "'Ello! w'ere do you come from? The Stites?' or, 'I'll bet a tanner you're a Yank!' I decided to make a confession, and I have been glad ever since that I did. The boys gave me a warm and hearty welcome when they learned that I was a sure-enough American. They called me 'Jamie the Yank'. I was a piece of tangible evidence of the bond of sympathy existing between the two great English-speaking nations. I told them of the many Americans of German extraction, whose sympathies were honestly and sincerely on the other side. But they would not have it so. I was the personal representative of the American people. My presence in the British Army was proof positive of this.

Being an American, it was very hard, at first, to understand the class distinctions of British Army life. And having understood them, it was more difficult yet to endure them … I had to accept, for convenience sake, the fact of my social inferiority. Centuries of army tradition demanded it; and

Private James Hall, 9th Royal Fusiliers (City of London Regiment)

I discovered that it is absolutely futile for one inconsequential American to rebel against the unshakable fortress of English tradition. Nearly all of my comrades were used to clear-cut class distinctions in civilian life. It made little difference to them that some of our officers were recruits as raw as were we ourselves. They had money enough and education enough and influence enough to secure the King's commission; and that fact was proof enough for Tommy that they were gentlemen, and, therefore, too good for the likes of him to be associating with.

Second Lieutenant Arthur Heath, 6th Royal West Kent Regiment

I was put into B Company. They are in their sixth week of training, though some of them turned up later, and the programme is fairly extensive – squad drill, musketry, physical training, company drill, route marching, night operations, and a few odds and ends. As soon as they found I knew how to form fours they put me in control of the platoon, fortunately under one of their regular officers who was recalled from the transport ship at Southampton to command this company, and I have been spending a good deal of the week in learning the general control of my platoon: inspecting their feet and their boots and their rifles and their dinners and their invisible

Above: On the rifle ranges in Devon: an instructor shows a recruit in the 11th Devonshire Regiment how to shoot accurately.

Right: A young officer of the King's Own Scottish Borderers tries out his Short Rifle Magazine Lee-Enfield.

toothbrushes, urging doctors to discharge a man with only one kidney, signing their passes for Saturday night, looking after blankets and boot polish, recovering marriage certificates for a man who could not get his separation allowance, and all sorts of little details like that. Military discipline is a queer thing and I do not altogether jump to it.

If you are a second lieutenant your lot depends a good deal on the temper of your Commanding Officer – luckily mine is suave. But the other side is what you have to insist on in other people. I shall soon be saying to men, as my captain said the other day to one unfortunate creature who had fallen out during a route march – 'There's no such thing as falling out on march. In my regiment no man ever falls out unless he falls down unconscious.' I find it difficult to talk like that at present, but no doubt it will come with practice. The route marching, by the way, was pretty good. We did twelve or thirteen miles between 9.30 and 2 [p.m.], and could certainly have marched seventeen miles in the day without too great an effort. As far as I gather no ordinary recruits would do anything like as well.

Bayonet fighting is a highly amusing pastime – if you stand by and watch other men doing it. It is a very breathless form of exercise, and a very dangerous one – more especially when, as sometimes happens, a large squad of men received instruction in it in a small hall. The consciousness that all around you and within a few feet of you are men brandishing heavy rifles, and not very certain of what these weapons will do in their not too dexterous hands – the sudden exclamation of a man adjacent to you as the butt of a rifle gets him wallop on the posterior – the half-smothered expletive of another as he gets a violent prod in the ribs – the crash of glass as the shade of an electric light falls to the floor – all these things do not conduce to your ease of mind, and they take much of the pleasure and 'pith' from your own efforts. And even the sergeant's assurances that all these lunges and points and parries wouldn't hurt a fly in mid-air, let alone kill or disable an enemy, don't help you much.

Private Thomas Lyon, 1/9th Highland Light Infantry (Glasgow Highlanders)

If anyone had told me three months ago that I should be celebrating the arrival of autumn by sleeping on a river marsh and getting up at five every morning, I should have given the man up for an idiot But here I am doing

Second Lieutenant Arthur Heath, 6th Royal West Kent Regiment

Lunchtime: a territorial of the 1/16th Queen's Westminster Rifles swigs from a bottle while out on manoeuvres.

it: and in the intervals I'm drilled and I drill others, I teach all men in my platoon to use a very dangerous and scientific weapon of destruction and I inspect men's boots, feet and toothbrushes as if I were a school prefect, a bootmaker, a chiropodist and a police inspector all rolled up together. I never hear any music, and I never read anything but the paper and little military textbooks. I make no jokes and sit in solemn silence while my commanding officers explain the truth. Discipline, my boy – that is what I have always needed. By the time you see me again I shall never open my mouth except to jerk out a command and a curse, and my only interest in life besides arrangements for killing other people will be food and warmth. Warmth is deficient here, but food quite admirable – and overeating is now not only a pleasure but a duty, for otherwise every kind of disease is produced by the superb riverside climate.

It was interesting to note the physical improvement in the men wrought by a life of healthy, well-ordered routine. My battalion was recruited largely from what is known in England as 'the lower middle classes'. There were shop assistants, clerks, railway and city employees, tradesmen and a generous sprinkling of common labourers. Many of them had been used to indoor life, practically all of them to city life, and needed months of the hardest kind of training before they could be made physically fit, before they could be seasoned and toughened to withstand the hardships of active service.

Plenty of hard work in the open air brought great and welcome changes. The men talked of their food, anticipated it with a zest which came from realising, for the first time, the joy of being genuinely hungry. They watched their muscles harden with the satisfaction known to every normal man when he is becoming physically efficient. Food, exercise and rest, taken in wholesome quantities and at regular intervals, were having the usual excellent results. For my own part, I had never before been in such splendid health … My fellow Tommies were living, really living, for the first time. They had never before known what it means to be radiantly, buoyantly healthy.

Private James Hall, 9th Royal Fusiliers (City of London Regiment)

Not every battalion was as well fed, not every battalion as well catered for. Men complained about irregular pay, and married men bemoaned the slow payment of separation allowances to their families back home, darkly threatening to desert if matters did not improve. Kit of almost every kind remained thin on the ground and even in December there were plenty of men who had seen nothing more than a cap, puttees and boots, sometimes an old coat perhaps with buttons missing. Living in bell tents cheek by jowl with comrades of every hue had been all right in the summer; it was acceptable even as the leaves fell from autumnal trees. But as the days closed in and the first frosts arrived, so the glossy sheen of soldiering was tarnished. Huts were being built but not at the speed required. Men sloshed around in ankle-deep mud, tents leaked and comrades no longer seemed such mates for life.

Gunner Cecil
Longley, B Battery,
South Midland
Brigade, Royal
Field Artillery
(Territorial)

Last night I was on picket [duty] on the horse lines again. It comes round oftener now. Rain, high wind and cold, each in superlative degree, made it the most miserable night we have yet spent, and without wishing the horses any serious harm we wished they would all drop down dead to save further trouble. Twice the ground ropes burst on which thirty horses were strung; luckily the rain was beating down so hard they were too miserable to stampede, but it was an hour's job in the pitchy blackness untying the wet knots and releasing the horses from the rope, tying them up again to guns and wagons, splicing the rope and once more re-tethering with our hands as numb as stones. One or two tried to bite and kick, but on picket you don't feel like a merciful man who is merciful to his beast, and they got badly tickled up for their trouble.

We feel rather sore that Kitchener's Army is being better equipped than our own. We have no uniform yet … consequently we have no change of clothes and are still in thin summer flannels, and frequently get wet through and have to let them dry on our bodies. This is not grousing but just airing facts of very poor management … Another thing is that we have only had ten shillings pay advanced out of nearly thirty-five shillings due; they don't pay regularly at all, and we are not to get *any* this Friday, but to get another advance next Friday. I should be glad to feel the War Office authorities, also the government MPs and officials, were receiving only one-quarter of what was due to them and an indefinite promise of a little more to be advanced in a few days. The RFAs, [Royal Field Artillery] other than the newly arrived recruits, have almost been in a state of mutiny, as we have a beast of a Colonel, and they have been at meal-times shouting in chorus, to the tune of 'Holy, holy, holy', the song:

Starving, starving, starving, always bloody well starving,
From reveille to lights out we're always bloody starving
Starving, starving, starving, always bloody well starving.
We shall be glad when our time's up, we'll starve no bloody more.

These fellows, I may say, are those who have *not* volunteered for foreign service. The Colonel in addressing them, before we came, said that 'they might think of their wives and children; but damn your wives and damn your children, if you put them before your country, you deserve to be called "cowards". This upset them, and a lot refused to volunteer who might have done.

As the Territorial Force was established for home service only, on the outbreak of war each Territorial would have to agree to serve overseas and could not be compelled. Not every man in every battalion was amenable, particularly those who had family and business commitments. A number of Territorial units struggled to reach the numbers required when the order came to proceed overseas and many relied on boys under the permitted age to go on active service.

Our little story of misfortune continues daily. We were under canvas till 3 December. We then came into huts here, and, after a desperate struggle with them, we are now leaving them for billets. The huts were badly built and not half finished. The rain comes in through the roof and the windows, and the leaks have become worse and worse, till now it rains as fast inside as out in some places, and drips everywhere. Also, it does this every day now for a fortnight. It is a dreadful waste of money over the huts, which we probably shan't be able to occupy till February now – about a month or six weeks before we are sent off to France. But there's really nothing for it. Neither the health nor the morale of the troops can stand against winter in wooden shower baths sunk in a quagmire of mud.

Second Lieutenant Arthur Heath, 6th Royal West Kent Regiment

It isn't pleasant to awaken from a dream of peace and home and discover that your shoulders are cold and clammy and your blankets sodden. Drip-drip-drip! You move your head slightly and a big drop of water hits you – splosh! – in the eye – and then another – and another. That refreshes you and thoroughly awakens you, and you sit up amid your blankets, and your head strikes the canvas of the tent, and immediately the dripping of rain increases in volume. You put up your hand to the spot where the water is coming through and run it down the canvas so that the water may find a channel to the foot of the tent instead of creating a miniature Niagara just over you. And in doing this you discover that the rain has caused the canvas to tighten considerably.

Private Thomas Lyon, 1/9th Highland Light Infantry (Glasgow Highlanders)

You wonder if you should bother to rise and go outside and slacken the guy ropes. This course calls for a good deal of courage, for the night air is chilly. You cannot summon up the necessary courage, so you lie still in the hope that somebody else will do the needful. Nobody moves. At last you mutter, 'The selfish pigs! Won't do a thing to help themselves. They'd lie and sleep even if the tent went on fire. Always me that gets the dirty work!' And you rise and stumble over the inanimate forms of your comrades towards the tent flap. It takes you ten minutes to undo this, and you inwardly curse the man who tied it – then suddenly remember that it was yourself, and start to cursing the others for lazy, useless dogs. Immediately you step outside a sheet of water is shaken from the flap, and gets you on the neck, and it trickles down your spine and you feel mad. A moment later you stub your big toe violently against a tent peg and you feel madder still. Then you trip over a guy rope and fall heavily against the wet canvas, and immediately there is a loud 'ouch!' from the interior of the tent, and an angry voice asks who the blinkety-blank is playing fool tricks outside. The tent is leaking like a sieve, and the owner of the angry voice is half drowned and he'll punch your fat head when he gets hold of

Winter 1914: snowballs pepper the outside of a hut belonging to men of the 1/16th Queen's Westminster Rifles.

you, etc., etc. And as you slacken the guy ropes you think thoughts about man's inhumanity to man, and you are the chief mourner among all the countless thousands whom man's inhumanity makes to mourn.

You are cold and wet and miserable, and sleep has forsaken you, yet when you re-enter the tent and awaken your messmates to tell them of your altruism and of the service you have rendered them they don't seem a bit grateful. And when you descant on your miserable wet condition the only consolation you have thrown at you is, 'Serves ye right. Ye should never hae jined!'

The Retreat from Mons had been a heroic shambles but despite the best efforts of the pursuing German army, the BEF remained largely intact when, on 6 September, the German advance was brought to a juddering halt. German soldiers were exhausted, too, their supply lines woefully overextended. When the French launched a surprise counter-attack on the right flank of the German army, the effect was immediate, forcing the Germans to retire onto the first defendable position, a ridge known as the Chemin des Dames, north of the River Aisne. Here all sides dug in and momentarily stared at one another. Then began the so-called 'race for the sea', as the French and Germans fought a series of heavy engagements, each side moving steadily north-west in an attempt to outflank the other. The BEF temporarily held the line on the Aisne. Only as the French and Germans fought on did the British take the opportunity, with French agreement, to remove themselves from the line and move by stages, in secrecy, round the back, to reappear, much to the Germans' surprise, on the left flank of the French forces close to the coast between Ypres and Béthune.

11 September: I rather like this dirty nomad life, trekking every day, always fresh scenes and fresh faces, no luggage, no washing or shaving or changing of clothes, and up every morning at the latest by four. And the fighting is of course exciting and commanding is great fun. Things have gone awfully well the last week. The Germans seem to have lost all heart and sting and to be thoroughly on the run. Yesterday was a great day … we more or less surprised them in a hollow. Under shellfire their formation broke up at once and in a few minutes nothing remained but a mob of several thousands

Lieutenant Colonel Philip Howell, 4th (Queen's Own) Hussars

bolting in all directions and rushing like rabbits for the woods. We lost no one till the time came to clear the woods, and then poor [Lieutenant James] Sword and two others were shot dead by men they could not see …

13 September: This had to stop rather suddenly. I was writing under a haystack, in black, pouring rain, when suddenly the Germans came on again, and we had a merry little fight in a thunderstorm – rather picturesque with the shells bursting in the middle of lightning and rainbows and the little French soldiers buzzing up on our left – little tigers they are now that they've got their tails up. So the Allemands were driven back and we billeted in the most delightful farmhouse chateau where the Germans had just been, and I slept in the German General's bed – 'His Excellency', they say he was called.

Trooper H. J. Dyer, 4th (Royal Irish) Dragoon Guards

15 September: We are not disturbed until 6.30 a.m. when a large shell burst on the road among the transport and some artillery, killing five and injuring twelve men besides killing eight horses and smashing up a gun completely. Had a very narrow escape here; happened to be behind a haystack when a shell burst on the other side. It set fire to the rick. We then retired to a large private park (Madame Caillaux's) and put up in the house. We are still at the house – a beautiful place, but gradually being blown to bits … Shells are falling – about twenty per minute – and many are dropping in the field next to us. One has just struck a cow and blown it up. We are off saddled, and I've just cooked some bacon, made some tea and pinched a pot of jam – so I am in for a good blow-out if the shells don't get too uncomfortable. I hear our orders are to capture their position at any cost. About five hundred more Germans have just been marched down the road. Damn! Just because one shell came rather close, we have to move up into the park – and I've not yet finished my tea!

22 September: Back again to support the infantry. Shells again dropping uncomfortably close. Am waiting for orders under the shelter of a hill. A horse that was struck by a Lyddite shell lies very close here. Its forequarters are completely blown away, and a large piece about the size of a saucepan is blown out of the centre of its back. God only knows what happened to its rider. A grave under a tree has also been blown open, exposing the man who was buried there. The smell here is awful.

30 September: Got shelled out of billets. Their big guns had found us out. Shells did much damage; killed eighteen and wounded thirty of the 9th Lancers. One fellow was blown completely to pieces, while another had seventy-eight wounds. Another fellow who was not quite dead was bandaged from his toes to his head. A sack brought up to the hospital on a barrow was believed to contain two bodies, but they were not sure whether two or three – they were so mutilated.

We had been in our billets in the village behind the Aisne a week when the order came to move. It came suddenly one evening at seven o'clock, as orders do at the front, and by 7.30 we were on the march. Where to, why, or for how long no one had any idea. Perhaps we were moving to a threatened point of the line, perhaps troops were being concentrated for an attack, perhaps the whole division, which had suffered heavily since the outbreak of war, was being replaced by a fresh division and was being sent back to the base to refit, reorganise and fill its gaps. As we marched along we attempted to make deductions from the direction we were taking. One thing was plain: the road led directly back from the line of the river [Aisne] and the enemy …

Captain Arthur Mills, 1st Duke of Cornwall's Light Infantry

The result of a shell landing among troops of the Welsh Regiment, at Kruisstraat, south of Ypres.

The 1/14th London Scottish during their brief sojourn at Fère-en-Tardenois on the Aisne, September 1914.

The battalion entraining for the trip north to Abbeville. The battalion would take part in one of the epic confrontations with the enemy at Messines, 31 October – the first territorial battalion into action.

One young artillery officer was very sarcastic about the mystery which was being made of our movements – the marching by night and hiding by day with no hint as to destination – and said several unflattering things about red tape, brass hat rims, and other insignia of staff. He was an amusing fellow with his wit sharpened to the point of acidity by the cold cheerless night he had spent in the open, and I stood listening to him for some time …

Our second night march was longer than the first, and we covered eighteen miles. We appeared still to be going farther and farther away from the enemy, but at one point, nearing the end of the march, we heard faintly the sound of guns. They were the French guns, we were told, so we gathered that we were somewhere behind the French lines.

The infantry boarded trains and were sent north, the men of the 1st Duke of Cornwall's Regiment arriving at Amiens, where they resumed their march through unspoilt countryside. Very soon, though, a new name, Ypres, would enter not only the British vocabulary but the British psyche. This Flemish market town was occupied by British troops on 14 October. Within a week, Ypres and the villages that lay beyond became the targets for a sustained month-long German campaign, as the enemy sought in vain to break through the thin British lines ultimately to threaten the strategically important coastal ports, the lifeline of the BEF in France and Flanders. The British troops dug in. The destruction of homes and property began in earnest, to the evident sadness of some.

From the Aisne we travelled in the usual fashion, thirty-six to forty in a horse box, via St Denis to Boulogne, where we stopped until 3 p.m. on the Sunday afternoon of 18 October. As usual, many rumours were afloat, the strongest being that we were going on garrison duty to some quiet little place, to pick up strength once more. That quiet little place turned out to be Ypres!

The reason of our stoppage in Boulogne was that a train in front of us, also a troop train, had met with an accident; seventeen men had been killed: so we had to wait whilst the line was being cleared. We were supposed to stay with the train, but a good many men went into the town. Consequently

Private Frederick Bolwell, 1st Loyal North Lancashire Regiment

Overleaf: 12 October 1914, a seething mass of transport and infantry belonging to the 2nd Scots Guards crowds the market place of Thielt, just prior to the First Battle of Ypres.

the train moved off suddenly, leaving one hundred men and three officers behind in Boulogne. They eventually joined us, each man receiving fourteen days Number One Field Punishment.

Leaving Boulogne, we travelled some way up the line, detraining at a small station called Arneke. Early next morning they marched us on to Cassel, where we stayed one day, marching out next morning in brigade order. We proceeded via Beaulieu and Poperinghe, resting for the night a few miles north of the latter place.

The following day we proceeded very slowly, and scouts were sent out to our right into a wood on the lookout for the enemy. Evidently everything was in order, as we advanced through that wood during the night. On the way we met many horse ambulances returning filled with wounded. Emerging from the wood, we arrived at the town of Boesinghe, and that night we found billets there.

Moving off early the next evening in a south-easterly direction, after marching the whole of that night with fixed bayonets and hushed voices, we went into action the next morning [23rd].

5th Division Field Ambulance stopping for lunch close to the important Allied rail junction of Hazebrouck.

23 October: We advanced under heavy fire at daybreak, and at once attacked. It was apparent to me that it was going to be another coffin shop, which means a warm time. The enemy were in a village opposite, and they were firing through the roofs of houses, and from all manner of things. We gradually beat them back, and at a given signal our flanks closed in, and then we charged. Queens, Black Watch, Kings Royal Rifles, Northants and North Lancs. We surrounded the whole village, and soon we were using the bayonet. We captured about seven hundred, but lost a lot ourselves, as the shrapnel burst on the ground, which is the worst. It simply raked our chaps down. One fellow who got shot in the neck was swearing, and then another came and finished him. All day we were fighting.

At night the country for miles around is lit up with ruined homesteads and stacks on fire. A remarkable thing was the number of cattle grazing placidly, not bothering in the slightest.

Sergeant Bradlaugh Sanderson, 2nd King's Royal Rifle Corps

The Germans have set fire to many houses and ricks in the vicinity by shellfire. Most of the houses have been hit, places that had been vacated only a few hours previously by peaceful inhabitants. Birds were singing in their cages as if nothing unusual was going on; pigs were grunting for food in their sties; horses were neighing for fodder; remains of a hasty meal are left on the table and hot embers are still burning in the grate. The furniture is still orderly except where a hostile shell has penetrated the room and disturbed it. The houses have the appearance of being hastily abandoned with the hope of returning again in a few hours. God only knows if they will ever see their homes again, or what is left of them …

We are having fine feeds off the cattle and poultry left behind. One day we had a rare stew in a large pot. We found a pig wandering about and decided to kill it but no one seemed game to do the deed. At last it was suggested to put him in a sack and shoot him. We burned him off and sliced and divided him up. In the meantime some fowls and rabbits and a goat were found and all went into the pot together. My word, it took a lot of cooking as Jerry kept on shelling and we had to run for cover, leaving the pot to carry on stewing. The best of it was when Fritz just missed putting one shell right into the pot, which threw up a lot of dirt and settled in our stew. But we didn't mind a bit of dirt – we were not going to lose that stew,

Lance Corporal Arthur Cook, 1st Somerset Light Infantry

and it turned out to be excellent! I had two or three helpings. We also nearly had a calf. It was wandering along the road behind us, and one fellow said 'here, bring me a rifle, I'll have a pot at him'. It was about fifty yards off so he had his pot but with no fatal result, it just swished its tail, looked round as much to say 'Who did that?' and wandered off again, this time into German lines. I think he must have been a spy!

Sergeant Bradlaugh Sanderson, 2nd King's Royal Rifle Corps

25 October: In Ypres. It is a lovely town, and one wouldn't think to see the people talking and walking about, the shops lit up, etc., that fighting was going on five miles away. The Germans haven't been right in. Our chaps got here just in time. We are ordered to wash and shave, to make the spies think we are fresh from home. I got a Belgium refugee to do the needful. He charged 2½d., if ever a fellow earned it he did.

26 October: Marched out of Ypres at 9 a.m. We looked clean, and a sergeant with the Army Service Corps insulted me, and asked if we were Kitchener's Army. The answer is unprintable. That night we're in the thick of it again, and making acquaintance with the old Jack Johnsons [5.9-inch howitzer shells]. Had a charge. One old fat German at the last trench put up his hands, and said something like 'merci', I thought that he meant thanks in French, but I was surprised when he pulled out his watch, a safety razor, money, and laid down his arms. Whilst I was picking it up, he scooted, but didn't get very far. Evidently he meant the English mercy.

27–29 October: Our telegraphists tapped the enemy's wireless today. By all accounts the Kaiser had given orders to take Calais at all costs by 1 November. Three or four army corps are up against us. We have orders to hold on at all costs. That order is quite needless. We haven't given way yet, and we never shall. It's quite an unwritten law that if a certain regiment loses trenches, the same regiment has to retake them. No regiment likes the words 'driven out of trenches' after its name.

I have to see about the issue of rations to the section, and if anyone wants to try a Chinese puzzle let them try to issue 2½ loaves of bread, about 11 small tins of bully [beef], 223 biscuits, 3½ tins of jam, cheese, and a lump of bacon with a bone in it, in a wood where no lights are allowed, to 15 men, each to have an equal share, otherwise there's ructions. This has happened since the early days of the Aisne. Sometimes there is one tin of Vaseline, a piece of soap, a pipe, chocolate, a pair of bootlaces, so we raffle them. One consolation, we get plenty of food, and Tommy has always some to spare for the kids.

The fighting around Ypres intensified. If the telegraphists had really picked up such a message, then the Germans were doing everything in their power to confirm it by launching one desperate attack after another. The villages within the rapidly tightening Allied salient in front of Ypres were being dismantled and Ypres was being shelled incessantly, the medieval Cloth Hall and Cathedral slowly succumbing as heavy shell after heavy shell slammed into their elegant edifices. The Germans outgunned the British, and they had a distinct superiority in manpower, at least in numbers, for while they could call on numerous regiments to attack, those pushing forward in suicidally close formations were no match for the thinning line of regulars in front of them. These regulars were

Houses burning in Ypres. The destruction of the town was remorseless.

highly trained in musketry, and equipped with superior rifles, and their fire proved devastating. The Germans failed to break through at Ypres, and perhaps their best opportunity to win the war had gone.

Corporal William Watson, 5th Signal Company, Royal Engineers

I first saw Ypres on 6 November. I was sent off with a bundle of routine matter to the 1st Corps, a couple of miles NW of Ypres. It was a nightmare ride. The road was pavé in the centre – villainous pavé. At the side of it were glutinous morasses about six feet in width, and sixteen inches deep. I started off with two 2nd Corps motorcyclists. There was an almost continuous line of transport on the road – motor lorries that did not dare deviate an inch from the centre of the road for fear of slipping into the mire, motor ambulances, every kind of transport and some infantry battalions. After following a column of motor lorries a couple of miles – we stuck twice in trying to get past the rearmost lorry – we tried the road by Dranoutre and Locre. But these country lanes were worse of surface than the main road – greasy pavé is better than greasy rocks – and they were filled with odd detachments of French artillery. The two 2nd

A man stands in the hole made by a shell in a stone-paved floor. The floor is level with his elbow. Note the blast marks on the wall behind him.

Corps motorcyclists turned back. I crawled on at the risk of smashing my motorcycle and myself, now skidding perilously between wagons, now clogging up, now taking to the fields, now driving frightened pedestrians off what the Belgians alone would call a footpath …

Beyond Dickebusch, French artillery were in action on the road. The houses just outside Ypres had been pelted with shrapnel but not destroyed. Just by the station, which had not then been badly knocked about, I learnt where to go. Ypres was the first half-evacuated town I had entered … Half an hour later I saw the towers of the city rising above a bank of mist which had begun to settle on the ground: then out rose great clouds of black smoke.

We encountered evidence of the destructive effect of warfare. Seen for the first time, it seemed unreal and dreamlike. Suddenly, on the right of the road appeared the shattered remains of a small villa which had been struck by a shell. A large hole gaped in one wall below which was a heaped mass of bricks, tiles and other debris. Blackened rafters protruded through the roof, window shutters hung drunkenly on their hinges, while the garden was littered with broken glass, tiles and dilapidated pieces of furniture, which in their unaccustomed environment presented a very melancholy appearance. On past the villa. Nothing relieved the heavy silence of the bleak winter's day except the clatter of boots on the greasy pavé, and the rattle of rifles and equipment.

Private Frank Hawkings, 1/9th London Regiment (Queen Victoria Rifles)

Further along the road more farms and cottages in various stages of ruin were observed amongst the trees and copses. The abandoned sheaves of harvested corn stood upright in the fields. A few herds of stray cattle, already semi-wild, were the only sign of life. Moisture pattered down from the trees overhead – our breath hung momentarily in the still air. On we plodded. Now came shouts from the front of the column: 'Ware shell-hole on the right.' The files swerved to the left to avoid a gash in the pavé about ten feet in diameter and three or four feet deep. These holes soon became numerous and the poplars on the sides of the road began to show white splintered holes in their trunks, some in fact had been reduced to splintered stumps. More shouts 'Ware wire!' Each section ducked as it approached the field-telephone wires stretched across the road.

Kindly dusk finally settled on the scene, but as a result the ordered march degenerated into a stumbling advance. We formed into double file, and proceeding in this manner we eventually clattered into the silent village of Wulverghem, and were brought to a halt alongside the church. In response to low words of command we loaded our magazines, the tinkling of cartridge clips and rattling of rifle bolts breaking the silence as we did so. By this time it was as dark as pitch.

Winter was well and truly on its way. Each side continued to probe the lines of the other, but the fighting was nothing in comparison with that of weeks earlier. The opposing forces were settling in, although that did not make life any easier; on the contrary, the weather would now become a new and formidable enemy.

Captain Edward Hulse, 2nd Scots Guards

20 November: It has been snowing hard, after two nights' sharp frost, and it is lying about two inches deep, except in the foot of the trenches, where by the continual passage of men up and down, it has become a freezing cold slush of mud, and chills one's boots right through. We have not changed our boots or socks even, and far and away the worst part is the cold in one's feet at night, which makes sleep impossible for more than half an hour or so at a time. Otherwise we are keeping pretty warm in our dugouts, and are gradually getting a bit of straw into them, where it keeps dry and is warm to lie on. We get a certain amount of charcoal served out, but not much, and with old mess tins, with holes punched in all over them, get the charcoal going, spread two or three oilsheets over the trench, and with three or four men sitting round, they can get quite a degree of warmth out of it. I believe blankets are coming up, but we must get them into the trenches dry, or they will be no good at all; even so, they can only come in by driblets, as so few men are allowed to leave the trenches at a time, and of course only by night.

The three-quarters of a mile or so of slush, across churned-up ploughed fields with deep ditches and well sprinkled with dead cattle, etc., is a trying journey, and none too easy on a dark night. The first night the ration parties and watering parties on their way back got lost, were sniped at by the enemy and promptly 'panicked'. Instead of crouching and keeping stock still, they dropped the rations and doubled about the place like lost sheep, and finally arrived in helter-skelter, by twos and threes, into the trenches without any food or water; and the result was we went hungry for the next twenty hours. I cursed them to heaps, and had all NCOs up and explained everything all over again and took them out and back the next night myself.

Corporal Arthur Cook, 1st Somerset Light Infantry

29 November: Had a lovely hot bath and change of clothing this morning. On arrival at the brewery where we were going to have our bath, we undressed in a room, taking off everything except our shirt and boots, our khaki coat, trousers and cap less the chinstrap were tied in a bundle and

placed in the fumigator, and our vest, pants and socks were carted off (lice and all) for boiling. We then had to go out in the open and proceed along the canal towpath for about fifty yards, in full view of the ladies on the canal bank. Remember, we only had a shirt on and it was bitterly cold, so we did not loiter for the benefit of the Mademoiselles much, but high winds did not help conceal our modesty! We were glad to get inside the bathroom which was nice and warm. Our bathtub consisted of large beer vats and ten men were allotted to each vat, so on discarding shirts and boots we clambered up into the vats like a lot of excited kids. Every now and again we peeped over the side to see if our boots were OK for we had been told to keep our eye on them as they were likely to be pinched. By this time we were a very lousy crowd, the lack of washing facilities had bred louse by the thousand, and the surface of our bath water had a thick scum of these vermin. But we didn't care, we helped scratch each other's backs (which already looked as if a lot of cats had been scratching them) to ease the itching. We were of course given a piece of soap and towel, and after ten minutes we were ordered out and dried ourselves and given a clean shirt. We then had to retrace our steps along the towpath to the

Overleaf: C Squadron, 2nd Dragoon Guards, climbing on board a requisitioned London B-type bus that will ferry them towards the trenches. Around 1,500 buses were taken to the Western Front during the war. Army Service Corps' hessian ration sacks have been adapted to carry a blanket, rain cape, spare shirt and socks as the cavalry did not have the infantry-man's large pack.

Section cooks of the 14th Field Ambulance prepare a beef and vegetable stew in dixies.

dressing room where the girls were still waiting. It must have been cold for them but I suppose they thought it worth the while! We were then issued with clean vest, pants and socks, then out came our clothes all steaming hot which we put on. My! What a sight we looked with all our creases and our hats all shapes.

Captain Cecil
Brownlow, Royal
Field Artillery

One morning after breakfast found me walking up and down the battery, stamping on the frozen ground to warm my feet, and smoking my morning pipe, whose fragrance was enhanced by the clear and sparkling air. Above me rose the massive hill of Kemmel, which, for the time being, was free from the rude attentions of the heavy howitzers. As I was off duty, I decided that I could not pass a spare hour better than by climbing the hill and seeing the magnificent view that it afforded. So, slinging on my glasses and stuffing a map into my pocket, I commenced the ascent. I left the main road and went up a steep, moss-grown path which led through a wood of beech and oak and fir. Here, amid the silent colonnades of trees and amongst the frosted undergrowth, glinting in the sunlight, I felt myself far away indeed from the drab monotony and sudden terrors of war, until a turn in the path would bring me upon a ten-foot hole blasted in the ground or a sixty-foot tree snapped off by a shell as a finger snaps a match.

At length I reached the ruined tower on the summit, which stood in an open field pitted with great shell-holes, and the view of the country that lay stretched below me was ineffable in its beauty, its interest, and its grandeur. Away to the north, a plain, fertile and populous, stretched to the pearl-grey horizon twenty miles beyond, and in the centre of this plain, beyond the gleaming waters of Dickebusch lake, the spires of Ypres showed clear and white above a dark belt of trees. Three miles to the eastward lay a ridge seamed with ever-growing trenches, and crowned on either flank by the villages of Messines and Wytschaete, while beyond, etched against the sky, were the tall chimneys of the great manufacturing towns of northern France. To the south spread the plain of the Lys, in the centre of which, a contrast and a counterpoise to Ypres in the north, lay the ugly and industrial city of Armentières. From left to right across this picture wound the opposing lines of trenches, which marked the boundary

Exposed to the harsh winter weather: horse lines of 1st and 4th Troops, C Squadron, 2nd Dragoon Guards, out in the open near the Mont des Cats.

between the hope of freedom and the faith of power. To the eye the whole countryside appeared deserted; only here and there the spark of a gun flash or the smoke of a bursting shell proved the contrary, that here was War.

With the settling in of winter a definite system of reliefs was instituted, so that the troops could get rest and change from the monotony and discomfort of the trenches. It would be difficult to exaggerate the hardships endured by the infantry during this period, for they were without those materials and articles which time and experience have shown necessary to cope with the ravages of cold and wet and inanition. There were no boards to floor the trenches, nor material to rivet the sides, and a sandbag was a precious thing. The bottoms of trenches were mires of cold and tenacious mud in which men would sink to their waists and remain immovable for hours. On occasions the parapets on either side would disintegrate and disappear, exposing the defenders, who would gaze at each other, smile grimly and set to work to build them up again. Cases of frostbite and 'trench feet' were far more numerous than wounds.

There was not much to look forward to, except Christmas. Come what may, officers and men were going to have as good a time as humanly possible. However, no one could have imagined quite what was going to happen.

Captain Ronald Fellowes, 2nd Rifle Brigade

Christmas Day: We all went to Church at 9 a.m. in Fleurbaix. I then went out with the General to attend a conference to decide what was to be done about getting rid of the water that is getting a serious menace to our trenches. We have got to clear out a lot of the ditches behind us and cut a lot of extra drains, and thus try and divert the flow of water.

After this we went down to the trenches to see how things were getting on – in the left section things were very much as usual – everyone at work digging and clearing away fallen-in trenches, etc. The usual sniping was in progress, and the General and I got shot at when we made a dash across the open for a few yards to escape a lot of water that was lying in the trench.

When we got to the right section a very different state of affairs was in progress – an armistice was on and the whole of the neutral ground between our trenches and the Germans was covered with men – they were mostly over the ground where the night attack took place a week ago, and they were busy collecting the dead bodies that had been left out there all that time – it was a weird sight seeing English and Germans all hobnobbing together perfectly friendly – our fellows were digging three enormous graves, and the Germans were collecting the bodies and bringing them along. It was a beastly sight seeing all those poor frozen bodies lying about in every kind of attitude, just where they had fallen.

Private Bertie Hutchings, 1st Hampshire Regiment

A Saxon cap badge was given to me with a cigar in exchange for my own in Xmas 1914 at Ploegsteert Wood. The German trenches were roughly 200 yards from ours. Our Company Officer's name was Captain Unwin. The Saxons were beckoning with their hands for us to go over to their trench but we shouted over that we would meet them halfway so Captain Unwin asked for a volunteer. I happened to be standing by the side of him at the time and it fell to my lot to go over and meet one of the Saxons and a nice fellow he was. We shook hands and his first words to me was there any Scotch Territorials out yet, as he was himself a waiter in Glasgow. After that I cannot remember what was passed between us as there was quite a crowd of us, but we were the best of friends for the next seven days. We used to walk about on top of the trench or in front of it without anything happening. I remember one day during the truce they accidentally killed one of our HQ signallers and they sent over and apologised and the last day of the truce one of their fellows brought over a message to say they had orders to open fire with their automatic machines but their first shots would be fired high. Captain Unwin in return gave him a box of chocolates. And they certainly acted according to message.

This armistice went on till 3 p.m., and is to be continued tomorrow to finish the collection and burial of the dead.

Captain Ronald Fellowes, 2nd Rifle Brigade

It was too weird walking about overland and seeing our trenches from the top – after having lived in them and walked in them for six weeks underground, and when the only view we got from them was from ground level. Everything seemed so different and the distances so short when one was not threading one's way amongst a labyrinth of zigzag trenches, going round traverses and up and down endless communicating trenches. It was quite an experience, and the whole thing made it difficult to realise that we were at war.

27 December: There is no firing to our front, what a change has come over it. A few days ago we were trying our hardest to slaughter each other, and here today are our men and the enemy walking about together in no-man's-land laughing and joking with each other and shaking hands as if they were old friends meeting after a prolonged absence. You had to see it to believe your own eyes. After exchanging cigarettes for cigars they would stroll along arm in arm. Not to be done out of this little armistice, I too went out and had a chat with several of the Germans, most of whom spoke very good English. I had a cigarette off one man. They all looked extremely well and assured us that they would not shoot as long as we didn't, so I don't know who will start the ball rolling here again. Anyway, we are making the most of this fantastic situation while it lasts. There appear

Corporal Arthur Cook, 1st Somerset Light Infantry

to be no shortage of Germans here judging by numbers out here in front. This truce had its advantages for it enabled us to collect our dead which had been lying about here since 19 December, and give them a proper burial in the cemetery near Somerset House (Battalion HQ) in Ploegsteert Wood. The Germans themselves handed over the body of Captain C. C. Maud, and told us he was a very brave man.

Captain Edward Hulse, 2nd Scots Guards

I hope to be able to send you shortly some small photos of self, Pip, servants, etc., in billets, and also, if they come out, a photo of us and the Germans together on Xmas Day. Swinton took them with a little pocket-camera, and the padre is taking the films home to get them developed. If the latter negative comes out, it will be a unique incident well recorded.

We had another comic episode on New Year's Eve. Punctually at 1 a.m. [German time] (German war time is an hour ahead of ours), the whole of the German trenches were illuminated at intervals of fifteen or twenty yards. They all shouted, and then began singing their New Year and patriotic songs. We watched them quietly, and they lit a few bonfires as well. Just as they were settling down for the night again, our own midnight hour approached, and I had warned my company as to how I intended to receive the New Year. At midnight I fired a star shell, which was the signal, and the whole line fired a volley and then another star shell and three hearty cheers, yet another star shell, and the whole of us, led by myself and the platoon sergeant nearest to me, broke into 'Auld Lang Syne'. We sang it three times, and were materially assisted by the enemy, who also joined in. At the end, three more hearty cheers and then dead silence. It was extraordinary hearing 'Auld Lang Syne' gradually dying away right down the line into the 8th Division. I fired three more star shells in different directions, to see that none of the enemy were crawling about near our wire, and finding all clear, I retired to my leaking bug-hutch. I had warned all sentries as usual, and had succeeded in getting about a quarter of an hour's sleep, when the platoon sergeant of No. 12 (my platoon number from 9 to 12) burst in and informed me, most laconically, 'German to see you, Sir!'

I struck a light, tumbled out, and heard a voice outside saying, 'Offizier? Hauptmann?' and found a little fellow, fairly clean and fairly superior to

Two images taken of the Christmas Truce by Lieutenant Robin Skeggs, 3rd Rifle Brigade. He was furious with himself for not holding the camera still to get clearer pictures.

Below: Germans pose for the photographer, the Commanding Officer of the 1st East Surrey Regiment.

the average German private, being well hustled and pushed between two fixed bayonets. The minute he saw me he came up, saluted, covered in smiles, and awfully pleased with himself, said, 'Nach London, Nach London?' I replied, 'No, my lad, Nach the Isle of Man', on which the escort burst in loud guffaws! He could not talk a word of English, except 'Happy New Year', which he kept on wishing us. He was a genuine deserter, and had come in absolutely unarmed. I went rapidly through his pockets, which were bulging on every side, and found no papers or anything of any value, but an incredible amount of every kind of food and comestibles. He had come in fully provided for the journey, and was annoyingly pleased with himself. I ordered him to be marched up to Battalion Headquarters under escort, and telephoned up to George and had him woken to tell him that I was sending him a New Year's present.

Captain Cecil Brownlow, Royal Field Artillery

In December, rumours were current that we were to be granted seventy-two hours' leave, and at 5 a.m. one cold morning I found myself with many others in the cobbled square of Bailleul, boarding one of a row of London motor buses whose advertisements flared out blatantly even in the darkness, and the glass of whose windows had been replaced by boards. As the buses lurched steadily on their long journey to Boulogne, the occupants related personal experiences for which editors in England would have sold their very souls. With a laugh and in a few flavoured words they told of the fighting of the last two months from Ypres to Béthune; of bombardments that stunned the senses, blotted out the trenches and shredded friends to pieces before their eyes; of German attacks in mass which faltered and collapsed before our rifle fire; of hand-to-hand struggles in the blackness of night in which bayonets slipped so easily into bodies that squealed for mercy; of the hardships of the trenches, that were but miry ditches in which men stood to their waists in mud and grew numb as they gazed across a litter of decaying dead at the ever-growing earthworks of the enemy. About 10 a.m. the bus descended steeply into the town of Boulogne and stopped on the paved quayside. In another hour I was leaning on the ship's rail, with the salt spray beating on my face and the coast of England growing clearer every instant.

With a clang of the engine-room telegraph, a curving sweep astern and a churning of waters, we brought up against the Folkestone pier, where a train was ready and waiting. Soon I was leaning back on the cushions of a corner seat, with an unopened paper on my knee, and England as prim and neat and lovable as ever rolling by the windows. With a roar and a flash of water we were across the Thames, sliding to rest in the echoing vault of Victoria Station.

I threaded my way in a taxi through the traffic of London. I had imagined there would be a change, some outward mark of the war stamped on the face of the great city, but it was all the same as ever – buses and taxis and luxurious limousines streaming down the roads, and countless people hurrying 'hither and thither' along the pavements and in and out of the houses and shops.

No sign of war – and I was amazed. Did they not yet realise what was in progress out there? And then, as if in answer to my question, there swung down the street and past the windows of my taxi a column of men, wearing caps and bowlers, carrying dummy rifles and drawing a dummy gun. 'The new armies,' I said to myself, 'the jest of Germany, the hope of Britain.'

Overleaf: The 1/14th London Scottish resting in what appears to be a schoolroom, early 1915.

Private Ellison, 14th Field Ambulance, looking resigned in the freezing weather. His injury was caused by an accidental collision as he left his snow hole.

Ough. Remember little Belgium! It's impossible to forget it when you've got about half of it clinging to your boots, and the other half splashed all over your person.

Lieutenant Cecil Down, 1/4th Gordon Highlanders

——— ——

A Happy New Year to everyone! The Germans, a few hundred yards away, have been wishing us all seasonable wishes by turning on a friendly and harmless fire of Maxims and rifles across the intervening field, to which demonstration, accompanied as it was with choruses, cheering and a cornet playing the Austrian Hymn and bits of other things, we did not even pay the compliment of standing to arms; except that a Scotch regiment, which also keeps New Year's Day, cheered and fired with great enthusiasm. It was a curious effect, looking over the parapet: our lines, silent and dark, the men standing about very much amused; the German lines one big roar of jovial sound, with fires blazing in places behind them, and the constant crackle of bullets going overhead. This was soon after eleven o'clock [British time]; but their time is an hour ahead. Now all is absolutely still. A single shot came over then; beyond the parapet it is all grey mystery.

I think everyone would have felt it wasn't playing the game to attack them tonight. That is one of the odd features of this. There is really a great bond of sympathy between the two sides, because no one can understand the sufferings of the one like the other.

Captain Harold Bidder, 1st South Staffordshire Regiment

9 January 1915: The trench troops have established a sort of truce. Certain things are tabooed. No one shoots at ration parties; or at parties collecting wood and straw; or at reliefs. Neither side can use their communication trenches now, so that if they did shoot at parties marching openly down the

Lieutenant Colonel Philip Howell, 4th (Queen's Own) Hussars

Seventeen-year-old Ben Glover poses for a snapshot. Later, as a captain, he would be killed on the first day of the Battle of the Somme, aged eighteen, serving with 55th Trench Mortar Battery.

road in fours both sides would soon, I imagine, be utterly destroyed. Every now and again some idiot breaks the rules and then there are profuse apologies! A day or two ago the Germans sent a message that a general was coming round their line, so would the English kindly hide their heads because for an hour or so a certain amount of shooting would have to be done just to show their zeal.

When it came to the appalling winter weather, British and German troops were comrades in misery. There was sympathy in abundance for any man who had to cope in such treacherous conditions. British trenches were, by contrast with those that came later, primitive: wood ripped from the floors of abandoned civilian houses was used to create some semblance of a firm footpath. Greasy, waterlogged earthen walls were not tied back or supported and, as a consequence, collapsed under their own weight. Simple breastworks or unconnected trenches were in contrast to the deeper and narrower complex of defined defensive lines and communication trenches that soon became a feature of the landscape and vital to survival. The men were ill equipped to stand sub-zero temperatures and prolonged exposure without adequate cover of any kind. The British Army was learning hard lessons through endurance.

Private Robert Harker, 1/1st Honourable Artillery Company Infantry

Marched off at 4 [a.m.] and relieved B Company – a very small trench with no cover to it and marshy and wet. I was next to Kenneth [a friend] and we had an awful time – the snow came down and froze us – there were no dugouts here and no covering of any sort – our feet were in a foot of marsh all the time and we both very nearly cried of cold feet – I couldn't feel mine – the enemy were about 200 yards away and as the trench had fallen in from the wet we had to lie nearly flat to get any cover at all – if we moved about we got bogged up to our knees – about 3.30 p.m. I was so cold I couldn't stand it any longer so, risking bullets coming over, I started moving about to get warm and at once sank in up to my knees.

Anonymous Private, 1/1st Honourable Artillery Company Infantry

The greatest writer of the day cannot describe the wretchedness of the trenches – we exist for letters only … Our trenches, made by the French, were nothing but ditches full of liquid mud, no wire in front, no communication trenches. The only way the front line could be approached was over the open through a sea of mud and across a bullet-swept area. Bullets came through the parapet as though it had been butter. In some places the parapet was only breast high and in order to get cover during the daytime the men had to sit in the mud on the floor of the trench, and very often a man would find himself sitting on the chest of a mutely protesting Frenchman who had been lying there for a month or six weeks.

2 January: Took over trenches at Bois Grenier from Shropshires. Ghastly night and wicked trenches. The whole place a river. No sleep.

Lieutenant Graham Hutchinson, 2nd Argyll and Sutherland Highlanders

   3 January: Waded to Headquarters up to my waist. Bailed all day without avail. Water gained two feet. No sleep. Rained all day.

   6, 7, 8, 9 January: Life in these days too hideous to write. Continuous rain and disappointment. Bitterly cold.

   10 January: Impossible to cook anything. Mud, rain, sickness. Trenches washed away. Have abandoned my kilt and wear it as a cape.

   13 January: Bitterly cold night. Freezing hard. Working party 9 p.m.– 1 a.m. High, cutting wind made it almost too cold to work. Royal Engineers sent no material worth having … Rubbed each other's feet with oil. Could not lie down. Huddled ourselves in a blanket and prayed for morning.

   15 January: Feel pretty rotten. Visited company squatting under odd bits of corrugated iron and in miserable earthworks. Not connected anywhere … Legs and feet getting cramped with wet. Rub each other for half an hour every few hours.

   17 January: Bright sunshine. Stood to at 7 a.m. Allemands all running about in the open. We did the same thing and started on the breastwork. No shooting. A sort of unwritten armistice. Each minding his own business. Fires and braziers going everywhere with clouds of smoke on both sides of the line, and everyone walking about.

   29 January: Owing to the fact that the water has reached the level of the tops of the parapets of both the German and our own trenches, and snow is beginning to fall, we are sitting on the parapets looking at each other.

   30 January: At dawn we commenced work on a new breastwork line. Large working parties approach both our own and the German lines carrying engineer material and timber. The Saxons opposite the Buffs are

sharing a heavy iron-headed hammer which is thrown across the barbed wire. Two imitation Buckingham Palace Guards with fixed bayonets have been mounted, one British, one German, some twenty yards distant from each other.

Private Frank Hawkings, 1/9th London Regiment (Queen Victoria Rifles)

2 January: Last night C Company was shifted into support trenches. As soon as we had been allotted our positions, we all made for the farmhouses in order to get doors and shutters to make shelters from the pouring rain. Scrivener and I succeeded with much trouble in bringing along a spring mattress. Having made a roof of this and covered it with earth, we put down faggots with the idea of bringing ourselves up above the level of the running water. All this we accomplished with much labour, but hardly had we finished when we were suddenly removed to another trench … There are now six of us crowded into one tiny shelter, it is pouring with rain and we are utterly fed up. Scrivener is almost in tears.

3 January: Last night a few of us made a raid on the livestock in the farm, just behind our trench. Scrivener caught a cockerel by the tail, but it wriggled free, leaving a bunch of feathers in his hand. Another fellow and myself tried to catch a pig, but after a short tussle we were left sprawling in the mud. We then gave it up and started to return, but a goat persisted in following us, bleating loudly. It made a bee-line for the sergeant major who tried to shoo it off, but it stuck to his heels. When we got close to the trench the sergeant major began to fear that the Germans would hear the bleating and would open fire, so he shot it. We were all rather sorry for the poor brute, which was obviously only pining for human company once more.

Keeping warm was imperative. Where men could not be observed, in reserve trenches, they scrounged around for anything they could get hold of to burn. The war had forced most civilians to abandon their land, leaving houses empty and ripe for salvage, men carrying or dragging items that might prove useful in the front line. Tables and chairs made their appearance behind breastworks and were used for their intended purpose unless broken up for fuel.

My fellows went out one night to get firewood, and came in with a beam about 30 × 3 foot, which they put on a fire. About five minutes later, the house fell down and the Germans cheered, and we joined in. In daylight, the place was seen to be flat. It is better like that, as it won't draw fire so much ... There are several smaller cottages about, all rather depressed, some with only one wall, others with none at all, but only heaps of bricks. A lot of the work of destruction is due to our men pulling down beams for firewood after the walls have been partially knocked away by shells.

Lieutenant Denis Barnett, 2nd Prince of Wales's Leinster Regiment (Royal Canadians)

9 January: Yesterday I rode to the firing line just to see what the trenches looked like. There was a good deal of traffic on the road – carts, motors, ambulances and odd soldiers: after that the road becomes increasingly empty. I rode on and on and on, wondering where the trenches were, with McBride, when suddenly 'ping, ping' and we found ourselves about 100 yards from them, and about 500 yards from the Germans. Till I dismounted and searched round with glasses there wasn't a soul to be seen: nothing but a shambled sort of rabbit warren-looking place with smoke appearing here and there. The trenches are so close up against the Germans that they can't be shelled: and therefore there is no necessity to make them either inconspicuous or narrow. So they dig out a sort of vast embankment with a regular promenade below it – just as they did in the days of old ...

Lieutenant Colonel Philip Howell, 4th (Queen's Own) Hussars

The 1/14th London Scottish shivering behind breastworks.

As there was a certain amount of sniping going on I half hid behind a house till I was put to shame by an aged Frenchman quite openly collecting straw, and a charming little girl who came out to see what I was doing. The family have been there throughout and seemed quite callous. 'Yes, some of them had been killed,' they said, 'but where else were they to go to? Anyhow, the shooting was not half so bad as it used to be, and during the last fifteen days only a few bullets had hit the house, and no shells.'

Throughout that winter, Territorial units continued to arrive in France. One man embarking overseas for the first time was the indomitable Cecil Down, a twenty-one-year-old officer serving with the 1/4th Gordon Highlanders. His wonderfully natural humour and extraordinary verve were captured in a collection of letters written over the following eighteen months, in which he described life in France in detail.

Lieutenant Cecil Down, 1/4th Gordon Highlanders

22 February: France is a fraud. Here have we been led to believe for the last six months that it is a land flowing with fair maidens, free wine and flower-strewn paths. And what do we find? First of all, horrible cobbly roads that hurt your feet. You have to march on the wrong side of them, too. The roads, not your feet. The free wine is in reality very bad beer, for which you have to pay the fair maiden (generally about fifty years old) a wholly exorbitant price. And they don't even seem to understand their own language. At any rate they could not 'compree' my servant when he asked for 'twa bougies', which he assures me is correct French for two candles. He knows this because a kind lady presented him with a book of 'Useful French Phrases' before we came out.

Our debut on foreign soil was marked by a pleasing incident. Our Commanding Officer had never been in France before. Neither had the adjutant. So, when they saw a figure approaching them arrayed in gorgeous uniform, they jumped to the conclusion that it was some French general come to greet us. Accordingly we marched past him at attention, with eyes left, and the band playing 'Hielan' Laddie'. We found out afterwards that he was a private in the local gendarmerie. Still, I expect he enjoyed the experience.

It was a brute of a march to the rest camp – five miles and all uphill. Poor little W., who prided himself on the completeness of his kit, began to have doubts about it after the first mile. At the end of the second he presented a small boy, who asked for 'bulleebif', with his 'bivouac, portable, one, officers, for the use of'. Another mile saw him part with a Thermos flask, which he presented to a French soldier by the roadside. In the next mile a patent stove and a French dictionary went, and a spare electric light and two tins of chocolate rations also disappeared before the end of the journey. When we reached the camp we hoped to be allowed to throw off our packs and rest our aching limbs, but instead of that we were kept at attention for three-quarters of an hour, while some old gentleman had a look at us. S'pose that's why they call it a rest camp.

The next morning was spent in dishing out fur coats. Mine is rather quiet, black fox with musquash sleeves, or thereabouts, but some of them are the very latest mode. Lance Corporal McGregor, for instance, looks very smart in his leopard skin with collar of skunk and cuffs of polar bear. He is a fish porter by trade. The CO's is rather a nice little thing in Persian lamb, touches of domestic cat about the yoke giving it a very chic appearance.

In the afternoon some of us went down into the town, which, by the way, is Le Havre – the men insist on pronouncing the 'Le' to rhyme with tea, but it's a dull place for all that. They say that we are off for the front tomorrow, but you never know. Several of my men put in their letters that they could hear the distant thunder of the guns, but as we are about a hundred miles from any fighting they must have keen ears.

The tent is becoming very cold, so I am going to turn in.

We were 'dished out' with sheepskin coats, commonly called 'furries', of varied hue, and comic figures strolled the platform. Here, too, we heard first the Franco-Belgian woman's war cry, 'Chocolat, good for English soldiers'. We agreed – at a price.

After a great deal of undecided bustle, serving out of rations for twenty-four hours, and the inevitable order to clean up (for which reason some of the more unfortunate hunted the dirty platform and underneath trucks for infinitesimal scraps of orange peel and wayward paper, hiding them again where we hoped the Colonel's eye would not reach), we entrained. The

Anonymous Private, 1/9th Royal Scots (Lothian Regiment)

French engine gave its funny squeak, the guard blew his bugle, a jolt, then more jolts, and we were really off. We started about eleven, we detrained after ten the next morning – roughly twenty-four hours with thirty-six to a horse box.

That journey remains unforgettable. As the short winter afternoon passed and we settled for the night on the straw before it got too dark, it seemed like a gigantic puzzle. Legs had to be fitted to opposite chests, bodies curved to make the most of corners. Legs underneath a criss-cross clump had to be violently released for cramp and a new clump made, unquiet sleepers had to be sternly dealt with, endless arguments that fifteen at one end had the same floor space as eleven at the other, accusations and reproaches, endless turning, twisting, and writhing, and the long night passed. Even Sergeant Ellis gave up in despair, and, ensconced in his own little niche by the door, left his flock to grin and groan and dispute as they pleased. Which we did. Crabs in a barrel on their long ride to London must go through the same, but with no hope from the dawn … It is possible some slept; to most it was a nightmare.

4 March: Muddy View Villa is a leaky wooden hut completely surrounded by moist Europe, ankle-deep. It has a door which also serves as window, but most of the light comes through the cracks in the walls. Several hundred draughts swirl round and round inside, filling your throat with foul smoke from a brazier. A brazier, by the way, is a tin can with holes in it. It contains coke, which gives forth smoke and gas but no heat. In one corner of the hut there is an ornamental lake several inches deep. The other three corners are occupied by eight of us. This is a great life.

Lieutenant Cecil Down, 1/4th Gordon Highlanders

We left Havre on the day after my last epistle. The manner of our going was thuswise. We left the camp at 2 a.m. and marched down to the station (goods department). The station was deserted save for one voluble porter who declared (quite truthfully) that our train was to start about noon. Dawn as seen from Havre Station on a frosty February morning is disappointing. About 6 a.m. a coffee stall opened. It was run by four English girls and proved a great blessing. Without it we should most certainly have turned to pillars of ice. As it was, my platoon sergeant's balaclava helmet froze on to his moustache, causing him pain when he tried to talk …

Goatskins were issued from late 1914 and were found to be both waterproof and windproof. They were much loved by those who wore them, though they proved difficult to carry.

Half an hour before the train was due to start, it made up its mind to go, leaving about three hundred assorted officers, NCOs and men on the platform. We started after it on foot, running hard. It must have been quite a spectacle. Before it had gone half a mile most of us had caught up with it and boarded it. Then, again without warning, it stopped with a jerk, and didn't carry on till 2.30 in the afternoon. Once it really got a move on, though, we kept up a pretty steady six miles an hour. Of course every time we came to a wayside estaminet the engine driver descended for a glass of vin blanc and a chat, but we all realised that this was war at last and no one complained. As you have probably gathered, we were not on the main line. There had been a big smash somewhere, so we were sent a circular tour round a very hilly and altogether rural loop line. At each little station the villagers crowded round the trucks admiring our kilts and bare blue knees – the kilts I mean. There seemed to be no signals or controls of any sort on the line, and at one time no less than four trains could be seen behind us. Downhill, steam was turned off and we ran along by the force of gravity at a great speed. We tore through one station on a down gradient at eighty miles an hour at least. This must have distressed the stationmaster who I am sure wanted to have a talk with the engine driver. The stationmaster, by the way, was a woman.

The train began its slow arduous journey via Calais and then up to the Belgian frontier where the battalion was eventually disgorged and sent into what Lieutenant Down was told was the biggest glasshouse in the world. For a day or two the men kicked their heels around the unnamed town until ready to be sent up the line.

Lieutenant Cecil Down, 1/4th Gordon Highlanders

The chief amusement was to watch the traffic in the square. Very early in the morning it is filled with bedraggled groups of men plodding home from the trenches, and with horse transport back from carrying rations up to the firing line. Later comes the hour of the supply column, when the little square vies with Charing Cross. Unending streams of lorries pass and re-pass, muddy and unkempt in their coat of dingy grey, under which you can still make out the faint outline of the peace-time owner's name. Allsopps, Harrods, and many another firms' lorries jostle each other here in just the same way as six months ago they did in dear old London. A car flashes through full of 'red hats', and every now and then an ammunition column trots by. A motor bus pants along, its windows boarded up and its grey coat all smeared with mud. Only the noticeboard on the top still proclaims that once upon a time Camberwell Green was its destination. Slowly and silently through it all glides a convoy of motor ambulances. You begin to feel that there is a war on. All the houses in the main street are splattered with mud up to the windows of the second storeys.

Just as we were settling down to enjoy ourselves we were pushed off to join the brigade of regulars of which we are now members. The march was not long, but arduous for all that. While we were in France the roads were fairly good, but once the frontier was crossed and we were in Belgium they became too awful for words. For the most part Belgian roads are straight, and run through avenues of tall spiky trees, which resemble more than anything telegraph poles trying to pass themselves off as Brussels sprouts. The middle of the road is made of small square stone blocks, and has a very abrupt camber. This is called pavé, and is generally only just broad enough for one cart to pass along at a time. It is very slippery in wet weather. The sides of the roads are a quagmire of reddish-brown mud, ankle-deep if you are lucky, and waist-deep if you aren't. When a lorry comes along you have to get off and wade through the slush. Ough. Remember little Belgium! It's impossible to forget it when you've got about half of it clinging to your boots, and the other half splashed all over your person. At one place on the road there was a group of Belgians trying to bolster it up, under the guidance of a Royal Engineers corporal. I think that Flemish must be the ugliest language in the world, a mixture of Low German and bad French, with a liberal flavouring of Billingsgate.

1 April: We are in a barn here [Caestre, near Hazebrouck], 120 or thereabouts of us, together with two young calves; happily a low rail does confine the actions of the latter to a six-foot-square portion of it. But, like the barn – they smell …

8.30. Just turned in. My sleeping place and that of two other men is the two calves' inner room, six feet long by five feet broad, the two little rooms being partitioned off from the rest of the interior of the barn; but as regards

Gunner Cecil Longley, B Battery, 1st South Midland Brigade, Royal Field Artillery room we are better off than the rest, who are packed so tight they cannot straighten their limbs and there is much interlocking of boots. I remember when acting Trinculo in *The Tempest* at one of our school plays, it fell to my lot to say that 'Adversity acquaints a man with strange bedfellows'. I little thought that the words were prophetic and that I should fulfil them myself fourteen years later! Certain of the other fellows talk of rats running over them. This afternoon we had to ourselves, and I spent it buying small things at the three or four small epiceries just for the practice at French. I can get on very well myself, but either I am getting a bit deaf or else they don't speak their own language properly, for I have to make them repeat it all.

A private of the 1/4th Royal Berkshire Regiment undergoes a medical inspection in a barn in Belgium, April 1915.

Most other ranks had never been abroad and their introduction to the Continent, though frequently cold and grim, was also an adventure, and letters were often full of detail, curiosity and excitement. The most significant moment for any soldier was to go up the line. Feelings of trepidation were natural, although most tried to hide their fears. Typically, a new battalion to the front was sent into a quiet sector to learn the ropes from those who knew the routine and the potential pitfalls.

The officers and sergeants had gone up to the trenches for instruction, and we followed the next night and had our first uneasy experience of bullets flying over and about us. Every night thereafter we were out on these 'fatigues' (and they fully justified their name) working to the wee small hours. In three parts of the line between Voormezeele and St Eloi we dug trenches, filled sandbags, put up barbed wire, and each place was hotter than the last. Some nights we stood in water putting in barbed wire; others we dug in sopping trenches. One night we filled sandbags when the snow lay on the ground, making the whole scene ghostly.

Luckily our first casualty was slight, and we were broken in gently. We were digging a trench, and the man had put down his spade (probably fed up, for it was wet), and a moment later felt a whack high up on his leg. 'Who hit me, you blighters?' and he turned wrathfully to smite the joker. Nor was he convinced till he felt the blood trickling down and the tiny hole, and straightaway became the hero of the night. The rest of us found this first shock passed easily, and very soon we were wishing we might be as lucky. 'Oh, for a cushy wound!' – how often we said it, half in jest and half in earnest, and discussed with care in our slack moments just where we would like it to be.

Yes, actually here! There, visible and tangible before me is 'The Line', for a few hours I myself, in my own proper person, am holding a few inches of the Allies' 200-mile front.

After all, there isn't much to see. The country is very flat and dreary. Some hundred yards or so of our trench can be seen snaking away on either side. In front, if you look over the parapet, is our wire entanglement, an abandoned cart, a dead horse or two, a long puddle gleaming in the moonlight, and there, 300 yards away, a dark smudge that marks the German line …

I wonder if you'd recognise me now? The only clean thing about me is my rifle (that, out of necessity, must be kept clean and oiled). I haven't had my trousers off since I left Southampton, or my boots since leaving billets; I'm smothered in mud from head to feet, and I haven't washed, shaved or brushed my hair for a week. When I come home you'll have to let me sleep in the scullery …

Anonymous Other Rank, 1/9th Royal Scots (Lothian Regiment)

Private Leslie Sanders 1/9th London Regiment (Queen Victoria Rifles)

One very quickly gets used to stray bullets flying around; they make the most various sounds. Some hurtle violently into the distance; some go 'crack-plud!' as they bury themselves in a parapet; some whine plaintively, some shriek overhead and some have a most vicious hiss. Several times I have seen a bullet hit stones or bricks near me, making a trail of sparks. Then there are machine guns, which go 'tap-tap-tap-tap-tap'. Shells, unlike bullets, travel more slowly than sound, so you can hear them coming – all except the trench mortars, which give no warning but just go 'zip-bang'. Other sorts make a sort of whistling noise, not very loud or suggestive of speed, which increases and culminates in a most resounding 'pom', almost musical in tone.

A quick snap taken looking over the top towards the German-held farm in the distance. Many men could not resist the temptation to have a quick look over the parapet.

Ronald Poulton Palmer arrived in France a month after Leslie Sanders. As well as being heir to the Huntley and Palmer biscuit fortune, he was famous for his sporting prowess, for he was not only a rugby international but also captain of the England team. Palmer served with the 1/4th Royal Berkshire Regiment, disembarking on the last day of March 1915. He sent the following letters to his parents, while the accompanying photographs were taken by the battalion's Commanding Officer, Lieutenant Colonel Oswald Serocold.

7 April: This morning we left billets and proceeded by the main road towards Armentières. We, my Platoon, No. 13 of D Company, acted as rearguard to the whole brigade. This meant marching behind all the train and field ambulance: and it caused a long series of checks. We marched through Bailleul, where there were thousands of soldiers resting, and through Meteren, where the Warwicks suffered so severely in October. Then we turned to the left, and arrived at Romarin in Belgium [two miles west of Ploegsteert], about three miles behind the firing line at Messines. There was any amount of mud and water about, and the billets were very close, but my platoon was lucky in having a good barn. We had quite a nice little house, but the woman was a shrew. And so to bed.

10 April: At 6 p.m. the company paraded to go into the trenches. Platoons were taken and intermingled with companies of the Dublin Fusiliers. We had a long, slow march down an avenue road. The Dublins were very humorous all the time and quite cheerful. We were a bit apprehensive! We then had a long march on what are called 'corduroy' roads. These are short pieces of boughs fastened to planks, to make a rough pathway over the mud … We passed several ruined cottages, which are full of dead, and the whole atmosphere was tainted with the smell of death.

11 April: We all stood to arms at dawn, and the Germans started a tremendous fusilade, as is their custom. But soon after all was quiet, and you could see the smoke rising from the fires all down our line, and the German line. About 11 a.m. our field guns put twelve shells on to the German trenches in front of us. Immediately the German guns opened on us … The result was eight feet of parapet blown down, another bit shaken down, one man with a dislocated shoulder of ours, and five men of the Dublins wounded, one seriously. As they were all within three yards of me, I was lucky. The brass head of a shell shot through the parapet, missed a man by an inch, and went into a dugout where we obtained it. The shelling is very frightening – the report, the nearing whistle and the burst, and then you wonder if you are alive. Crouching under the parapet is all right for the high explosive, but for shrapnel it is no good, so that is why they mix them up. The men – the Dublins – were quite as frightened as we were as a rule, but some didn't care a damn. Some were praying, some eating breakfast, one was counting his rosary, and another next door was smoking a cigarette

Lieutenant Ronald Poulton Palmer, 1/4th Royal Berkshire Regiment and cheering up our fellows. After a prolonged pause, we rose from our constrained position, and went on with our occupations; but it unnerved me for a bit.

21 April: The work is the most important thing, as I am in charge of it, and my time is filled up with it by day getting the work organised for the night. This has got better and better, and now I have a good system. Of course it is nearly all done at night. It is curious, at 'stand to', at about 8 p.m. to hear the sniping dying down, and then suddenly the 'tap tap' of the German [working] party starting. Then we know we are safe, as there is a kind of mutual agreement not to fire on each other's working and ration parties. So out we go and hardly a shot is fired. The men betray the usual good humour at it all and are in perfect spirits … They have grown quite callous, and you hear them whistling and shouting while working on the parapet, in the full moonlight.

24 April: We came out, after four days in, last night, and immediately went off digging, after an hour's rest. The whole thing as a war is a screaming farce. This is honest fact. We went up to a part of the line near here which has a gap of 200 yards in it. Here Territorial engineers are building a magnificent breastwork and parados, and Territorials supply working parties. The joke is we are 120 yards from the German trench and about 80 from the German working parties. And we make the hell of a row, laugh, talk, light pipes, &c., and sing and *nobody fires a shot*, except one old sniper who seems to fire high on purpose; and yet when the flares go up, we stand stock still so as not to be seen!! If you were here now, 1½ miles from the firing line in one direction and 900 yards in another, you would never know there was anything unusual on. There is no sound of guns or rifles.

The Germans are about 550 yards away [from our front trenches] and are very quiet. They sometimes blow a motor horn, and sometimes sing the 'Marseillaise' and 'Tipperary'. They started firing a Maxim just before we filed out last night, but they let us go in peace.

27 April: I think they [German snipers] have had the advantage of knowing the ground. We can't trace their whereabouts yet at all. There is a house just behind our lines, and we can get there in daytime, and we have men in the roof for hours with telescopes trying to trace them. But they can see nothing. They [snipers] must come out at dawn and go back at dusk,

if they are in front of their trench. But that is not certain. If we can't find them by movement we shall go out at night, and try and see if they come out, and generally reconnoitre the ground in front. This ground is getting very thick with long grass, and will soon be very good cover. It is quite absurd to see the quite immovable landscape, with no movement of any kind on it, and yet to hear the most accurate shots on our parapet, shots which have killed two men dead in the last two days, who foolishly put their heads up in a low part of the parapet to look back. Don't worry about me in this respect. I am in charge of the work and the parapet is being raised, and immensely strengthened and thickened.

29 April: We are in a beautiful wood about 1,700 yards back. It is perfectly lovely here, absolutely boiling. I bathed today in a very dirty pond just outside the wood. We live in log shanties, and eat all our meals out of doors. Our only diversions are making various wood things, such as hurdles, chairs, bowers, shelters, and pegs and stakes, and watching the aeroplanes being fired at overhead, and hearing the German shells buzzing

Major Francis Hedges (looking at the camera), commanding A Company, in the line near Ploegsteert. Behind are the ruined barns noted in Ronald Poulton Palmer's letters.

leisurely over the wood to burst beyond us, trying to find our guns who reply as leisurely. It is funny hearing them buzzing gently overhead and then bang! Yesterday the Germans shelled a big farm about 600 yards behind us, and set it on fire. It was a fine sight to watch. Yesterday was a most extraordinary day. I went out of the trench after breakfast (you can get out along a communication trench by day) to see some bomb-throwing and then came back, watched this shelling, then a poor fellow [Private Frederick Giles] was shot and fell right on to me. Then I stayed behind to show the relieving company the work to be done … Then I came back here, and in the wood I heard a nightingale singing more perfectly than I have ever heard it before. And so home to bed in this lovely spot.

I am awfully well, and quite safe … Yes, Battcock and a man in my company have had a cap shot through …

4 May: We are now in our third day in the trenches, and go out tomorrow. We have had a quiet time, only having about fifteen shells the first evening, aimed at the house which lies just behind the middle of our

Officers at Battalion Headquarters. Second left is Lieutenant Battcock, wearing the cap holed by a bullet. Fourth left is battalion commander Lieutenant Colonel Oswald Serocold, with whose camera the pictures were taken.

England rugby captain Ronald Poulton Palmer (top left) sitting outside a wattle hut in Ploegsteert Wood. He was killed a few days later, the first officer in the battalion to die.

line. They suspected a sniper in there, and gave it book [hell]. They did no damage much but one or two fell short, and one went straight into the dugout of our junior subaltern who fortunately was on duty. Another fell into the cook's dugout, and he was peeling potatoes five yards away! Otherwise we have been very peaceful only it rained a lot, and that doesn't make things very pleasant. But we have installed a splendid French oven, stolen from [a] farm, in a kitchen dugout, by the officers' mess, and we have all kinds of roast joints and red wine and Apollinaris water! at 1 franc 15 a bottle!

Ronald Poulton Palmer was killed next morning as he supervised trench repairs, hit either by a sniper's bullet or by a stray shot. He had served for five weeks in France and was the third man in the battalion to die and the first officer. Curiously, it was a death he himself had foretold. In March 1915, in conversation with an old friend, he spoke of those he knew who had fallen in the war. His friend noted: 'There was a long silence. Then he said, "I don't want to be killed yet; there is such a lot I wanted to do, or try anyhow." I asked if he felt that he would be killed; "Oh yes," he said, "sure of it." I said nothing and again there was a long silence. Then he suddenly said, "Of course it's all right; but it's not what one would have chosen."'

Telegram from Hazebrouck received by Ronald's parents, 6.12 p.m., Oxford, 6 May: 'Regret your son killed last night. Death instantaneous. Colonel Serocold.'

Captain and Adjutant Gerald Sharpe, 1/4th Royal Berkshire Regiment

He [Ronald] will be an awful loss to us as he was a fine officer and the most popular officer in the regiment with officers and men, and his place cannot be filled again. I shall miss him horribly and feel his death acutely. I liked him the best of all the officers: he was such a real good chap without the slightest bit of conceit and always ready to do anything to help anybody.

He died the finest death any man could wish for and he suffered absolutely no pain. I saw him yesterday a few hours after his death and he looked quite peaceful and happy. We buried him this evening, 6 May, in the cemetery. We have suffered and he is now at rest.

The Bishop of Pretoria who is out here conducted the service and gave a most beautiful address about him. He knew him quite well and said that he was a man of superb character and that whenever he was with one, one felt that you were in the company of a man who was doing you good (which is absolutely correct). He also said that if there was anyone in the regiment who was absolutely prepared to meet death at any moment, it was he.

I wept like a child at his funeral, as did many of us, and the regiment to a man will mourn his loss to the end.

Ronald Poulton Palmer was very unfortunate. Not only had he been serving in a quiet sector of the line where a policy of live and let live had been tentatively established, but he had been killed just hours before the battalion left the front line to go into reserve.

As a matter of course, the army rotated troops so that every battalion took its turn in the front-line trenches. The routine was normally three days in the front line, three days in support trenches, three days in reserve, and three days in rest, although on many occasions such routine was put aside, leaving men to spend longer in the trenches before being relieved.

The rumour was true after all, and on Wednesday night we were relieved. We marched all the way back not arriving at our billets till nearly 2 a.m. We had a long halt in one place, where tea was served – close to the line and well within sound of the firing, but very comfortably in dead ground. The scene was picturesque – the long snake of the whole battalion covering nearly half a mile of road, a medley of packs and rifles by the wayside, men lying down or sitting drinking tea, a cheerful buzz of talk; all along the line the clear flames of candles burning steadily in the still night: in one place the red glow of the field-kitchen fire, and for background the sombre depths of the wood. We marched at first by devious by-roads in threes, twos, or even single file: here and there men were carrying candles stuck on bayonets' points, so that the whole procession looked rather like a torchlight tattoo. But when we reached the main road and formed fours – well, we were tired, but we'd spunk enough to set a decent step and to make the night hideous with marching songs ... As we passed through the sleeping hamlets not a soul took any notice of us. Only a mile or two behind the line – but secure!

We did not reach our billets till about 2 a.m. It was bad marching, for I don't think we covered more than eleven or twelve miles; but then we were heavy laden ... You can understand we were glad to reach our destination; and almost the first thing to greet us was the accumulated post of the past few days, neatly laid out by platoons. Tired as we were, there

Private Leslie Sanders, 1/9th London Regiment (Queen Victoria Rifles)

Above: Before the introduction of more memorable trench names, the army used a system of letters and numbers to identify the location of trenches.

was not a man but claimed his mail, lit his candle and settled down to read his letters and open his parcels.

Anonymous Private, 1/9th Royal Scots (Lothian Regiment)

We were relieved in Trench 71 by the 9th Argylls, the other brigade Territorials, whose speech proclaimed them as Glasgow as we were Edinburgh – a cheery lot. We gave them a 'good luck, boys' as we filed out and started across the open to the rendezvous at Glencorse Wood. There we had the weary wait which seems incidental when a whole battalion moved, but annoyed us excessively, lying on the chilly mud with the excitement of our relief from the trenches oozing out and the reaction of sleeplessness setting in. Then we went through Westhoek to the railway, and that put (in vulgar phrase) the tin hat on it. Stumbling along over the rails or sleepers or the edge of the embankment in pitch dark, in full marching order and a great weariness, it was a cross and sleepy battalion that finally came off the line on to the broad Menin road a mile from Ypres. In our early nights of fatigue we had often passed companies of men who slouched along in the dark, spiritless and depressed, who rarely answered our eager queries of 'Who are you?' or 'Where are you from?' or, if they did, merely with a growl and went on with their heads still sunk on their chests. We had wondered then, but we understood now. At our first halt we dropped on the road, and in a moment a steady chorus of snores told its own tale. For those who sat awake it was weird, almost ludicrous.

Opposite: Lance Corporal Norman Edwards, 1/6th Gloucestershire Regiment, enjoys a dip in a barrel. His friend and photographer, Private Arnold, smuggled this and other images back to England in a slot cut into the bottom of his water bottle.

Dawn found us still on the road, walking mechanically on with one dim thought animating us, of the moment when we would arrive, drop our packs, and sleep, which we did at last about 5 a.m. at the black huts beyond Vlamertinghe. We only kept awake to have a hot drink of tea, get our teeth into a solid meat sandwich, and bless the quartermasters who had had them ready. Then we got our boots off and slept the round of the clock.

Gunner Cecil Longley, B Battery, 1st South Midland Brigade, Royal Field Artillery

Even out of this war one keeps on getting a lot of humour and fun out of the thing – quaint situations, oddities of horses and queer fixes we get into and makeshifts we have to put up with. I often lie on our smelly straw and chortle with amusement to hear, for one thing, the variety of tone, calibre and timbre of the snores and other methods of breathing which men use when sleeping with a tunic and greatcoat buttoned tightly up to their

necks, or the midnight imprecations when a muddy foot meets the head of a man beneath it in the tiers of human sleepers, and we cover the floor of our barn as closely as the pieces of marble in a mosaic, and are often in as queer shapes!

I had a rare luxury the other day – a bath in a bucket of water. It had to be done on the instalment plan, and I may say that our daily ablutions, though meagre, are a source of unbounded astonishment to the woman and her man who still stay here! It is a phase of daily life that doesn't enter into their domestic economy, and for anyone to try and get clean when they will presently be as dirty again is mild but innocent foolishness. Madame certainly does wipe her hands on her soiled apron before bringing you half a franc's worth of butter in the palm of her hand, but whether with the object of cleaning the apron or the hands we have never yet been able to determine. From the state of the butter, however, expert opinion leans towards the former. Monsieur does not wear braces, but there is a button of tremendous responsibilities which just keeps his bifurcated garment hooked round his hips. He works hard with a flail; we look on shaking with apprehension. I know it will happen one day. Apart from that, they flourish, as they charge 'Inglis soldats' very firm prices on the constantly reiterated principle, 'You plenty money, me nix'. Yes, heaps of it, my good woman, one shilling and twopence halfpenny a day – highly skilled labour at that!

Anonymous Private, 1/9th Royal Scots (Lothian Regiment)

We were billeted in Ypres, and to the lot of A and B Companies fell the Convent of Irish Benedictine nuns, which had been vacated by French troops. Our first job was to clear the little wood-partitioned cubicles of dirty straw, and generally clean up. Cubicles were portioned off, one to three men, and we got off our superfluous gear. Then we all started on a tour of inspection, which degenerated for most into a hunt for souvenirs. What we expected to do with them none of us probably thought as we ransacked the bare attic rooms into which the sisters had evidently gathered everything in great haste. One brought back in triumph a branching brass candlestick, another a crucifix and a small image of the Madonna, still another a small painting which he fondly imagined *might* be an Old Master – the most impossible things were secreted in packs to be quietly got rid of when we realised the folly of it. One or two lingered longer over

the papers and ledgers strewn about the floor; the daily housekeeping of seventy or eighty years ago written in a clear, fine, old-world hand touched us to the quick. What a peaceful, sequestered life – what an awakening and an end! …

But how comfortable we were! A sacrilegious horde of kilted heretics! The days we lay within the high-walled garden in the sun; the afternoon teas we gave when some of us 'struck it lucky' with parcels; the rosy sleeps close together with shared blankets in the wooden floor of our little cubicles – what days of content and comradeship those were!

Troops were surprised by how close many French and Belgian civilians remained to the front lines. In the early days, rapidly decreasing numbers of farm animals wandered the battlefield, domesticated dogs and cats making their home in officers' dugouts or curled up in another rank's scoop made in the side of the trench wall. Soldiers who looked over the top through a periscope saw abandoned farm buildings in various stages of ruin and farm implements rusting in the fields among untended and rotting crops. Just behind the lines, farmers clung on to their land, determined to hold what was theirs while keeping a keen eye out for any pilfering Tommy or Fritz tempted by a chicken.

Private Thomas Lyon, 1/9th Highland Light Infantry (Glasgow Highlanders)

I am seated on a little patch of grass at the foot of Madame's garden, my back resting against the trunk of a tall and stately poplar. Blue is the sky and bright the sun, and a grateful little breeze pleasantly rustles the yellow corn in the adjacent field and the poplar leaves overhead … Madame's seven-year-old son is playing in the garden with little Georgette, whose grand-père keeps the estaminet just across the street. The sound of their prattle and laughter reaches me.

A little while ago a dozen or so of the enemy's shells ploughed up the earth with a great roar at only a few hundred yards' distance. Madame ran out into the garden and looked around. When she saw that the shells were too far distant to do her harm she immediately returned indoors. Pierre and Georgette paused in their play for a second or two after the first shell burst, and then resumed their game as though nothing had happened.

It is a picturesque hamlet, but when I look more closely at it I see that many of the houses are but roofless shells, the interiors mere heaps of bricks and mortar. And other houses, still inhabited, have great gaps in the gables and the roofs, and there is not a single house among them that has all its windows intact. Boards, pieces of tin, or sackcloth do duty for the missing panes …

You wonder perhaps why these people continue to live here, immediately in front of the enemy guns. But whither would they go? And is not this home to them? The French peasant is deep rooted in the soil that bore him; he does not so much dread change, but rather esteems it a thing inconceivable … To let all go to wrack and ruin because the Boches choose to disturb [their] slumber by sending over their horrid shells occasionally! – *mais non*, the thing is unthinkable.

On 22 April 1915, the Germans launched another concerted effort to break the British and French line in front of Ypres. The offensive began with a release from cylinders of chlorine gas which, when blown into Allied trenches, inflicted terrible casualties among French and French colonial troops who were holding the line, utterly unprepared for this new form of chemical warfare. Panic spread and momentarily the line gave way. However, the Germans hesitated, and British and Canadian soldiers filled the breach. For the next six weeks the Germans hammered away at Ypres' creaking door, failing to appreciate how close they were to a breakthrough as every Allied unit was rushed to its defence. Days later, as the Germans persevered with gas attacks, the British pulled back, thereby shortening their lines around the city. By 24 May the Salient had been reduced to a third of its former size, but the Germans had been kept at bay. This offensive would be the Germans' last effort against the British for three years on the Western Front. Gas had been introduced for the first time to the fighting and there was alarm about how to combat its deadly effects.

Even we, where we were, were just able to smell it and our eyes began to water. Incidentally, too, it is a bit of a nuisance, as since the attack we have been deluged with conflicting instructions, and things which the men insist on calling 'perspirators'. The first thing to turn up was a collection of body belts, that woolly article of underwear which every British soldier

Lieutenant Cecil Down, 1/4th Gordon Highlanders

is supposed to wear round his lower chest, but which none do wear. These had to be cut up into suitable lengths and tied over the mouth in case of a gas attack. Next day we were told that they should be dipped in hypo, a solution [to counteract the effects of chlorine gas] which should be kept in the trench. We had to certify that this had been done by midnight of the same day. Naturally there was none to be got. Next day hypo was a washout, and ammonia was all the rage, but it didn't matter much, as there was none of that either. Then along came a new sort of gag, made somewhere down the line, with little tapes hanging all round it. Now we have just had the third variety, a mixture of cotton waste and gauze smeared in something which tastes very nasty. The men don't know where they are. First they are told to breathe in at the mouth and out at the nostrils, and then an order comes cancelling that and recommending the exact opposite. Hardly has the significance of this order been impressed on the men than along sails another billet-doux to the effect that the nose should be gripped firmly by the thumb and first finger of the right hand to prevent any air reaching the lungs or being expelled there from by way of that limb. Is the nose a limb? Just as you have read this out aloud along comes an orderly with still another missive, to be read to the troops on

Primitive gas masks issued to British soldiers in response to the Germans' first use of chlorine gas in the Ypres Salient, April 1915.

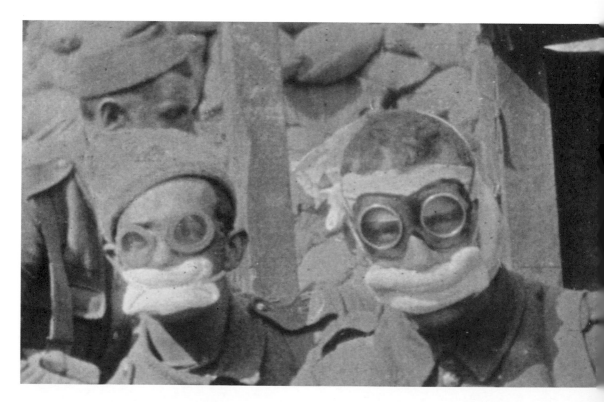

three successive occasions. According to this the mouth must be firmly closed, and everything done through the nose. Personally, to be quite safe, I have decided not to breathe at all.

The losses in Belgium hastened the arrival of the first Kitchener Divisions. Lord Kitchener had not wished to deploy his New Army piecemeal but as one concentrated force. However, circumstances dictated that at least some divisions would be required overseas earlier than originally anticipated. Not that these men were not ready to serve. They had had the best part of nine months' training, and, if not quite the finished article, they became increasingly irked by the endless routine and repeated practice and felt not only fit but ready to go.

Inevitably, there was some banter, not always light-hearted, between the Regular Army, the Territorials and, as they appeared, Kitchener's Volunteers, as to their relative strengths and worth as fighting soldiers. Regular soldiers looked down on Territorials as 'feather bed' part-timers, and could peer scornfully at Kitchener civilians whose training was, by force of circumstance, shorter and less professional than their own. Yet Kitchener's men had pride in what they

had achieved and, indeed, they had reason to feel superior, too, for they were volunteers, not men dragged to the colours by hunger, criminality or unemployment.

Second Lieutenant Arthur Heath, 6th Royal West Kent Regiment

We have been 'tightened up' since Christmas. At Hythe nothing but enormous field days in battalion and brigade training … We are all really very proud of ourselves. Here are our regular officers who have been jeering at us for months and boring us to death by stories of what the first battalion did [in 1914]. Then a week or two ago a sergeant arrived who had fought with the first in France and come back wounded. Almost his first remarks were about the awful difficulties they had there. And he actually went on 'Of course it will be quite different with these men – you can see that. They joined because they wanted to help, but over there they were all unwilling.' No doubt he meant the reservists – still these men were praised to the

skies by Smith-Dorrien, and generally placarded all over Kent as the heroes of the twentieth century ...

On the whole I'm quite happy and it doesn't matter a scrap whether I am or not because we shall get away in anything from three to six weeks unless the signs are deceiving us; and, once away, in my own opinion we shall all be casualties before very long. When we are all dead they will make peace and the only thing that annoys me is that I shan't be alive to grumble at the terms.

Men of the 1/10th King's Liverpool Regiment fighting near Ypres. These dramatic 'action' shots were widely reproduced in the British press, despite the ban on taking such images.

The restraints of discipline and the very exacting character of military life and training gave them [the men of Kitchener's Army] self-control and mental alertness. At the beginning, they were individuals, no more cohesive than so many grains of wet sand. After nine months of training they acted as a unit, obeying orders with that instinctive promptness of action which

Private James Hall, 9th Royal Fusiliers (City of London Regiment)

is so essential on the field of battle when men think scarcely at all. But it is true that what was their gain as soldiers was, to a certain extent, their loss as individuals …

Discipline was an all-important factor in the daily grind. At the beginning of their training, the men of the new armies were gently dealt with. Allowances were made for civilian frailties and shortcomings. But as they adapted themselves to changed conditions, restrictions became increasingly severe. Old privileges disappeared one by one. Individual liberty became a thing of the past. The men resented this bitterly for a time. Fierce hatreds of officers and NCOs were engendered and there was much talk of revenge when we should get to the front. I used to look forward with misgiving to that day. It seemed probable that one night in the trenches would suffice for a wholesale slaughtering of officers. Old scores were to be paid off, old grudges wiped out with our first issue of ball ammunition.

But all these threats were forgotten months before the time came for carrying them out. Once Tommy understood the reasonableness of severe discipline, he took his punishment for his offences without complaint. He realised, too, the futility of kicking against the pricks. In the army he belonged to the government, body and soul.

As the men prepared to go overseas, special leave was normally awarded to allow them to go home and say goodbye to their families. Such leave was not guaranteed and in some cases the first news that a son was going overseas was a card posted from the Channel ports.

Second Lieutenant Arthur Heath, 6th Royal West Kent Regiment

My dear Mother,

I've packed and labelled my things for home, I've seen the men draw their ammunition, I've stuffed my pack, my haversack and my pockets full of all imaginable articles, and in an hour or so we shall move. So my last thoughts in England are to you. I had myself photographed this morning. Enclosed is the receipt for a dozen, and the proofs will be sent to you in due course. One is just to amuse you by showing what my hair looks like now. The rest I hope are more flattering. If I never see you again, this will show you what I was like at the end of my time in England, and if I come back and settle down to civilian life again, it will be a memento of my curious past. I wish I could tell you how much I love you. But you know already. As I told you, don't bother if letters get through irregularly. We shall have a busy time till we get up into the trenches, and it won't be all leisure even there. So always take no news to be good news.

My love to you all,

Arthur.

Some of us have bought extra haversacks, and we have also been served out with white bags for the iron ration. We have in addition to carry 120 rounds of ball ammunition on us (an incredible weight), a big army blanket and waterproof sheet, as well as full equipment and rifle; and then there is our wardrobe! I shudder to think how many things I have bought lately, which 'exactly fit the breast pocket'. There is a large tin cigarette case (I thought it might protect my heart or something), a looking-glass, a writing case, a collapsible knife, fork and spoon, a pocket medicine chest, a tobacco pouch and a tinder lighter. All these things, as well as a bulky pocket-book, a soldier's pay book, pipe and matches, have to fit into the very small pockets provided in the tunic. I shall hardly be able to stand up as I am, so I think you will understand that a suit of [chain] mail would be just about the last straw.

Private Robert Sturges, 19th Royal Fusiliers (City of London Regiment)

That was written before the actual struggle began – the struggle of packing, I mean. Men were to be seen with perspiration pouring down their faces, vainly trying to cram into their packs and haversacks twice as much as they would hold. Desperate decisions had to be made as to whether this or that quite indispensable article should be left behind. Finally it was done somehow. When I tried on my various accoutrements, the weight, which hung upon my shoulders, pressed against my hips and glued my feet to the ground, was tremendous. A friend of mine weighed himself in full kit before starting and turned the scale at nineteen stone! One's appearance was rather comic; the pack was bulged out by the blanket and waterproof sheet, which it contained in addition to socks and shirts, etc.; the two haversacks, filled to overflowing, stuck out like saddle bags on either side; the overcoat was rolled and looked like a horse-collar worn bandolier fashion, and finally the iron ration bag, suspended from any odd buckle, banged against one's legs at every step.

Next day the 19th Royal Fusiliers were ordered to leave for France.

We woke all Tidworth with our band, our songs and our shouting, and heads came out of every window, and everywhere hands were waved. While we were entraining, the band went on playing on the platform: 'Keep the home fires burning', I think it was. But that most sentimental of songs failed to rouse an atom of sentiment in us, especially as many of the performers were suffering from a superabundance of spirits, not all their own.

Soon it was all left behind, and, wearied out with our exertions and excitement, we most of us slept through the journey to the coast. There we were shepherded on to one of the smallest Channel steamers I have ever seen. We filled every corner; staff officers returning from leave, and one general, who made his name famous earlier in the war, had to stand in the crush with all the rest.

I had often pictured myself in the position, in which I then was, actually leaving England for the front. I imagined myself taking a last long lingering look at the white cliffs of the old country as they melted into the haze of the horizon astern, and wondering if I should ever see them again. These thoughts suddenly occurred to me as we were pounding through the water, and I hastily turned to take my last lingering look, but it was too late; 'the old country' was out of sight. I then tried to do the 'wondering if I should see them again part', but something distracted my attention, and the whole thing was a hopeless failure.

The size of the British Army in France grew exponentially. At the end of 1914 approximately 270,000 troops were in France and Flanders; by the summer of 1915 this figure had doubled and it would more than double again the following year. For all the troops in the line, of whatever hue, normality was a daily grind that rarely stopped; if there was a 'start' for Lieutenant George Miall-Smith, it was as daylight approached. At least it was summertime and no longer bitterly cold, although rising was never easy.

27 August: 'It's three o'clock, sir.' I wake up with a start and realise that through the darkness opposite to me my servant, his head through the entrance of the dugout in which I lie, is endeavouring to wake me.

Without the slightest attempt to hide my impatient resignation to circumstances I just manage – my eyes still closed – to jerk out a sulky and hasty 'right-ho!'. In this manner I put my servant in the position of an offender, but with a rustle he is gone, once more allowing the curtain in front of the door to shut out the chill air of the early morning.

For a brief few seconds I persuade myself that I am justified in remaining where I am. I magnify my comfort. My right leg and my right arm are both asleep and have no feelings in them, all sorts of undiscovered hard projections stick into my back, my feet ache from the tightness of my boots and I am stiff all over.

However! Warm I am, and when I think of the grey chill morn which awaits me the other side of that curtain, I shudder and pull my overcoat more tightly round my neck. I curse the Kaiser and wish *he* had to turn out in a cold early morning and trudge round the trench. I picture him lying between the clean sheets of some cosy bed – fast asleep.

Lieutenant George Miall-Smith, 8th Norfolk Regiment

That early morning feeling: an unknown officer of the 183rd Tunnelling Company, Royal Engineers, wakes in his dugout.

I convey my thoughts to my fellow officer (in so many grunts and groans) who is lying by my side. But he pretends to be fast asleep, and but one grunt escapes his lips. But stay! As if repenting his lack of sympathy towards me he tells me to 'Remember Belgium'. This remark I consider is one too many at the present moment, and, now wide awake, reply that I don't suppose I shall ever forget her as long as I live after this …

My hands deep in my pockets, my chin thrust as low down in my collar as possible, and shivering all over (chiefly from lack of circulation), I begin my stroll round the interminable trenches winding in and out. In the semi-darkness I can just see sleepy men in the narrow traverses, rifle in hand, standing silent and motionless. I bump past them without a word, treading on many toes and tripping over more. The moon still hangs in the fading sky, and on my right can be seen the low pink of the coming sun. Miscellaneous rifle shots bark out and whistle over our heads, otherwise there is complete silence. I trudge the trench from point to point wishing it would get light. Minutes pass like hours, and still I shiver. Still it seems as dark as before. My head is heavy and I find it hard to keep my eyes open.

Sentries report 'All quiet'. It is now quite light. I hurriedly stamp back to my dugout, thinking of that wire bed all the way. Once in, I flop upon it, and am asleep in two shakes, to wake at 10 a.m. on a bright sunny day.

Private Thomas Lyon, 1/9th Highland Light Infantry (Glasgow Highlanders)

After a couple of weeks of this subterranean existence a man comes to regard the surface of the earth as unnaturally elevated. It seems quite right and proper that one should be hemmed in on either side by earthen walls that rise to a height above one's head. Custom robs the circumstance of its strangeness, and it is the green, specious world that the periscope reveals which seems remote and strange.

In the merciless glare of the day the trench seems as unlovely and unromantic an abiding place as the insane mind of man could devise, but, veiled in the kindly shadows of the night, its appearance is transfigured. It was while I was on sentry duty the other night that I discovered the mystery and beauty in the trench. The sky was marvellous with stars and a languid moon lent a further sorcery to the night. Away to our left the guns boomed intermittently, but on our front was a nervous silence.

I glanced along the trench, and lo! It was an enchanted place, compact of mystery and fantastic beauty, its walls – wet with recent rain – gleamed silvern in the light of the moon, and the upper part was composed of great blocks of shining marble, speckled here and there with the more brilliant lustres of pure jewels. There were strange purple and violet shadows that touched the imagination, and in one place a long, golden needle of light stretched from side to side of the trench. It was merely a ray of candlelight projected through a pin-hole in the waterproof sheet hung over the entrance to a dugout. And the red and fiery eye that glowed hatefully from the dense gloom at the end of the traverse was but the light of a cigarette – when one knew. From time to time the stars were blotted out by a white glare that filled all the world, and in this desolating light the trench lost its weird beauty and mystery and was discovered in all its stark unloveliness.

You have the feeling that your trench is the limit of your nation and its power – an outpost of empire. There is a little strip of no-man's-land, and then the enemy in his outpost of empire. If you show yourself, he kills you; so you don't show yourself. You live most of your days seeing only the two walls of the trench and the sky, and when you do look over, or go out at nights to see your little world, your horizon even then is only some hundred yards away.

Lieutenant Denis Garstin, 10th Prince of Wales's Own Royal Hussars

You see by day a ragged field, pitted with shell holes, in each of which there is always a bully-beef tin. The grass is lank and untidy, where it has been allowed to grow. There are some bodies lying stiffly about, the skin dark brown from exposure, and the clothes rotten. There is a look of a refuse heap about the field. Even the barbed wire, mended and strengthened in the darkness, helps the impression of disuse. Beyond this no-man's-land you see a low line of sandbags – coloured sandbags. And that is all. What is happening behind those sandbags you can only guess.

By the summer of 1915, the old system of trench letters and numbers had changed to the new almost universally remembered trench names. Bald letters and numbers had proved confusing to the men and difficult to recall. The trench system was becoming ever more complicated and memorable names made it easier for a man to navigate his way around especially if there was a pattern to the names, while also giving a human touch to the general environment which was home to these men.

Private Thomas Lyon, 1/9th Highland Light Infantry (Glasgow Highlanders)

The names borne by the various trenches have an interest of their own, inasmuch as they usually give some clue to the identities of the battalions which dug them, or at least to the districts from which these battalions were recruited. In this neighbourhood, for instance, there is Glasgow Road – ('we done that', a Highlander told me with pride) – Hertford Street, Finchley Road, Strathcona Walk and Harley Street – the last-named being that in which the advanced field dressing station is situated.

Opposite: Dr Eric Marshall, RAMC. In 1909 he accompanied Ernest Shackleton on the expedition to reach the geographic South Pole, where he suffered severe frostbite to his left hand. Note the change from trench letters and numbers to names by this stage.

Similarly, the numerous dugouts with which the sides of the trenches are honeycombed, and which are as varied in their architectural features as the buildings of any city, have their distinctive names set forth on little name-plates attached to the front of each – or perhaps the name may simply be printed with a copying ink pencil on one of the sandbags forming the upper part of the walls. Feminine cognomens are legion – there are Mary and Nancy and Violet Villas by the dozen; while others have such fanciful appellations as Kensington Palace, The Leicester Lounge, Vale of Avoca, Burlington Arcade … From all of which it may be deduced that Tommy is a sentimentalist as well as a humourist.

Lieutenant George Miall-Smith, 8th Norfolk Regiment

At this part of the trench some curious earth caverns are dug from the parados, and contain numerous khaki-clad figures deep in slumber. Some have quaint boards put over the entrance, such as the following:

THE SNIPER'S NEST
Beds 4d., 6d., and 8d. per night
Bring your own KEATING'S

Or

'Hotel de Flea'

They chiefly refer to the bugs and rats which abound. At night-time the tops of the trenches seen against the light sky seem alive with rats in some parts.

I have managed to keep clear of the 'little strangers' [fleas] so far, save for one hopper which I caught, tried and executed yesterday afternoon. I am hoping it will be an example to the rest.

Captain Lionel Crouch, 1/1st Oxfordshire and Buckinghamshire Light Infantry

The men have made a garden on the side of a communication trench. It is labelled 'Kew Gardens – Do not pinch the flowers'. All our spirits are reviving under the influence of the better weather. The trenches are beautiful and quite like old times. The apple trees and hedges are budding; some of the hedges are quite green …

I have started a garden at my Company Headquarters. Will you please send as soon as possible two packets of candytuft and two packets of nasturtium seeds? My daffodils and hyacinths are topping. I told you about 'Kew Gardens'. The men have now put on the grass two bones labelled, 'Here lieth all that remains of the last man who walked on the L'hawn'.

Tommy humour: 'Strand Palace Hotel' with a 'Garage [for] 40 Cars'.

At times, briefly, it could almost feel as though the trench was the world and, by extension, that there was no enemy across the field. So rarely were they ever seen that the noise of shells and bullets could feel almost disconnected from actual human endeavour.

It was a weird experience. Rifles cracked, bullets zip-zipped along the top of the parapet, great shells whistled over our heads or tore immense holes in the trenches, trench-mortar projectiles and hand grenades were hurled at us, and yet there was not a living soul to be seen across the narrow strip of no-man's-land, whence all this murderous rain of steel and lead was coming. Daily we kept careful and continuous watch, searching the long, curving line of German trenches and the ground behind them with our periscopes and field glasses, and nearly always with the same barren result. We saw only the thin wreaths of smoke rising, morning and evening, from trench fires; the shattered trees, the forlorn and silent ruins, the long grass waving in the wind.

Although we were often within 200 yards of thousands of German soldiers, rarely farther than 400 yards away, I did not see one of them until we had been in the trenches for more than six weeks, and then only for the interval of a second or two. My German was building up a piece of damaged parapet. I watched the earth being thrown over the top of the trench, when suddenly a head appeared, only to be immediately withdrawn. One of our snipers had evidently been watching, too. A rifle cracked and I saw a cloud of dust arise where the bullet clipped the top of the parapet. The German waved his spade defiantly in the air and continued digging; but he remained discreetly under cover thereafter. This marked an epoch in my experience in a war of unseen forces. I had actually beheld a German, although Tommy insisted that it was only the old caretaker, 'the bloke wot keeps the trenches tidy'.

The strain of constantly watching and seeing nothing became almost unbearable at times. We were often too far apart to have our early morning interchange of courtesies, and then the constant phtt-phtt of bullets annoyed and exasperated us. I for one welcomed any evidence that our opponents were fathers and husbands and brothers just as we were. I remember my delight, one fine summer morning, at seeing three great kites soaring above the German line. There is much to be said for men who enjoy flying kites. Once they mounted a dummy figure of a man on their parapet. Tommy had great sport shooting at it, the Germans jiggling its arms and legs in a most laughable manner whenever a hit was registered. In their eagerness to 'get a good bead' on the figure, the men threw caution to the winds, and

Private James Hall, 9th Royal Fusiliers (City of London Regiment)

stood on the firing benches, shooting over the top of the parapet. Fritz and Hans were true sportsmen while the fun was on, and did not once fire at us. Then the dummy was taken down, and we returned to the more serious game of war with the old deadly earnestness. I recall such incidents with joy as I remember certain happy events in childhood. We needed these trivial occurrences to keep us sane and human. There were not many of them, but such as there were, we talked of for days and weeks afterward.

Second Lieutenant Arthur Heath, 6th Royal West Kent Regiment

Pivoting on his left leg, this man takes a quick potshot at the enemy, probably at the behest of the photographer.

The thing I hate is the artillery. I detest them and all their works. They stay three or four miles behind in the most comfortable billets imaginable and just amuse themselves by loosing off their instruments of torture at the infantry. It is all very well to talk of a clean death in battle, but it's not a clean death that the artillery deals. It means arms and legs torn off and men mangled out of recognition by their great hulking bullies of guns. I would sweep them all away and settle it by the quiet and decent methods of the infantry.

Well, the whole thing is tit-for-tat. We break their parapet one night – the next morning they break ours. They drop some rifle grenades into our trenches – we set up an infernal machine to do the same to theirs. I had great fun finding out how to work it. Most of these grenades on both sides fail to go off, I fancy. In general, if one side is quiet, the other waits a long time before provoking him. The real depressing thing about this trench warfare is plainly that you know your own casualties, but you have very little idea of theirs. It's not like fighting in the open, where you know at least that you have gained a mile or lost it. It spoils the beauty of these wars of attrition so much not to know which side is being worn away most.

There has been a lot of wit about in the trenches lately. When the news of the Russian – or is it the English? – naval victory in the Baltic came through, we got it from General Headquarters (sent all along the line). A few minutes later I went along the trench and discovered my sergeant shouting in a very shrill squeaky voice through a megaphone 'Fritz, your navy is destroyed'. Elsewhere in the line a board was put up:

'The following German ships have been lost –
1 Superdreadnought. Hoch!
3 Cruisers. Hoch! Hoch!
7 Destroyers. Hoch! Hoch! Hoch!'

One of the Germans was heard replying indignantly 'Schwein'. But a more dignified reply was made by a board from the Germans saying that in August 80,000 Russians, and I do not know how many guns, had been captured. Down our way they put up a board with 'Mr Grey' written on it, and a dreadful face that most resembled Mr Gladstone disguised as a monkey. However, my men have now constructed the most hideous German figure on Guy Fawkes lines – face rather like a drooping turnip, and in course of time that shall be exhibited to them. It cheers them up a bit, and that's a blessing.

During the day the men rested, reading, writing home or sleeping before work started in earnest under the cover of darkness. Thoughts of a hot meal

consumed soldiers' minds, as they waited for fatigue parties to bring food up the communication trenches.

Each platoon has detailed a certain number of men to go back out of the trenches, in charge of an NCO. This fatigue party meets the transport at the appointed place, and the CQMS hands to each man a couple of bulky sandbags, and the party starts back for the trenches. There each platoon sergeant divides the platoon rations among his four section commanders, and the section commander distributes them among his men …

First and foremost comes the bully, forever famous. This is compressed corned beef packed in small tins. The opening of these tins is a labour of Hercules to the inexperienced, as we soon discovered. Some of them are provided with keys, wherewith one is supposed to wind off a strip of metal round the top of the tin. The strip invariably breaks halfway, however, and the novice is usually compelled to resort to the tin opener fitted in the clasp knife served out to him. Thereupon, if successful, he gouges about the tin and the meat inside, until he is able to scrape out fragments of the latter on to his plate, or substitute for a plate, and finally makes a most unappetising meal. If unsuccessful – well, I remember a man in our section opening a tin for breakfast that first morning at Boulogne. After cutting his finger badly three times, he flung the tin on the ground, stamped on it, and went for a brisk walk round the camp.

The jam tins are circular and not so difficult to negotiate. The army jam was plentiful and excellent. The French were even more fond of it than we were, we discovered, and I venture to predict that for some time after the conclusion of the war the English traveller, who asks for confitures anglaises with his tea, will be served out of a small cylindrical tin. I had always heard that the British Army specialised in plum and apple jam, but I never saw any myself. Apricot was the commonest with us, though marmalade, of which we never tired, was fairly frequent.

The biscuits rather staggered us at first. They are exactly like dog biscuits to look at, though not so brown perhaps. They are very dry and tasteless, and we never thought that morning at Boulogne, when we opened a case of them marked 'Spratts', that a time would come when they would be more valuable than gold and precious stones.

Private Robert Sturges, 19th Royal Fusiliers (City of London Regiment)

Opposite: A 'whizz-bang', a small 77mm German shell, lands in B Company's sergeants' mess, 9th Rifle Brigade, probably in the town of Ronville, south of Arras.

A Tommy enjoys a cup of tea. In his right hand is his hot lunch while two rum jars sit at his feet. No wonder he is smiling.

A word about the bacon and the stew: the former was of excellent quality but was spoiled by being boiled instead of fried. The stew – I suppose it was good enough really, but I found that after four months of stew for dinner I had to be very, very hungry to eat it.

To assist him to eat his food, and if necessary cook it, every soldier is served out with a canteen or mess tin. The lid, which contains a folding handle of its own, acts as his plate or frying pan, while the bottom is his cup or saucepan. The mess tin, with its sharp angles and internal handle, is a most difficult thing to clean inside. It is usually impossible to get hot water to wash it out with after a meal, and the grease gets into all the cracks and stays there. Rubbing it with earth was the best method of getting rid of the grease, we found; but that tended to make the next meal of stew or cup of tea a trifle gritty.

Where there was food there were bound to be rats. Rats were universally hated and universally hunted. Their ubiquitous presence in and around the front line proved almost intolerable for some men, no more than an occupational hazard for others. The numbers of rats proliferated near the trenches as food was plentiful. The rats did an efficient job of stripping the dead of flesh, a useful activity, but one for which no one could be grateful. The rations were also targeted, and sleeping men did well to place out of harm's way precious food parcels from home.

Private James Hall, 9th Royal Fusiliers (City of London Regiment)

As for the rats, speaking in the light of later experience I can say that an army corps of Pied Pipers would not have sufficed to entice away the hordes of them that infested the trenches, living like house pets on our rations. They were great lazy animals, almost as large as cats, and so gorged with food that they could hardly move. They ran over us in the dugouts at night, and filched cheese and crackers right through the heavy waterproofed covering of our haversacks. They squealed and fought among themselves at all hours. I think it possible that they were carrion eaters, but never, to my knowledge, did they attack living men. While they were unpleasant bedfellows, we became so accustomed to them that we were not greatly concerned about our very intimate associations.

All enemies to slumber might be overcome, however, but there is one I cannot master. It is the rat. As soon as I get settled and begin to feel drowsy, I hear a rustling just by my head, then something patters across my chest, across the next man, on to the third who gives a convulsive jerk which flings the rat back heavily into my lap. This happened two or three times last night. It is like one of the forgotten sports, 'Tossing the rat'. At other times they waltz on the top of your head, or screech most horribly in your ear. I can't get accustomed to the beastly things. I believe they are attracted by the warmth of human bodies. One man I heard of woke up one night to find a rat lying curled up against his neck. He put up his hand to brush it away and was bitten through the finger.

Private Robert Sturges, 19th Royal Fusiliers (City of London Regiment)

Today I was fast asleep when the time for an observation came round. And I should infallibly have overslept it if a mouse had not relieved me from the toils of Morpheus. I had two traps set side by side on a shelf. A mouse trod on one and it clicked off and caught him by the very tip of the tail. Swinging round in his agony, he knocked down the other trap, the fall of which awakened me. I was saved. It was just time for the observation. I regret to say that I killed the mouse brutally while the sleep was still on me. What will happen to me for such ingratitude? I shall never be able to look a mouse in the face for the rest of my life. If only I could hypnotise myself into believing it was a German mouse.

Corporal Frederick Goodyear, Attd Special Company (Meteorological Section) 5th Division, Royal Engineers

One of the bright young officers sent to the front in the late spring of 1915 was a nineteen-year-old Liverpool-born second lieutenant, Kenneth Brewster. Although the ban on cameras had just come into effect, he either chose to ignore or was ignorant of the new rules forbidding their use while on active service. Over the following four months until he was wounded, Kenneth not only took many images, but openly disclosed in his letters home the pictures he had taken and how they were developed, ordering prints for some of the men under his command.

Second Lieutenant Kenneth Brewster, 1st Royal Fusiliers (City of London Regiment)

4 May: We have been having splendid weather out here for the last week, the place has quite dried up, and all the trees are coming out, to look behind the trenches you would hardly imagine that there was a war on except for the ruined houses and the occasional bursting of a shell. It is very interesting watching the aeroplanes being shelled and fired at by machine guns and rifle fire, there was a German one hit the other day. He flew very low over my trench, his engine had been put out of order by shellfire, but I do not think the pilot was hit because I could see him sitting up in the aeroplane. He came down over the German lines, then we burst shrapnel over him. I expect he was either killed or wounded with four others who rushed up to help him. I wish I was in the Flying Corps. It is much the safest place, they are always flying about, but it is very seldom that one is hit.

I have built myself a splendid house just behind my trench. It is about six foot high and about eight foot square. It is all made of wood except for the iron roof with earth on top. It has a glass window and a folding spring bed which was blown out of a farm near here when it was shelled … I wish this war would end though. I do not think it is possible before another two or three months at the earliest.

Your loving son, Kenneth

18 May: My dear mother and father. Thank you very much for the cake which I have received, have you received the German rifle grenades which I have sent you? I do hope they are not lost because they are rather hard to get and it is only a few that do not go off. If you get the *Daily Mail* of 15 May you will see some photographs of the trench I live in. They were taken by the captain of the regiment that relieves us when we go into billets. My house is only about twelve yards away from the bridge you see in the photo. There is also a good photo of the trench mortar, and one of the German bombs thrown by a trench mortar which fell in the trench on my left and did not go off. It was about two feet in the ground and had to

be dug up. The man in my platoon found the picture you see hung in the trench. I took some photos of the trench myself. The officer standing in the water was taken two or three months ago. The trenches are not like that now. I will write again soon.

Your loving son

Kenneth.

1 July: My dear Mum and Dad. I expect you will receive some photographs which I asked a fellow going on leave to post in England, will you get some printed from the negatives which I took with my camera because I want to give the men some prints … will you let me know when you receive another lot of photographs from the Kodak Co. They are photos of our old trench that took us four months to build and make comfortable, then we were moved out of them.

As day turned to night, so the working day began. Fatigue parties brought supplies up to the line; other men went forward of the trench to affix or mend the belts of protective barbed wire. Patrols were also sent into no-man's-land and no man, except those on watch, was left idle. It made sense, for not only did the darkness shield all activities, but there was nothing like strenuous work to keep the debilitating effects of the cold at bay.

The painting 'hung in the trench' referred to by Second Lieutenant Kenneth Brewster in a letter home to his parents.

Lieutenant Cecil Down, 1/4th Gordon Highlanders

The man who is going to win the war is the poor old lance corporal of the unpaid variety. General A wants something done. He acquaints Col. B of his wishes. Col. B notifies Capt. C, who in his turn passes on the good news to 2nd Lieut. D, who skilfully shifts the burden to Sergt. E. Sergt. E, intent on obtaining a disproportionately large issue of rum for his platoon and himself, details Lance-corp. (unpaid) F. Lance-corp. (unpaid) F takes six men, three shovels, a pick and a tin of chloride of lime and the job gets done. Then he returns and reports the completion of the job to Sergt. E. Sergt. E steps up to 2nd Lieut. D, salutes, and reports – 'I've done that job, sir.' 'I' mark you. No mention of Lance-corp. (unpaid) F, with his six men, three shovels, pick and tin of chloride of lime. 2nd Lieut. D wires to Capt. C, 'Have done job.' Capt. C sends a message by orderly to the effect that he, 'he' mark you, has completed the allotted task. Col. B takes pen in hand and writes, 'Ref. your B.M. 3427 I beg to report that this work has been brought to a satisfactory conclusion by me'. Still no word of Lance-corp. (unpaid) F. General A, replete with a good dinner, receives the message. 'Good fellow that Col. B,' he murmurs. In due course Col. B becomes Col. B, c.m.g. Lance-corp. (unpaid) F remains Lance-corp. (unpaid) F, until a kindly shell carries his head away.

Private Robert Sturges, 19th Royal Fusiliers (City of London Regiment)

The night before last a man came up to me – he was a scout NCO – and asked me if I had heard about the patrol that night. I hadn't. 'Oh,' he said, 'you and I are to go out at 2 a.m. to examine the German barbed wire'. My blood turned to water and my tongue clave to the roof of my mouth, for as you know barbed wire entanglements are quite near the trenches, so that this meant crawling right over to the German trenches. Moreover, the moon was at the full and you could see quite a distance from the trench.

I tried to get some sleep before starting, but it was difficult, as my head was filled with all sorts of fancies half-thoughts and half-dreams. What should I do if the other man got hit out there in the open? What would happen to me if I were hit? What should we do if we met a German patrol? And so on. But I flatter myself that I slept a bit. At 2 a.m. I turned out feeling very cold, and as I went down the trench all my friends shook hands with me and wished me luck. I was awfully frightened. Then I and the other man climbed over the parapet and crawled forward. Almost at once all

feeling of nervousness left me. Once we got started, I felt excited of course, but not at all in a funk as I had expected. Rather strange; I suppose it's the same with every one else. We got through our own wire easily – it was in a very bad state – and then began to crawl towards the German trenches which were about 130 yards away at this point.

A tricky and often painful job: putting out barbed wire in front of reserve trenches.

Fortunately it was rather cloudy, and so not quite so light as it might have been. We crawled literally on our stomachs, propelling ourselves along by our elbows and toes, a slow, laborious and dirty method of proceeding which I can't recommend. We passed close to two or three dead bodies, and at our approach two big birds flapped up around us, uttering harsh cries. I should like to be able to say that these were vultures and had been tearing the bodies of our soldiers, wallowing in their loathsome orgy and all that sort of thing. But as a matter of fact I think they were only owls, watching for mice and rats.

Every now and then a star shell would go up making me feel as though I was on a large empty stage with the limelight full on me. At such times we flattened our noses into the mud, kept perfectly still and made a noise like a corpse. A few stray bullets flew about over our heads – men always shoot high at night, thank goodness.

We crawled and crawled and crawled and then we rather lost our bearings, at least we weren't at all sure how the German trenches ran. We had been sent out without having seen any plan of the trenches or having had them explained to us, which was rather a mistake. Now if you imagine that the British and German trenches are simply two parallel straight lines, with a salient here and there, at Ypres for instance, and corresponding re-entrant or dent in the other side, your idea is not quite accurate. You have only to stand in the front line at night and watch the star shells to see your mistake. You can see them shooting up and down all round you, owing to the continual writhing and twisting of the trenches. So it isn't surprising that we got a bit muddled. We saw spurts of flame from various rifles and machine guns to our front, our left and rear – cannons to the right of them, cannons to left of them, sort of idea.

I and the other fellow had a bit of an argument out there in the middle, as to which side the rifle fire on our left came from. He thought it was German, and I thought it was British. However, he was in charge, so we made towards it. But after crawling for some time we never seemed to get to the trenches. So then we had another argument, and this time more considerations influenced our decision.

First and foremost a machine gun had begun to erupt uncomfortably close from that point of the enemy's trench nearest to us, so that if we had gone on we should have had to advance straight on to those rapid spurts of flame. Moreover, being under machine-gun fire, even at night, when you are in the open gives you a feeling of utter helplessness and insecurity. To listen to the smack, smack of the bullets from the bottom of a trench is a different thing altogether. So the machine gun was a fairly strong argument. Secondly, we had had orders to stay out till three o'clock, and I found on looking at my watch that it was already past that time. So we decided to turn back, though we had not accomplished our object of examining the German wire. Our homeward journey was accomplished with greater speed than the outer (I was leading!). We passed several full haversacks and things on the way, I came across an old rusty rifle with the bayonet fixed and examined it eagerly, hoping it would be a German one, but I found it was British, and belonged to a body lying close by, and so not worth carting back as a souvenir.

I heaved a sigh of relief when I dropped over our parapet again and was once more safe back in the trenches. We had only been out an hour and a half, but from the greeting accorded to us by everyone we met we might not have seen them for several years. Our half-hour's overtime had worried them a bit, I think.

In our brigade a man is damned lucky if he gets a dozen hours' sleep in three days in the trenches. It's working and carrying parties whenever it isn't sentry and listening post, and trench mortars and whizz-bangs on and off all day and night in the intervals of bombardments by crumps. I don't pretend to have been through anything like as much as men who have been out here eight months and never missed the trenches, but I have been through enough to know what they have been through. And then people think it is mud and wet we mind; that is nothing, absolutely nothing, compared with the nerve-racking hell of bombardment. Of course, people at home can imagine that more easily than the bombardments, so that is what they talk about. I can't think that human nature ever had to stand in any kind of warfare in history what the modern infantryman has to stand. The strange thing in a way is that there doesn't seem to be any limit to what you can make human nature stand.

Corporal Frederick Keeling, 6th Duke of Cornwall's Light Infantry

Two of my boys had their dugout blown in on top of them yesterday. At first it looked as if they must have been killed, but we worked like demons to dig them out, in the hopes of finding them still alive. After a quarter of an hour we managed to drag them out, covered with bruises and hardly able to breathe, but whole. We tried artificial respiration, brandy, and all sorts of things. At last they came round, and one of them – we had always thought him a bit of a weed before – turned round to the other where he lay and gasped, 'Man, yon's gran'. D'ye ken we've escapit th' efternoon fatigue?'

Lieutenant Cecil Down, 1/4th Gordon Highlanders

If nothing else, the British Tommy survived on his ability to turn the darkest moments into instances of humour. Maintaining the capacity to laugh saved soldiers from breaking down or going mad and is, in many ways, one of the forgotten stories of the war. In all the degradation found among the most sickening sights and in the worst and most physically demanding conditions, humour was maintained. It may have appeared in bad taste; it may have seemed ridiculous and out of place, but being able to turn to humour as a last resort helped win the war.

Lieutenant Cecil
Down, 1/4th
Gordon
Highlanders

I was going round the trenches with a certain officer, who shall be nameless, and who has a reputation for being rather 'windy'. He is my superior officer, by a long way, and so, as becomes the perfect little Company Commander, I was escorting him round with honeyed words, in the hope that he would remember me favourably when next there was mention of a soft job. We came to a nice secluded corner and my companion sat down. So did I. He tilted up his tin hat from his forehead and wiped the perspiration from his brow. So did I, for it was hot, and he had been walking fast, either in the laudable intention of seeing a lot, or in the less laudable but more natural desire to get back to his hole in the ground. 'Phew,' he remarked, 'it is hot.' I assented. Silence. Then he broke out again. 'There's one thing I do like about these trenches,' said he, 'you always know where the Hun is going to drop his shells. What! Now this place, for instance, the Hun has never shelled, and never will if the war goes on for a hundred years. What! What!' Before I had time to reply there was a familiar swwwwish, and then whizz-bang, whizz-bang, whizz-bang. We picked ourselves up from the bottom of the trench where we had gravitated by some natural instinct and grinned at each other. 'What a …' Whizz-bang, whizz-bang, whizz-bang. When we were quite sure that the salvo was at an end we hopped it in the most approved Derby-winner fashion. It was amusing, as the trench boards had been laid down very badly, and every time the large foot of the rapidly receding figure in front of me came down with a flop on the nearest extremity of one, the other end would jump up and hit him in the eye. That happened three times, and each time he picked himself up I had to pretend to stumble so that he should not see my face. There was a large grin thereon. Poor chap, he really is as brave as they make them, but he's a dugout and hasn't quite grasped the fact that this is an ungentlemanly war. He judges things by the Crimea or whatever the medieval scrap was in which he played so dashing a part.

Opposite: 'Always smiling' says the accompanying caption. Private Rogers, 1/7th West Riding Regiment, taken outside a dugout on the west bank of the Yser Canal.

Lieutenant Oscar
Viney, 1/4th
Oxford and
Buckinghamshire
Light Infantry

When I was going the round of the sentries at about 3 a.m., I noticed a light appearing time after time in the middle of a field. I carefully stalked it, getting the revolver I had ready; but on getting close I found it was one of our own sentries lighting matches. I asked him what on earth he was doing, and he said: 'Please, sir, I sneezed and dropped my teeth, and I'm trying to find them.'

We laugh, but it was a tragedy – stark tragedy. I imagine the poor beggar groping about a muddy field at three o'clock on a bitter winter's morning, black as pitch. His hand strokes something solid – nothing but a bit of frozen mud. He grasps another, and another, and still another piece of the same substance. Hope dies down, and mental agony racks the wretch, for he simply must recover those teeth; they are not like the things on the list of official stores procurable at the canteen.

Lieutenant Cecil
Down, 1/4th
Gordon
Highlanders

The toffee you sent was very good but a trifle sticky. In fact its stickiness was almost my undoing. I was on duty at 2 a.m. and to keep myself awake inserted a large portion into my mouth. Almost at once a signaller appeared and told me that I was wanted on the phone. I went to the signaller's abode, took up the instrument, and tried to say 'Hello', but could not open my mouth. My jaws were stuck tight. At the other end I could hear the CO cursing my lack of promptitude. Again and again I tried, but to no purpose. The toffee had me in its grip. At last the CO got wild and started to shout 'Hello' and other less polite remarks down his end of the machine. This time I managed to answer with a long drawn –

'o-o-o-m.'

'That you? '

'o-o-o-m.'

'Why haven't you come before?'

'o-o-o-m.'

'You've been to sleep. You're half asleep now.'

'o-o-o-m.'

'You have, I can hear the sleepiness in your voice', and thereupon he delivered me a lengthy lecture upon the subject of falling asleep at one's post, and the penalties involved, among them Death. All I could reply to his diatribe was 'o-o-o-m,' and it was not till morning that the matter could be satisfactorily explained.

My experience of the trenches has taught me several things. First the humour of it, which may sound strange but is quite undeniable. It may be that one is rather highly strung at such a time, but things strike one as awfully comical sometimes. To see people running into each other with their heads in the air and rushing around corners in frantic efforts to dodge rifle grenades is extraordinarily funny. I remember one man getting his foot caught in a floorboard when running to escape a grenade; the look of tense anxiety, as he struggled to get his foot free, made us laugh for the rest of the morning. Curiously enough, fear and humour can exist together, as I discovered when those trench mortars came over that night. When the second one went up I rushed and dived into a shelter which was already full of people, to their great annoyance. I couldn't help being amused, though I was in terror of my life at that moment.

I suppose every one imagines that he knows the meaning of fear and the sensation of fear. I always thought I did. Your heart beats rapidly and you perspire all over, I thought. But I find that before I had only been nervous, never afraid. The sensation of fear, which I have experienced and my friends, too, is first and foremost a sensation of cold. You have been feeling quite warm and comfortable, when something alarming happens; a trench mortar goes off or a whizz-bang bursts uncomfortably near. You feel as if a door had been suddenly opened, letting in upon you a cold draught. You actually begin to shiver; all the muscles in your body tighten and you are in a state of tension. If you aren't careful you will find your teeth trying to chatter.

Private Robert Sturges, 19th Royal Fusiliers (City of London Regiment)

Although the trenches were the safest places, soldiers were still assailed by a variety of deadly weapons. The machine gun and sniper's bullet could catch those who were momentarily lax or imprudent; a bombardment of enemy shells was brutal and blunt, forcing men to sit out the assault, incapable of effecting an escape. But often the most terrifying attacks were those that came periodically and unexpectedly and helped wear away at the nerves, and among the worst of these weapons was the *Minenwerfer*, a German trench mortar. This came just slowly enough to give men an opportunity to escape, but quickly enough to make hesitation almost certainly fatal. Men lived on their wits and their adrenalin.

Private Thomas
Lyon, 1/9th
Highland Light
Infantry (Glasgow
Highlanders)

There would be the shrill sound of a whistle blown by the man on lookout duty, followed by the cry, 'Bomb to right!'

Instantly your eyes sought the sky – indeed they rarely wavered from it – and as they caught sight of the ungainly missile (a trench mortar bomb) hurtling in a great arc through the air, you judged the place where it would fall and joined the other men in a wild stampede along the trench. *Whong!* You were stunned and deafened by the hideous roar that seemed to fill all the world; the earth vibrated in horrid fashion and a mighty wind blew; and then a shower of stones and earth and pieces of metal fell all around and about and darkened the air for a moment. You huddled – a dozen of you – close together in the lee of the parapet, your heads well down, and trusted to luck. A few minutes later, and just as you were regaining breath, the whistle sounded again and the cry, 'Bomb to left!' and away you went again in another mad rush, jostling the man in front, jostled by the one behind, trampling on each other's heels, bumping against the corners of the traverses – with only one idea, to get as far away as possible from the landing place of the mortar bomb.

All the afternoon and evening we spent our time scurrying backward and forward along the trench like so many frightened rabbits. No man thought of settling down in a dugout or a corner of a traverse. All were standing in the trench with anxious eyes straining constantly on the sky over by the enemy's lines, every sense alert, every fibre of feeling taut and tense. Our nerves were sorely jangled, what with the long-continued strain and the demoralising effects of the recurrent explosions. In the early evening several mines were exploded near to our lines, and the sickening heave of the earth that accompanied these, and the shattering roar that followed did not tend to soothe our mental agitation. 'This is pure hell,' said a white-faced, trembling-lipped boy beside whom I once found myself cowering in against the parapet …

In the day-time one can see the enemy's mortar bombs travelling through the air. During their flight they turn and tumble over and over in a curiously ungainly and erratic fashion, and look not unlike the big tin cans used for the transport of milk by railway. Indeed, by Tommy they are variously called 'milk cans' and 'old boots' from their clumsy progress through the air. At night one is warned of their approach by seeing the trail of sparks made by the fuse attached. The destructive effect of these huge bombs, many of which contain well over a hundred pounds of high explosive, is comparatively local. There is not the forward throw and scatter of metal that distinguishes shrapnel shell bursts. But their power of breaking down the strongest of trenches is terrific, and the shock of their explosion, with its accompanying inferno of sound, tends to unnerve the steadiest of troops. The fact that they can be seen in the air for a second or two before they explode, while affording a man a sporting chance to escape from their dire effects, also tends during any prolonged bombardment to put him into a highly strung condition.

'Stretcher-bearers to the right!'

The word was quickly passed along from mouth to mouth. In a few minutes two bearers staggered past me in the dark trench bearing between them the inanimate figure of a man whose low moans alone indicated to me that he lived. A moment later another stretcher-bearer passed leading by the hand a man stunned by shock and with sightless eyes.

And then, against the dark sky I saw a trail of sparks, and instinctively I sounded the warning whistle. The bomb seemed to be coming directly towards me, and I hesitated a moment before deciding which way to run. As I started off I heard another two men tumbling up behind me. We had just reached the corner of the traverse when – earth and heaven seemed to come together and to become one vast tongue of leaping flame; I felt myself falling through space and was conscious of a shattering roar.

The next I knew was that somebody was pulling me out from beneath a heap of sandbags and loose earth, and I heard him shouting in strange, faraway, agitated accents, 'Double up, men, there are three fellows buried here!' And others came with spades and entrenching tools, but ere they had begun work they had to run away again, and there was another flame that reached to heaven, another vast shaking of the earth, another roar, but not so loud this time. More sandbags and earth fell all round me, but I managed to wriggle out and was almost clear as the helpers returned. A minute later, and as I sat quite dazed on a fire-step, there was another rush of men along the trench, and another bomb burst near me. I felt the earth vibrate, I saw the wild flash, but I heard nothing. Soon, too, the sight left my eyes – my eyelids closed and no effort of will could open them. I was in a world all silent and dark. A stretcher-bearer half led, half carried me down the communication trench to the dressing station, but I was barely conscious of making the journey.

Another battlefield tactic that ate away at men's resolve was that of mining deep beneath no-man's-land, laying a charge and then blowing opposing trenches sky high. Both sides pursued this underground war with vigour, and for the infantrymen who occupied the line, any thought, any suspicion, that the enemy was digging beneath them caused understandable jitters. However, many mines were blown not directly beneath the trenches but in no-man's-land, a tactical explosion to block or destroy enemy galleries before they were completed. There was then a race to seize the resulting crater and fortify it, thereby gaining a local tactical advantage.

Private Robert Sturges, 19th Royal Fusiliers (City of London Regiment)

There was [a] distraction to prevent us getting bored that night, namely a succession of mine explosions: 'mining activity' I think they call it in the communiqués. If I remember rightly, no less than five mines went up that night. On each occasion we felt the preliminary shudder of the ground beneath our feet, heard the muffled roar and, in one case, received a good deal of earth: it is surprising what a time after the actual explosion the earth comes down. Apparently everything is over, when suddenly it begins to rain earth, or hail earth should I say? A mine going up at night always causes a great disturbance. Everyone within miles fires wildly in the direction of the crater, every machine gun comes into play and star shells are fired by the score.

Second Lieutenant Arthur Heath, 6th Royal West Kent Regiment

My platoon had the doubtful honour of being in the most dangerous part of the line we were holding, and had nearly half the battalion casualties, but they were not serious. Our welcome was a little unnerving. We were in a place where the lines run at curious angles, and in a sort of corner, where the trenches were about 120 yards apart, the Germans had exploded a mine nearly halfway across some months ago. About an hour after we had got in there was a tremendous explosion, the earth flew up, from a place that seemed quite near us, fifty yards or so

The moment a German mine was detonated beneath trenches occupied by the 1/5th Lincolnshire Regiment, killing 11 men and wounding 22 others.

into the air, and at once the German rifles and machine guns opened a heavy fire.

The men were a good bit scared, and for a moment or two I wondered if the Germans were going to rush. My job seemed to be to steady things a bit, and it would have been a fine occasion for a dramatic speech. The only remarks that came into my mind, however, were 'Sentries look to your periscopes and the rest keep low'. It was prosaic, but the opportunities for romance do not occur to you at the moment – at least, they didn't to me. After all, it is no use saying 'Remember Waterloo' to my men, for most of them have never heard of the battle, and would think that I was referring to the railway station. My job, however, really began later. There used to be a listening patrol in the old mine crater near which the new mine had been exploded. I had to go out, as commander of that part of the trench, and find out what really had happened, and what could be done about occupying the place or preventing the Germans from getting it.

Lieutenant Cecil Down, 1/4th Gordon Highlanders

It was a nice sensation going up to that crater, something like walking in your own funeral procession. When we reached it, after passing through a deadly sort of barrage with amazing luck, the crater was an awful sight. By the light of the moon you could see it all, the great yawning hole, a good fifty feet deep, with dead bodies stretched in ghastly attitudes down its steep sides. Every now and then one of the bodies, stirred by some explosion, would turn over and roll to the bottom, sliding down into a perfect shambles, where it would soon lose its identity among the jumbled heap of corpses and shattered limbs. Around the lip of the crater our men were trying to dig themselves in, but the earth was no firmer than sand, and in a second the crumbling foundations of an hour's desperate work would slide to the bottom, where at least they helped to cover up the awfulness which the first light of dawn was beginning to show up still more clearly. At one or two points, where old trenches led up to the crater, heavy bombing was going on, and it was only with the greatest difficulty that the enemy was being kept back. Our job was not in the crater just then and so we clambered over the lip and into another bit of trench which had been captured by us for some length, after which the Germans were still in possession.

Fighting over such craters was a grim, ugly business, and even Lieutenant Cecil Down's subsequent letter home, normally so upbeat and humorous, did not try to hide the horror. As the fighting died down, he had 'established' himself in a dugout in which a seven-foot mineshaft had been sunk. Exhausted, he fell into the shaft and woke three hours later to discover he had been reported 'missing, believed killed'. In his letter, he described in detail the fighting he witnessed but ended once more with the humour for which 'Tommy' was renowned. To stay alert at night he had penned a little poem, he said:

> At tea-time in the trench one day
> A shell took Bailey's brain away
> Said Thomas as he cut the bread,
> 'Look, there goes poor old Billy's head.'

Such ditties had kept Down awake and sane. However, even the blackest humour had curative limits.

Some of the men, in their suffering, forgot every one but themselves, and it was not strange that they should. Others, with more iron in their natures, endured fearful agony in silence. During memorable half-hours, filled with

Private James Hall,
9th Royal Fusiliers
(City of London
Regiment)

danger and death, many of my gross misjudgements of character were made clear to me. Men whom no one had credited with heroic qualities revealed them. Others failed rather pitiably to live up to one's expectations. It seemed to me that there was strength or weakness in men, quite apart from their real selves, for which they were in no way responsible; but doubtless it had always been there, waiting to be called forth at just such crucial times.

During the afternoon I heard for the first time the hysterical cry of a man whose nerve had given way. He picked up an arm and threw it far out in front of the trenches, shouting as he did so in a way that made one's blood run cold. Then he sat down and started crying and moaning. He was taken back to the rear, one of the saddest of casualties in a war of inconceivable horrors. I heard of many instances of nervous breakdown, but I witnessed surprisingly few of them. Men were often badly shaken and trembled from head to foot. Usually they pulled themselves together under the taunts of their less susceptible comrades.

At the close of a gloomy October day, six unshaven, mud-encrusted machine-gunners, the surviving members of two teams, were gathered at the C Company gun emplacement. D Company's gun had been destroyed by a shell, and so we had joined forces here in front of the wrecked dugout, and were waiting for night when we could bury our dead comrades. A fine drenching rain was falling. We sat with our waterproof sheets thrown over our shoulders and our knees drawn up to our chins, that we might conserve the damp warmth of our bodies. No one spoke. No reference was made to our dead comrades who were lying there so close that we could almost touch them from where we sat. Nevertheless, I believe that we were all thinking of them, however unwillingly. I tried to see them as they were only a few hours before. I tried to remember the sound of their voices, how they had laughed; but I could think only of the appearance of their mutilated bodies.

On a dreary autumn evening one's thoughts often take a melancholy turn, even though one is indoors, sitting before a pleasant fire, and hearing but faintly the sighing of the wind and the sound of the rain beating against the window. It is hardly to be wondered at that soldiers in trenches become discouraged at times, and on this occasion, when an unquenchably cheerful voice shouted over an adjoining traverse, 'Wot che'r, lads! Are we downhearted?' – a growling chorus answered with an unmistakable,

'YES!'

We were in an open ditch. The rain was beating down on our faces. We were waiting for darkness when we could go to our unpleasant work of grave-digging. Tomorrow there would be more dead bodies and more graves to dig, and the day after, the same duty, and the day after that, the same. Week after week we should be living like this, killing and being killed, binding up terrible wounds, digging graves, always doing the same work with not one bright or pleasant thing to look forward to.

These were my thoughts as I sat on the firing-bench with my head drawn down between my knees watching the water dripping from the edges of my puttees. But I had forgotten one important item in the daily routine: supper. And I had forgotten Private Lemley, our cook, or, to give him his due, our 'chef'. He was not the man to waste his time in gloomy reflection. With a dozen mouldy potatoes which he had procured, heaven knows where, four tins of corned beef, and a canteen lid filled with bacon grease for raw materials, he had set to work with the enthusiasm of the born artist, the result being rissoles, brown, crisp and piping hot. It is a pleasure to think of that meal. Private Lemley was one of the rare souls of earth who never lost his courage or his good spirits. I remember how our spirits rose at the sound of his voice, and how gladly and quickly we responded to his summons.

''Ere you are, me lads! Bully beef rissoles an' 'ot tea, an' it ain't 'arf bad fer the trenches if I do s'y it.'

I can only wonder now at the keenness of our appetites in the midst of the most gruesome surroundings. Dead men were lying about us, both in the trenches and outside of them. And yet our rissoles were not a whit the less enjoyable on that account.

It was quite dark when we had finished. The sergeant jumped to his feet.

'Let's get at it, boys,' he said.

Half an hour later we erected a wooden cross in Tommy's grave-strewn garden. It bore the following inscription written in pencil:

Pte 4326 MacDonald.
Pte 7864 Gardner.
Pte 9851 Preston.
Pte 6940 Allen.
Royal Fusiliers.
'They did their bit.'

Quietly we slipped back into the trench and piled our picks and shovels on the parados.

It was imperative that men were removed from the normal rotation of trench routine for a proper rest, a place where they could be away from the immediate sounds of gunfire, and the imminent threat of death and injury, to give time for body and soul to rest. They could not wait to come away from the line and they looked forward to it in just the same way that they feared the news that it was time to go back up again.

Lieutenant Cecil Down, 1/4th Gordon Highlanders

As was rumoured, a rest was in store for us. We were pulled out of the line without much warning, and here we are in a dear old village resting for all we are worth. We arrived at a station eight or nine miles away and marched here through the snow, first of all along the level, then through a great black wood as still as death, and then down into this village, nestling round the church, with the walls of the cottages almost as white as the snow itself, and the most gorgeous red tile roofs. Everything seemed so peaceful as we halted in the square and waited to be shown our billets. A perfect rest. Breathless rides through those grand woods. Pleasant afternoons round the fire. Of such things we thought. And there were rumours of a trout stream and a beautiful gamekeeper's daughter – the beautiful daughter of a gamekeeper I mean. Our hopes have been dashed to the ground. We are resting in the manner prescribed by the powers that be, and not in our own way. The result is that we have never been busier in our lives.

This is what happens. After many months of red war a division is withdrawn to recuperate at some spot in rear of the line. Officers and men are tired. They need a rest. Very well, they shall have one. And so they leave the guns behind them and seek repose. Now the land into which they come is a pleasant land, and a land where no Hun dwells. His place, however, is taken by the Arch-Hun, an old gentleman with a red band round his hat and nothing to do but to worry poor fatigued soldiermen. Before we have even had one good night's sleep Arch-Hun Number One descends upon us. He earnestly hopes that we shall have a good rest, but we must realise that we are where we are not only for the purpose of resting, but also in order to smarten ourselves up again, and recover from the discipline devastating effects of trench warfare. We salute and promise to do an hour's close-order drill every day. As he leaves the room, Arch-Hun Number One collides with Arch-Hun Number Two, who is on his way to impress upon us the need of long route marches for troops who have been unable to move about for the past few months. We give him our word for it that we had intended to have a route march every day, and we pray fervently that the other Arch-Huns have an offensive or something to keep them busy and leave us in peace. But we pray in vain. Number Three we never saw, but he spoke to us over the phone. He said that he was in command of the training area or something of that sort, and was no end of a general. We did not stand to attention as he couldn't see us, but when he rang off

Left: Two stooks of rifles belonging to men of the Honourable Artillery Company (HAC).

Right: Men of the HAC clean up after a spell in the trenches.

we were committed to an hour's running and rapid marching before breakfast. Arch-Hun Number Four was convinced that physical jerks were essential to the welfare of troops in rest, and Number Five thought that we must have forgotten how to skirmish and wouldn't it be a good thing if we did some every day just to freshen up the memories of the men. Arch-Hun Number Six was of the old familiar kind, from whom we cannot escape even when we are not resting. He desired the presence of fifty men every day at the Coal dump at B24C85 from eleven to two to unload coal. Arch-Hun Number Seven thought that another little inspection wouldn't do us any harm, and Arch-Hun Number Eight, who should really be classed as Super-Hun Number One, put the lid on it by stating that, as the training which must be put in by us during our rest period was so important for all ranks, leave would be stopped, but that as a special favour one per cent of the strength might be allowed to go on a jaunt to Calais for twenty-four hours. Aren't they good to us?

So here we are resting hard from about 3.30 a.m. till late in the day.

Corporal James Parr, 1/16th London Regiment (Queen's Westminster Rifles)

Oh! This army! At times I feel I could scream and put straws in my hair and I probably should if I didn't laugh. We are so messed about and badgered from pillar to post that I hardly know which way to turn; but it's all so childish and farcical that you can't help laughing at it when you can spare the time from swearing … You've no idea of what a rush it is to get off in the morning of a long march. Reveille 5.30, blankets to be rolled in bundles of ten and stacked at a certain place by 6, washing bowls, spades, lamps to be collected from the barns and taken somewhere else by 6.30. Breakfast 6.30, barns to be thoroughly cleaned and tidied by 6.45, battalion parades ready for marching at 7 – and then is generally kept waiting for an hour before it starts …

We march for fifty minutes and halt for ten, regular as clockwork. The halt just pulls you round and the first twenty of the fifty minutes go fairly easily, then time begins to drag and the last ten minutes, are done by sheer physical force. On and on, 'til it feels as if your neck muscles were being pulled out with pincers and your boots were soled with red-hot iron. You push your cap to the back of your head and the Colonel, riding down the column, calls out 'Put your cap on straight!' And all the time you have to smile, and joke, because the others are joking round you (when they aren't swearing) and you know that many of them are worse than you. That boy marching alongside you – it is his birthday and he's just nineteen – has got a swollen joint in his foot from frostbite last winter and dreads the halts almost as much as the marching because it means the pain of starting afresh; and that bugler in the platoon in front, who is having his pack carried by an officer, is sure to fall out about the tenth mile, for he is flat-footed and that is his limit. The dinner halt is very near now, thank God – only one more hill (and a nasty one) to be negotiated. I have seen nothing of the country, as my eyes have been fixed for the most part on the heels of the man in front.

In the autumn, British troops attacked near the town of Loos in conjunction with a French offensive to the south in Artois and Champagne. It was not an offensive that the British were entirely willing to undertake, preferring to wait until the new year when they would be better prepared. Nevertheless, the French, who had borne by far the biggest proportion of the fighting to date, were keen that their ally should play a significant part, and persuaded Sir John French to commit an army to the offensive.

Since the cessation of fighting at Ypres in May, the Germans had reduced their manpower in the west to redirect troops to the Eastern Front where they had had some notable successes. Those troops remaining on the Western Front were now in a defensive mode and were well dug in.

The Allied offensive would see for the first time Kitchener Divisions included in the Order of Battle. A four-day bombardment of German positions was ordered but the British did not have enough guns and so gas would be used to support the attacking waves of infantry. Although there was some initial success, including taking the town of Loos, the German second line of trenches was not breached. British reserves were held too far back and could not be brought forward quickly enough to maintain any forward momentum. Ultimately this failure was to cost the British Commander-in-Chief his command. The offensive struggled on for four weeks but to no avail, leaving a great many men dead and many more counting their blessings from their hospital beds.

Private Harold Butler, 6th The Buffs (East Kent Regiment)

10 October: No. 1 Temporary Hospital, Exeter

Well, matey it was Hell – simply Hell. I am lucky to be alive. On 27 September we marched to the attack. We had to march ten miles to the trenches with no food in our insides, some of the men fainted on the way; anyway we made the attack on the morning of 28 Sept, at ¼ to 10 a.m. The trenches were full of dead and we had to walk on them. We charged with fixed bayonets and I had got about twelve yards when I felt a blow at my shoulder like a sledgehammer, but I ran on with the blood oozing out like a fountain when I got bowled over with a bullet in the leg. I rolled into a small shell hole and laid there, trying to stop the blood which was pouring out. I was lying in a pool of blood.

Well, as I lay there a chap darted in and lay down beside me, he was frightened as he saw all the other men falling down and so he fell down near me, he wasn't wounded. Well, I lay there for hours with Maxim guns firing at me and Germans sniping but thank God they did not hit me again. And when it got dark the other chap crawled back to our trench but he never helped me so I was left weak and ill. I couldn't rise so I rolled over and over, dead bodies, German helmets etc. till I got to our trench then I dragged

Battle briefing: on the eve of going over the top, men of the 2nd Cameronians are given detailed instructions as to the following day's objectives.

myself along the communication trench for 1½ miles to the dressing station, and from there I went to several such places until I got to Rouen, that is the base and stayed in hospital there for five days. From there I came across to dear old England and I landed in this place, and now I am gradually getting better, but I'm going to be ill for some time (if possible). I am in no hurry to go out again (yet awhile). I have lost the dumdum bullet they extracted from my leg, but I hope to keep the one they get from my shoulder. Harold

As the British offensive at Loos was being pressed, the British Army, as part of its widening commitment to the war, was settling into vacated French trenches north of the River Somme. To British troops, the Somme appeared like a halcyon backwater in comparison to what they had experienced in the north, especially around Ypres, and indeed it would remain so for a further nine months. As autumn turned to winter the soldiers once again prepared for a general cessation of hostilities and a second Christmas at war.

On Xmas Eve we had lots of fun. Sgt Logan and I stuffed the men's socks with, first, two apples, then three handfuls of nuts, then a Xmas novelty from the Soldier's Comfort Association, such as a mouth organ or pipe, or game of checkers or a book, etc., etc. Then in the other sock we had a big package of candy and a pipe from me and two or three handkerchiefs from Walter and a stationery wallet and some tobacco and cigarettes. Weren't those lovely stockings! Some of the sections had a Santa Claus parade and handed them out. We at Headquarters hung them out over the chairs.

Walter got up some lovely socks for Madame's five little boys and girls. I put a piece of money in each and then Walter and I put in a nice box of candy for Madame and Lucie, the big Belgian girl. All the children came in on Xmas morning and presented us with bouquets and recited, in true childish fashion, some appropriate verses for Noel. It was sweet, in its way!

On Xmas morning, first of all, we arose at 7.30 and attended a communion service conducted very nicely by Captain Walker in my office –

Lieutenant Colonel William Harrison, 2nd Division Ammunition Column

Overleaf: Over the top: a very rare image taken of the London Rifle Brigade going through a gas cloud into action at the Battle of Loos.

quite a few attended and it was very impressive and inspiring. Captain Walker stayed to breakfast at which we had nice porridge and cream, kippered herring and coffee. A special cook from No. 2 Section aided in the preparation of our dinner. Don Pidgeon had been given charge of it and he ordered quite a lot of things from England, some of which arrived and some didn't.

Luckily we were able to buy a turkey. One of the doctor's civilian patients gave him a splendid goose, and they were both well stuffed. We had good soup of a prepared kind, excellent sardines on toast as an hors-d'œuvre, fresh vegetables, carrots, etc. and canned peas. Then we had one of Mother's plum puddings which came in gaily burning with brandy, and some small mince pies, and nuts and raisins, oranges, candies galore – also the best of champagne which is procured here at quite a moderate price. We had twelve in all and our table and room was beautifully decorated with quantities of holly with lovely red berries. We had a wonderful old candelabra and burned candles only. We had little flags of all the Allies and at each place a little present bought in London.

I drew a nice little pocket-book – others a diary or a shaving brush or some good little thing. Then we toasted the King, our Allies, our own Canadian home and ourselves and other toasts. It was a very successful affair.

Lieutenant Cecil Down, 1/4th Gordon Highlanders

Did I ever tell you that I am mess president? Anyone less fitted for the job could hardly be imagined … At present my chief trouble is the Christmas dinner. The plum pudding is all right, except that it will be hard to choose from the selection of them which is pouring in every day. The General has two, the brigade major three, the staff captain one, and the rest of us five between us. How I am going to make them all imagine that they are eating one of their own I don't know, unless I take a desperate plunge and use the seven-pound one sent by the *Daily News*. It should be a pleasing sight, half a dozen stalwart Tariff Reformers eating the gift of that paper. After the pudding we have plenty of preserved fruits, as well as almonds and raisins, but the turkey looks like falling through, and heaven alone knows what will take its place. There is a large haggis, but of course that is being kept for hogmanay night. I'd love to give them mutton, with sardines as the savoury, but I don't think I have the courage. We shall do all right in the liquid department, as we have been sent a dozen of champagne, and have some fine old port (à la Field Force Canteen) and a selection of liqueurs in our cellar. Our cellar, by the way, is a large packing case which travels about with us wherever we go. Each time we move, a bottle of port or whisky gets smashed – 'must have been the bumping on the road' – but it wouldn't look quite so suspicious if one of the bottles of mineral water got done in as well. Isn't it a terrible war?

Overleaf: A seventeen-inch 'dud' lying by the side of the Achicourt–Arras road.

There is a big attack coming off very shortly, and we are in it. And there is just a minute to scribble a line to you, with my love and greeting.

Lieutenant Malcolm White, Attd 1st Rifle Brigade

———

We were relieved last night just about the time that 1916 reported relief complete, and poor old bruised 1915 hobbled off to its permanent rest billet. The first sign of the relief comes in the morning, when the signalling officer of the other brigade arrives, and starts to take over the lines, and to go over those which have been newly laid. His signallers arrive soon after lunch, and half an hour later ours leave for camp, the first of the brigade to go.

During the afternoon the machine gun and bombing officers turn up, either on horseback or else on foot from the corner at which a friendly motor lorry has dropped them. Soon they are poring over maps in which lines in all colours radiate from points where machine guns lie hidden, and lists of grenades held in the trenches and at the main stores. Before long their relief is finished and two more weary soldiers hit out for home. With much splashing our mess cart struggles through the mud, loaded high with food and 'the cellar'. I am rather afraid, too, that when it turns the corner out of sight the packs of all the batmen will be added to the pile. The General, his work done, sits and reads *The Times* over again, while in the office the brigade major and staff captain are clearing up their papers and talking. Darkness is falling when, with much creaking, the baggage of the other people arrives, and soon from the direction of the kitchen comes the smell of frying onions.

The purr of a motor is heard in the distance, and then the k-lop, k-lop, k-lop of feet being dragged out of the mud. The door opens, letting in a blast

Officers serving with the 9th Rifle Brigade in winter billets 1915/16. The man standing is the adjutant, Captain Francis Gull.

Lieutenant Cecil Down, 1/4th Gordon Highlanders

of cold air and three muffled figures, the brains of our relief. The two generals retire to their room, where they discuss defence schemes and the programme of work. Our general is thinking to himself that he almost wishes that he hadn't to go, because he knows that the other people will thoroughly mess up the magnificent results of a week of real hard work. Their general, on the contrary, finds that his worst forebodings were only too true, and that during the week he has been away we have done absolutely nothing. That's the way in the army. Nobody ever does any work but oneself, and yet they do say that two million sandbags are used every week.

While the staff captain is handing over lists of stores, the correctness of which he certifies with his tongue in his cheek, the brigade major is explaining what has happened during the week, what work has been done, what strafing attempted, and, generally speaking, how the war has been progressing. Dinner comes on, and the mess president of the incomers apologises to the brigadier of the outgoers for the poorness of the dinner, which as a matter of fact he knows to be a particularly good one. Just as coffee is being served a message comes in to say that two of the battalions have successfully completed their relief, and gradually other pink slips arrive, telling that one lot of men have sat down to watch for another week and that ours are squelching down the long, long trail home. Ten strikes, and there are still the machine-gun company and one of the battalions unrelieved.

Our Brigadier yawns. He has had a long day. Soon we are all yawning. We have nothing to do, and are very tired; they want to get to bed and sleep so that they can be up early next morning. We both have to stay until that last battalion has finished its relief, for the machine guns reported shortly before eleven, and it is almost twelve now. The brigade major goes to the telephone and rings up. 'Haven't you finished yet – think the party for thirty-two must have got lost – try and hurry them up – yes, I know it's very dark – right – good night – what's that – oh, thank you, same to you', then hanging up the receiver and turning to the general, 'They aren't quite finished yet, sir, but they wish you a Happy New Year.'

We settle down again in our chairs and carry on with the yawning. An orderly brings in a pink form. The brigade major wakes up with a start.

'That's all now, sir', and goes off to wire to the division. We collect our coats and prepare to leave, when the Brigadier remembers a story he must tell. It is a very long one, but all stories have an ending. The door opens, letting out a ray of light into the dark night. Then it closes, and we plough our way towards the car, where the driver sits half frozen. Sleet stings our face and ears, and we bury our chins still further in our coats. A mile or so in front of us men will be standing out in it all night. We are the lucky ones without a doubt. And from the crossroads the Belgian battery bursts out into a new year's greeting. Ha-ppy-New-Year.

I am writing this quite comfortable on a bench with a [table]cloth of sandbags, and there is a wooden seat to sleep on. Unfortunately, there is no place for the servants, who have to live and cook on our brazier on the steep stairs! However, they are used to this. I have just got a new company cook; he is a great improvement on the last, who got slack. However, a week in the ranks will probably cure him as, though an officer's servant as cook has less leisure time and is more constantly at work, still he is assured of good shelter, plenty of food and is more certain of seeing the war through! He also has the art of making a decent stew; very often, in fact most days, the meat ration only admits of stewing, unless one is dining out at Headquarters, where one is sure to find a recognisable joint. But here in the front line, the less one eats the better; one is living for many hours a day in a stuffy dugout, the only outlet of fresh air being the short staircase which is always filled with servants who, besides cooking for us there, feed and sleep themselves.

Captain Eric Whitworth, 12th South Wales Borderers

Competent servants, especially those who proved a dab hand at cooking, were a valuable asset, often procuring food of a quality and freshness that astonished officers who eschewed questioning where the food had been obtained. Servants kept a note of officers' likes and dislikes and their fads, and could be trusted to take care of an officer's possessions, and to know where everything was at a moment's notice. It was a good job, with significant upsides for the incumbent. As one officer noted, a servant was often given permission to leave the line and, with mess money, given a roving brief to buy food wherever he could get it. He

Officers' servants preparing meat outside a billet.

might return with fresh bread, butter, eggs, perhaps a tin or two of fruit, maybe even of fois gras. And, of course, the more he bought, the more he cooked, and the greater likelihood of leftovers for him. Nevertheless, not every servant felt appreciated, and not every servant proved capable.

Private Daniel Sweeney, 1st Lincolnshire Regiment

You will be surprised to hear that I have stopped cooking for the officers. I have six new officers and one of them I did not like at all; they wanted me to do impossible things. I told them that I had satisfied other officers for two years and as I could not satisfy them they had better find someone else to do the cooking. Perhaps I have done a silly thing by leaving the job but I will chance it. I know everything will be a lot harder for me and I shall have to do sentry and all other horrible things. We are expecting to go back for a rest soon so if all goes well I may get another staff job.

We have two orderlies to do the waiting and that sort of thing. It sounds rather extravagant, but it isn't really, as one of them is too old to do anything else, and if we didn't have him he would have to go home as unfit. The head orderly stutters, but never smiles, and is constantly fighting with his helpmate, the infirm one, who goes by the name of Gibb. Gibb is a canny Scot, tall and skinny, with a flowing white moustache. He loves any sort of work which is unnecessary, and, though he is always at it, he won't do anything unless he does it in his own way. His chief jobs are to pick the tea leaves out of the sugar (somebody down the line always mixes them up before we get them), and to remove the hairs from the crust of the bread. Ration bread is always covered in hair, for some reason or another. It rather looks as if the bakers rub the loaves in sandbags while they are still warm. He does those two jobs quite well, but where he is a bit of a trial is waiting at mess. Of course he is much older than any of us, including the General, but that is hardly a good reason for his taking part in the conversation as he hands round the soup. 'My opinion,' remarks our guest, a mere major general, 'is that the Germans are not yet nearly done for, and that . . .' 'Mon,' breaks in old Gibb, 'd'ye no' ken whit yon Bottomley says?' and the major general, unaccustomed to being addressed as 'Mon' by a private soldier, collapses in his chair unable to speak or eat.

Lieutenant Cecil Down, 1/4th Gordon Highlanders

Chipping into the conversation as though Gibb were an officer was hardly the done thing and certainly not to a major general. Nevertheless, there were many among the rank and file who were being offered commissions, for the British Army was suffering from an acute shortage of commissioned men and many ordinary ranks were clearly of the right calibre. The losses among young officers in 1914 and 1915 had been grievous to the point that replacements as young as seventeen, and even sixteen, were sent to the Western Front. In searching for suitable candidates, the British Army found what they were looking for: Cambridge graduate Frederick Keeling was one obvious choice.

I was, in fact, anyhow very nearly, the senior sergeant in the battalion so many of the old hands had gone under. I feel I am doing all that I should be doing as an officer unless I happened to be in the exceptional position

Sergeant Major Frederick Keeling, 6th Duke of Cornwall's Light Infantry

of adjutant in an ordinary infantry battalion, and don't feel inclined to break the many ties by which I am bound for better or worse to my battalion. People at home who talk glibly about one's 'taking a commission' don't seem to realise anything about the hundred ties and associations which bind a man to his unit in any soldiering worthy of the name. It is a strange thing, but I feel that much of such pluck and fighting spirit as I possess doesn't come from my own self only it is born of the ties which I have with scores of individuals with whom my soldiering is associated. When you come back to a battalion after an absence you feel this very strongly.

Keeling refused a commission. He had soldiered in the trenches with his friends and could not envisage leaving them. Yet the feelings of loss were not replicated in units that had not shared such adversity and from which a large number of men were identified as suitable candidates for the officer corps. Throughout 1915, hundreds of men had been commissioned from the ranks of the Artists' Rifles and the same was about to be true of four public schools battalions of the Royal Fusiliers. The public schools and universities had supplied a large number of young men to the Fusiliers, men who had originally volunteered to serve as other ranks. They now appeared 'right' for a commission. By the spring of 1916 three of the four battalions serving in France would be disbanded, with men either being sent to cadet schools for officer training or moved on as drafts to other battalions. Private Robert Sturges was offered a commission earlier than most.

Private Robert Sturges, 19th Royal Fusiliers (City of London Regiment)

I think I have already told you the exciting news of four commission papers being given out and of the ensuing rumours. There really seems to be something in it. The story now goes, and most people seem to believe it, that another battalion has been sent for to take our place as soon as possible, and that we are to be withdrawn to the base. There we are to become OTC, from which batches of men will be taken from time to time for commissions. Everyone is bursting with excitement, as, if it is true, it means that this will be our last spell of the trenches for some time anyway. Part of the battalion is in the trenches now and part in reserve, our

Field Engineering Class.
Main Pillar Launched.

Same, showing process
of launching.

The RAFT, though faulty,
affords much amusement.

The BRIDGE more complete.
HENDERSON gets a trifle wet!

company being among the latter. I am to rejoin them tomorrow. We may have to relieve the companies in the trenches for a bit. It all depends on when the relieving battalion comes up. I hope it will put in an appearance soon as we have had snow for two days now and it's awfully cold; not weather for the trenches!

Officer cadets removed from the front line for officer training undertake a spot of bridge building, to evident amusement.

A few days later Sturges was ordered to return to England.

Saying goodbye is never a cheerful proceeding under the most auspicious circumstances. The circumstances on this occasion could scarcely have been more auspicious, but the contrast seemed all the greater in consequence. We were saying goodbye to men whom we had come to know inside out;

Rifleman Digby Freeman, 5th London Regiment (London Rifle Brigade), during his last leave in England. He was mortally wounded and died at 6.05 a.m., 12 October 1916.

more than that, we were saying goodbye to a life: a life, it is true, of squalor and dirt, a life of terror and hardship, a life which we hated, yet – shall I say it? Not one of us would have admitted it – thoroughly enjoyed.

We longed to get the journey over as soon as possible, but the train being French could not understand our anxiety, and refused to depart from its accustomed crawl. It was after dark when we reached Boulogne, and we rushed down to the quay lest we should miss the leave boat. We were in time all right, but the fates were against us, as, a minute before our arrival, the harbour was closed. The delay was tantalising. We spent the night in a neighbouring camp, and came down to the quay again early the next morning. This time the way was clear and, after what seemed a lot of unnecessary waiting, the boat slowly moved out of the harbour.

The crossing was much as other crossings, except that it was comparatively calm, and that we all wore life belts. I was told afterwards that just outside Boulogne harbour could be seen the masts of some ship which had been sunk there just previously. I did not see it myself, as when crossing the Channel I prefer to sit still and read a book, to rushing about and taking a lot of quite unnecessary exercise.

In due course we landed at Folkestone and got into an English train. We were half home again already. All the old things, the advertisements, the porters, the platforms, seemed like old friends. It was perfectly natural to see Beecham's Pills or Pears Soap, I suppose, but somehow we noticed them coming back where we had never noticed them going out.

In December 1915, two months after the failure at the Battle of Loos, Sir John French was removed as Commander-in-Chief of the BEF. Sir John's failure at Loos was the catalyst for his downfall, although in truth it was a catalogue of misjudgements and errors which put paid to his position. In his place was appointed Sir Douglas Haig. A firm believer that the Western Front was the theatre in which the war should be concentrated and where it would be won, he resolutely disapproved of other campaigns that had ultimately drawn away manpower from France and Flanders.

The battles of 1915 would appear, in retrospect, small affairs in comparison to the plans already under way in January 1916 to fight on the Somme. The size of the BEF would grow exponentially over the following months; it included a schoolteacher, Lieutenant Malcolm White. Soon after arriving in France, his battalion was inspected by the new Commander-in-Chief.

The arrival of Sir Douglas Haig down the road was rather picturesque. Unfortunately I had, like all Officer Commanding Companies, to give out that men *must* look straight to their front and not follow him with their heads, and therefore I had to keep my own straight. So it came about that I saw literally nothing except the great man himself when on the ground. But coming down the road, as I said, it was picturesque; the Commander-in-Chief and the Army Commander and their staff (or, rather, half a

Lieutenant Malcolm White, Attd 1st Rifle Brigade

dozen of them) and six Lancers and the corporal carrying the Union Jack, behind; it was this very medieval procession, trotting down the road a quarter of a mile from the field, that we could all have a look at and which was very striking. When he came on we had the usual business; the bugle sounded and we gave the general salute by battalions. Then he rode down past each battalion, when I could have had a good look at everybody if it would have been done: and as you may guess, I swivelled my eyes round a bit, only taking care to keep my head straight. However, the effect was that it was not until I found him bending down from his horse and asking me how long I'd been out, and 'had I been quite fit at the time?' that I realised he was upon me. I don't know at how many Company Commanders he stopped; quite likely all, though I don't think he did. It was fortunate that of two remarks, with which I have favoured the C-in-C, one was a lie! But the alternatives were:- (1) 'Yes, sir.' (2) 'Well, sir, now you come to mention it, I *did* catch a slight chill in the lines, and had a short spell in hospital in Hazebrouck; you know the place, perhaps, sir: very nice people they were indeed.' So rather than hold up the great man and the Army Commander and other brass-hatted gentry and the whole brigade with these truthful particulars, I chose (1).

Lieutenant Theodore Wilson, 10th Sherwood Foresters

I was sitting at my table – where I am writing this – when the door opened and in walked Sir Douglas Haig – the Commander-in-Chief!! The room was full of officers all discussing high tactics or swearing at the weather, or telephoning or consulting maps, and an 'awful hush' fell. Our General was with him and they walked round, talking to each officer in the room. They were all staff majors and colonels and I was the only New Army man in the room and the only subaltern at that, and I had a hole in the knee of my breeches! I tried to slip out (my table is near the door) but everyone was standing motionless to attention and the Colonel – my Colonel – frowned at me to stand still, which I did, feeling awful.

When the C-in-C came opposite me, the General said, 'This is Wilson, sir, who is helping us with staff work.' The C-in-C, to my great confusion, put out his hand and we shook hands. (Historic moment! Licks Nelson and Wellington hollow, doesn't it?) The C-in-C is a wonderful looking man, with a very firm chin, and dark blue eyes (or slate-coloured). He is rather short but very broad and strong looking. He looks at everything so directly and deliberately that you would almost think he was doing something difficult in just seeing – if you know what I mean. He never takes his eyes off the eyes of the man he is talking to …

I have had my leg pulled horribly about it here – as they all say I had bribed the General to put in a good word for me, and that I was the only man 'Sir Douglas' wished 'good luck' to, and that he only stood in front of me for so long because he had never see anything so odd to look at before in his life, and wanted a good stare while he was about it! They also say that I was polishing my hand on the back of my breeches before I shook hands and that I called him 'Duggie, old boy' and asked after 'Mrs Duggie! …' Everyone rags all day here. They are a most jolly crowd. Out of work hours we hardly ever stop laughing.

Catching up on home news, a young lad reads a letter from his family.

Officers both in and out of the line had to censor the post their men sent home. This was a task few officers enjoyed, not least because of the time it could take to read through scores of letters. Most chose to skim through them, looking for any mention of locations or other banned information felt by the army to be useful to the enemy.

Back in billets again and very busy doing nothing in particular. It is surprising what a lot there is to do and how very little there is to show for it. The morning after our return from the trenches the men write letters to all the people they have ever known or are likely to know. About midday your sergeant puts his head through the door of your hut and hands you a hundred or so to carry on with. They are a ragtime collection.

The first one you open will probably be one of the 'young hero' type and will contain some reference (untrue) to the constant thunder of the guns. The writer you gather is the only one of his section not suffering from

Lieutenant Cecil Down, 1/4th Gordon Highlanders

'wind up', which is not surprising considering the awful time we are all having. The food is awful and totally insufficient, only a pound of bully beef and several handfuls of biscuit per day, not to mention tea, sugar, vegetables and soup. Some men are never happy unless they are grousing.

Then comes the son anxious not to let his mother get an inkling that he is near the front. Either he gives lengthy descriptions of the surrounding country and little pen-pictures of the 'aeroplane flitting like a dove in the blue sky, surrounded by puffs of snowy smoke' variety, or else faute de mieux he recapitulates the salient features of his mother's last letter, dishing it up with an abundance of 'wells'.

'My dear mother,' it generally starts, 'your ever-welcome letter to hand. Also the cigs, which were fine. Well, you was saying that Sandy Ross had joined up at last. Well, it's about time he did. Well, this is a nice place but not very warm. Also the women are ugly. Well, little Andy is better, is he? Tell him I am glad to hear it' and three pages more in the same vein. I like that sort of letter, there's never anything to censor in it. But I guess the mother likes it more.

Then there's the 'old soldier' to his wife. Love for his family runs through an otherwise bald and unconvincing narrative, 'Dear wife,' he begins, 'It was good of you to send the socks as came yesterday. This place is all right, plenty of food, and rum every night. Give my love to Jock and Sally. There is a church here without no steeple which a German shell has blown away. Also little Tom. My officer gave me some cigs. to-day. Not forgetting baby Jean. Which was good of him. There is a terrible bombardment going on just now, so you might send me another tin of Keatings. I must stop now.
Your loving husband. Till Death. No. 13287
Pte. xxxxxxxx This for Sally and little Tom
xxxx also baby Jean xxxxx. Tell Jock he's got to be a man now and look after you.'

Lastly, there are the sort you read with one eye shut and the other one looking in the opposite direction. They generally begin, 'My own darlingest,' etc., etc., and end, 'your boy, Jock'. On the outside of the envelope are the mystic letters SWAK, but inside there is nothing of military importance.

Did I tell you of a rather nice boy in my platoon who writes a family letter daily always beginning

Second Lieutenant
Robert Vernede,
5th Attd 12th Rifle
Brigade

'Dear Mum and Dad, and dear loving sisters Rosie, Letty, and our Gladys, I am very pleased to write you another welcome letter as this leaves me. Dear Mum and Dad and loving sisters, I hope you keeps the home fires burning. Not arf.

The boys are in the pink. Not arf. Dear loving sisters Rosie, Letty, and our Gladys, keep merry and bright. Not arf.'

It goes on like that for three pages absolutely fixed; and if he has to say anything definite, like acknowledging a parcel, he has to put in a separate letter not to interfere with the sacred order of things. He is quite young and very nice, quiet, never grouses or gives any trouble, one of those very gentle creatures that the war has caught up and tried to turn into a frightful soldier, I should think in vain.

Censoring letters in billets might have been boring, but at least it was restful and comfortable. Billeting both officers and men had proved profitable for French and Belgian families, but as the war dragged on spirits began to flag and no longer were all temporary 'tenants' greeted with open arms. On the contrary, they were sometimes positively despised.

31 January: The old woman, my landlady, is about sixty, unmarried; her brother lives here, too. I have ascertained that they are notorious in the vicinity for their miserliness and ill temper. She springs out on you and bellows at you about your dirty boots and so forth. I admit she has put my back up, so sometimes I laugh and sometimes I rag her in English, which she doesn't understand, and sometimes I ask her what she is talking so loud for (in French), etc. etc. She then proceeded to complain to the Sanitary Officer that I was an undesirable and dirty person. It is true that I only wash my boots about once a week. I may say that in the whole house there is just about half a crown's worth of ancient matting and worn oilcloth. So there is no harm done. But she dislikes not having officers only in her rooms. This afternoon I was amazed to receive a visit from

Corporal Frederick
Goodyear, Attd
Special Company
(Meteorological
Section) 5th
Division, Royal
Engineers

two NCOs of the sanitary section. They were equally amazed at my manners and appearance. I don't know what they had been led to expect. It so happened I had washed the boots this very morning and hadn't worn them since. There they were, spotless. The room was also unusually neat and clean.

3 February: The landlady continues in good fettle. She is determined to shift me somehow. It turns out that there is some irregularity and she hasn't received any money for the room since it was first occupied on 27 Aug. And nobody seems to have any papers about it. But I refuse to worry about getting another billet. I have told her that an officer brought me here and I shall stay here till another officer orders me out. Then she goes raging away to the officer of the ADVS (Vet.) on the ground floor and relieves herself about me to the sergeant there, saying that her house is reserved for officers and that she won't have soldats in it. 'Les soldats – pf-f-f', with a disdainful wave of the hand. The sergeant, a stolid old chap, being a soldat himself, doesn't think this is quite tactful on her part.

I take great delight in suggesting to her ways of getting rid of me. I have recommended her to complain against me to the gendarmes, to the Mission francaise, and to the secretary at the mairie. These are various ideas I picked up in conversation with an interpreter. The only thing I won't do is to move without proper compulsion. I point out to her that she must arrange for my removal, as she wants it, but that, in consideration of the fact that we are foreign troops, so it may not be easy for her to know exactly how to act, I am willing to give her all the advice in my power, but that unfortunately I am not an expert in billeting and further that I am not certain who billeted me here, whether it was the meteorological people, or the signallers, or the camp commandant, or who. So for the moment there is a fine fog over the whole matter. However, I can trust her to send some lightning flashes through it. I expect hourly to be cast out on the street. – And I am wondering vaguely how to salvage all my stuff, if I have to move at a moment's notice.

5 February: The landlady has succeeded in getting rid of me. Having failed with the sanitary section she tried the gendarmes, and the Town Mayor came to the conclusion that, if we couldn't agree, I had better move. So they found me a billet a little way down the same street next door to

Opposite above: Resting in billets. Geoffrey Woodroffe (left) and Eric Vine, friends of John Polgreen in the Artists' Rifles. All three were commissioned and all survived the war.

Opposite below: All smiles now, but not every billeting family continued to welcome British soldiers with open arms.

where I feed. It is a much worse billet, but the people seem nice enough. It isn't really their house; they are refugees from the other side of the German lines … I clean forgot my rifle and a pair of pants, and my former landlady was seen bringing them down the street after me. Humours of war, I suppose!

When we got here this morning, the owner of our mess billet was ready for us with a marble chimney slab in three pieces, which she says we broke last week, when we were here. I should think she did it with a sledgehammer, myself. After a long shrieking argument with her, she getting in ten words to my one, I said I would make myself acquainted with some of the elementary facts of the case. She said that it was a matter of 100 francs.

Lieutenant Malcolm White, Attd 1st Rifle Brigade

Two days later Lieutenant White arrived at yet another billet. Here, too, all was far from well.

Arrived at an unlovable village, at about 11.30. The men's billets were bad. When we came to find our mess, we discovered a very angry, high-screaming woman, pushing our servants out of the door and depositing their rifles and their 'sacs' (packs) after them. It appeared that the servants had come in and taken possession in rather a cavalier fashion. Indeed, the lady brought in her husband clad in pants and a shirt, and thus arrayed he shouted 'Sortez; sortez', and gave us a spirited imitation of the exact song and dance which the servants had done, his wife providing the music. I've never heard anyone so loud as that woman. I remarked that there were 'des choses de plus mauvaises' – Q. 'Quoi donc?' A. 'Les Allemands.' – 'Allors, allez les chasser.' We assured them that, as usual, there would be money for all this. At that the man ceased to dance, but the woman is still shouting and comes to me with complaints against my servant, whom she calls 'celui-la'. Celui-la stands gravely to attention the while in the doorway, and I simply expire with laughter.

Opposite: Happier times: Lieutenant White's great friend and fellow teacher at Shrewsbury School, Lieutenant Southwell, possibly in the village of Simencourt, west of Arras.

She has just forbidden us to play with a tennis ball in the orchard at the back.

The issue of compensation was always a thorny one for the British Army, aware that it was occupying premises and land that belonged to a friendly nation but also that inflated requests for compensation were legion. Attempts to mollify angry civilians were often far from successful.

Captain David Hirsch, 1/4th Alexandra, Princess of Wales's Own (Yorkshire Regiment)

I've learnt quite a lot of French. I've also billeted the battalion twice, each time without an interpreter and once with a population that could only be mildly described as hostile, as they had suffered rather heavily from close billeting and slack supervision of hungry and cold troops, a fact that resulted in the disappearance of eggs and chickens, vegetables and beehives, butter and milk and in the burning of anything wooden up to window frames.

Compensation was paid to farmers who could prove financial loss, and sanction taken against any soldier caught pilfering. Much has been written about Courts Martial awarded to soldiers accused of very serious crimes, such as desertion or cowardice, less of the day-to-day, run-of-the-mill offences that were serious enough to be taken to court but not serious enough to warrant severe sanction. In all, over 163,000 Courts Martial took place overseas. The conviction rate for other ranks stood at over 85 per cent with the vast majority resulting in relatively minor punishments from fines or reduction in rank to field punishments.

Lieutenant Cecil Down, 1/4th Gordon Highlanders

The way that justice is dispensed in the army is wonderful. Imagine the private parlour of a small French estaminet cleared for action, the tile floor covered with sawdust and a bright fire burning in the grate (thank the Lord we are out of the land of stoves). In the centre of the room a table with three chairs at the fire end of it, and in front of them piles of blotting paper, foolscap, pens (but no ink), and a collection of books, foremost among which is the red-covered *Manual of Military Law*. So much for the setting of the stage. Now for the players.

Punctual to the recognised time for starting these shows, half an hour late that is, enters Second Lieutenant Dash, the junior of the three members of the Court. A few minutes later he is followed by the other two, Lieutenant Asterisk and Captain Blank, the President. They sit down on the chairs. Captain Blank in the centre, Lieutenant Asterisk on the right and Second Lieut. Dash on the left. The President lights a cigarette and offers his confreres his case, from which they also extract smokes. 'Have you the foggiest idea what it's all about?' he asks. The reply is an emphatic negative. They look through the papers in front of them, and the bunch with the requisite information is discovered. The President picks it up and glances through it. 'Seems a good bit of it, doesn't there?' They plod through the pile of documents. At last they have finished. 'Better get a move on now,' says the President. 'How do you begin?' Asterisk has been on a Court quite recently and remembers, or thinks he does, the wording of it. Dash takes one of the many sheets of paper and fishes an indelible pencil out of his pocket. 'Fire ahead,' he grunts, and writes to Asterisk's dictation.

'Proceedings of a Court of Enquiry assembled by order of Brigadier General A. Bhoy at ... – or should that come before the "enquire into" – anyhow, leave it at that – ... got that down, good!

'The Court, having assembled, proceed to take evidence.'

'Finished,' says the writer. 'Shall I tell the sergeant to call in the first witness?'

He does so.

From outside comes a roar, 'Private Sloper, Shun! Ri'turn, quickmarchlefwheelriturnalt', and the first witness is manoeuvred in. He stands in front of the table looking very sheepish, and out of sheer embarrassment starts to scratch his head.

'Stantenshun, Private Sloper', in stentorian tones from the sergeant.

'What is your name and number?' asks the President, and when this has been given, 'Well, what have you to say?'

The oracle speaks. 'I was acoming down the road from Sally Farm it might 'ave been Tuesday, sir, when I sees 'im.'

'See who?'

''Im 'oo's outside, sir.'

'He means Private Fowler, sir.'

'I sees Privit Fowler comin' out of the 'ennouse. I ses to 'im ses I, "'Ullo Bill, 'ave you seen Charlie lately?" "No," ses 'e, "I carntsayslave." "Wot, not seen old Charlie?" ses I. "Why 'e was askin' me for you las' night." Then 'e turns round to me, 'e does, and ses, "Wotdyerthink of the beer 'ere,

Tom." "Not much," ses I, "but the vinnblangs alrite."'

'Half a second. Private Sloper. Did you see Private Fowler carrying any hens with him or not?'

'Well, sir, I notices as 'ow 'e 'ad somethink under 'is tewnic, so I asks 'im, "Wot the 'ell 'ave yer got there?" and 'e ses to me, "Wot the 'ell's that gotter do with you?" "You've been pinchin' 'ens," ses I, "I can see them under your tewnic". "Aven't I told yer ter mind yer own bloo."'

'You haven't answered my question, Private Sloper. Did you or did you not see him taking away some hens?'

'Yessir, an' I ses to 'im.'

'That's enough. And had he his rifle with him?'

'Yessu–, an' I ses to –im, "Wot in the 'ell."'

'That's enough. Have you got all that down, Mr Dash?'

'I was hardly able to keep up, sir.'

'Well, write this down. I saw Private Fowler at four o'clock on the afternoon of 17 November. He was coming out of La Ferme Salle and was carrying his rifle. Several hens were secreted underneath his tunic. That right, Private Sloper? Right then, sign it', and the abridged version of his evidence is passed over to him.

His signature duly made, he retires, manoeuvred out in the same way as he was manoeuvred in. Outside he can be heard carrying on with his explanation of what he said to him, and what him said to he.

'Second witness', calls out the President, and from the outside comes the sergeant's voice, 'Corporal Biggs, 'Shun! Ri'turn, quickmarchlefwheel-riturnalt.'

Corporal Biggs is no end of a fellow and gives a terrific salute. He evidently knows what is expected of him, for, placing his head on one side and staring steadfastly two foot six above the head of the President, he starts at a terrific rate. 'Sir-on-the-afternoon-of-the-17th-hinstant-at-about-four-p-hem-I-was-proceed-in'-in-a-westerly-direction.'

'Half a moment, Corporal Biggs. Would you mind giving us your number and regiment? Right. You were passing the farm when you saw Private Fowler.'

'Yes, sir. I saw him hissuing from the hentrance, equipped with his rifle. Underneath his jacket I noticed a suspicious procumference which hon hin-vestigation proved to be three hens. Blood was dripping from newly formed hincisions, which, if my opinion be requested, were caused by bullets from a rifle or other such-like harticle. As he was unable to give any satisfactory explanation of how he came to be in possession of the aforesaid hens, I took charge of same and reported the matter to my platoon commander.'

'Thank you, corporal. Very clearly put indeed. Please sign this, and do you mind telling me if you have ever been a policeman? I thought so. Next witness, please, sergeant.'

The next witness is the owner of the hens. He is accompanied by the interpreter. After five minutes of the most frenzied word storm the interpreter speaks.

'Sir, zis is ze farmair to which ze chickens did belong. 'E ses zat zey vas prize hens and zat they cost him fifty francs each one. But I do not sink that 'e the truth tells. If you like I vill ze birds fetch.'

He brings them in, and they prove to be notable only for their skinniness. The owner is told that he will be repaid a fair price, and departs unhappy. The hens remain before the Court, lying on the table.

The final witness is Private Fowler. He comes in looking very sulky, and forgets to salute. Under the circumstances he can hardly help admitting that he had something to do with the lamentable end of the hens, but he tells a long and complicated tale of how he was trying a cartridge into his rifle, 'just to see if it fitted', when the rifle went off by itself and the bullet went through all three hens. When found with the hens he was going in search of the farmer to compensate him. When he has finished the President looks at him.

'Are you going to stick to that tale, Private Fowler?'

'Yessir, it's the truth I'm telling.'

'Certain? ... I should think of something better if I were you ... Or what about telling the truth? ... It is the truth ... Oh, all right, if you're going to put your money on it, come and sign.' And as the man goes out, 'Isn't it extraordinary what bad liars some people are?'

For a minute the case is discussed, and then, 'The Court, having considered the evidence, is of opinion that the three hens were shot by Private Fowler.'

A bird sits on the fuse cap of an artillery shell.

'Thank the Lord that's over,' from Captain Blank.

'But what about the hens?'

From the estaminet slunk the three members of the Court. Each carried something shapeless wrapped up in a large sheet of blotting paper.

The British had been firmly ensconced in the Somme region for six months. In comparison with the industrial region of Loos and Lens to the north, and the flat, uninspiring terrain near Ypres, the Somme, with its rolling chalk landscape, its charming gentle valleys and woods, its river and its pretty tributaries, reminded soldiers more of the Sussex Downs than France. Furthermore, this agricultural region remained largely unspoilt. As the spring and then early summer brought the land to life, so soldiers could enjoy, at least for a moment, all that nature and wildlife had to offer.

Corporal Frederick Keeling, 6th Duke of Cornwall's Light Infantry

It is pleasant to have a change, but it is not in all ways for the better. The spring is delightful in this rolling chalk country. Every morning when I was in the front-line trenches I used to hear the larks singing soon after we stood-to about dawn. But those wretched larks made me more sad than almost anything else out here. Their songs are so closely associated in my mind with peaceful summer days in gardens or pleasant landscapes in Blighty. Here one knows that the larks sing at seven and the guns begin at nine or ten.

Lieutenant Cecil Down, 1/4th Gordon Highlanders

It is at dusk, when the German lines are gradually fading away into the evening shadows, that I like to get out and wander through the padre's garden, which by day is in full sight of the Hun. Along deserted gravel paths, now sprouting with new green grass, borders of the most beautiful white narcissus on either side, through sheltered walks fragrant with violets, into the fruit garden, a mass of pink and white blossom. There I love to stay and watch the setting of the sun and the first gleaming white lights shot up by the anxious sentries at the foot of the hill. And when I begin to feel too sentimental I pull myself together and loot a bunch of spinach and the best of the rhubarb for our dinner. The spring onions are nearly ready, and the asparagus won't be long now. It is rather a find for me, as when an orderly comes along from Battalion HQ with a bit of a stinker in the way of chits, please explain delay and all that sort of thing you know, I send him back with a soothing answer and a prime cauliflower. They are beginning to count on me for their supply of 'vegs'.

A black-and-white kitten, about three-quarters grown, lives in our dugout, and forms a centre of common interest. While things are quiet it will run about outside but it will not go far away. It recognises the sound of travelling shells but what is really remarkable is its ability to differentiate between ours and the enemy's. Shells coming from guns behind us make a noise similar to that of Jerry's coming towards us. But this cat can appreciate the difference in direction and also understands that danger comes from one direction only. Batteries of all sizes are around us at distances of two or three hundred yards and they are tolerably active. But puss takes no notice of our guns firing nor of the sing and whistle of our own shells coming towards us from the rear and passing over us towards the enemy; but directly Fritz starts to send any over to us she makes a beeline for the dugout. She doesn't wait for the shell to burst; as soon as she hears its whistle she is off, no matter what she is doing; she will even leave her dinner and won't come out of the dugout until the shelling is finished although none of the shells may fall dangerously near us. There is something more than instinct in that.

Sapper Albert Martin, 122nd Signal Company, 41st Division, Royal Engineers

The trenches lie in a village and a wood, and grass, nettles and thistles grow very high along their edges. I have seen thistles six feet high. It makes one feel like Alice in Wonderland when she grew small – your head is about the level of the roots of the grass, and you go along looking up from that position at these great plants that you are accustomed to brush aside with your foot. One seems to have become an insect.

Captain Harold Bidder, 1st South Staffordshire Regiment

Corporal Frederick
Goodyear, Attd
Special Company
(Meteorological
Section) 5th
Division, Royal
Engineers

It is one of the ironies of nature that few animals are more unsteady on their legs than centipedes. I had one walking on a newspaper the other day, the lightest puff rolled it over. The legs are very feeble and set close to the middle line. As they move them in bunches of about ten at a time, when walking, I can't see that they get full value for the number they have.

I watched a cuckoo for about half an hour the other day. He was in a leafless tree. There is no more vain and absurd bird. Flutters and flirts about as if he were a flycatcher. If he'd only keep still, he might pass for a sparrowhawk, except that his tail is a bit too long.

Lieutenant
Cecil Down,
1/4th Gordon
Highlanders

Two swallows have started to build a nest over the fireplace in the mess room, and they carry on quite unperturbed by the other occupants. They fly in and out of the window, and if that is shut they bang their wings against the glass until someone lets them in or out. Our latest subaltern, who has to sleep in the mess room, feels rather bitter about this, as they keep flitting about all night long and they insist on using the window directly above him, and so he has the choice of getting out of bed to attend to their wants or of having the window wide open and getting soaked every time it rains. There is a telephone wire stretched across the room from the door to the window and the two sit on this while we feed, and look down at us with faint interest.

A good example of a privately taken snap of the sort an official war photographer would not take.

By the early summer of 1916, final preparations for the great Allied offensive were under way. The plan, devised as far back as December 1915, foresaw a great joint effort by British and French forces on the Somme where, unlike at Loos, the Allies would attack symbolically side by side.

In February the Germans launched a massive offensive at Verdun, derailing Allied plans inasmuch as the French commitment to this proposed offensive had to be scaled back, leaving the bulk of the effort to British and Empire troops. The losses at Verdun placed almost intolerable pressure on the French army which, in turn, placed pressure on the British to attack as soon as possible on the Somme.

Twenty-two today: John Polgreen takes a birthday dip behind the lines.

Such an offensive, it was hoped, would force the Germans to moderate their efforts at Verdun. Throughout the spring months of 1916, the British prepared not for a breakthrough, as has often been suggested, but for a battle which would weaken the enemy to such a degree that the war might be brought to a successful conclusion in 1917. There was no great strategic objective on the Somme other than that this would be a battle of attrition.

It was evident to all that something out of the ordinary was impending, for men and guns continued to appear in ever-growing quantities. Valleys that only a week before had been devoid of all occupants now began to assume an aspect of busy preparation. Huts and dugouts were being constantly erected, and the masses of materials assembled for the Royal Engineers became exceedingly great. Horse lines seemed to spread themselves across every fold in the ground, and batteries to spring from the soil in every direction. Once again, as on the eve of Loos, we lived in an atmosphere of endless speculation.

Second Lieutenant Geoffrey Fildes, 2nd Coldstream Guards

Certainly, many signs and portents gave credence to our belief that great things were about to happen. The construction of new roads along specially selected routes seemed hardly explicable on any other grounds; also, a new railway was being built across the countryside to the north of us. Though only a single track, it would be a valuable auxiliary to the permanent line down at our present railhead. Every ravine and hollow behind the Fricourt ridge was being converted into a battery position, and trenching and mining operations were being pushed on at all possible speed throughout the neighbourhood. Miles of wire cables were said to have been laid in trenches seven feet deep, these being joined up at certain points into a huge telephonic system.

Lieutenant
Cecil Down,
1/4th Gordon
Highlanders

They manage to keep things a bit more quiet than they used to, though a certain amount did get out concerning the 'Push'. The news would probably come up with the rations, the quartermaster having been told by the ASC supply officer. Your post from home would contain one or two references to it. From the casualty clearing station would come tales of extensive preparations to receive wounded. All these signs might be mere coincidences, but when you saw the cerise band on the hat of an elderly gentleman walking round the trenches you knew that the worst was in store. For the Deputy Assistant Director of Medical Services is the stormy petrel of the Western Front. Whenever he appears in the front system, there is trouble ahead. He comes into your dugout and says a few well-chosen words on the sanitation, or lack thereof, in your trenches, but all the time his eye is roving round your abode deciding how many stretcher cases could be accommodated in it. And sure enough an hour or so after he has gone there comes along a chit from Battalion HQ saying that your happy home is to be turned into an advanced aid post, and will you please clear

The Somme: looking across to the German trenches in the Schwaben Redoubt. On 1 July, men of the 36th Ulster Division attacked from Thiepval Wood on the right.

out of it forthwith. Then it's a foregone conclusion, and you are quite prepared for the summons to meet the CO in his boudoir with all the other officers, and have a large document, labelled 'secret and confidential' in blue pencil, read out to you on the subject of your assaulting the German trenches, marked in red pencil, on the near date and at a time to be communicated later by special messenger. But this time, though, everybody knew when it was coming.

10 June: Wet, of course! … Major Kirkland had a premature [explosion] today whilst firing High Explosive. Blew the gun to pieces – the wheels came off and the spokes flew out of the wheels. Three men, a sergeant and an officer laid out. It also set fire to the gun pit. Beastly luck. What the Huns do is enough, without any such mischance. We have now got three gun pits completed, two big dugouts and the mess nearly completed. I have got 1,800 rounds of the 8,000 we are to start with, stored now, and am to get the rest at the rate of eight wagons daily. Don't know where the devil to put it! 9 p.m., as I am writing, the Boche has started searching round the valley again, and it is simply packed with wagons and working parties.

Lieutenant William Bloor, C Battery, 146 Brigade, Royal Field Artillery

11 June: Wet and stormy. Worked twelve hours. French batteries keep coming in. The French here have come up from Verdun, where they have been for six weeks. They are known as the 'Iron Corps' and are the pick of the French army. The going is very heavy now for transport – in this district all the traffic is across country, and as all metalled roads are impassible, wagons are often axle-deep; and all day long the teams come struggling up the hill near us, the drivers using whip and spur and voice with all their strength. The French horses are a hardy smallish horse of a distinct type – they are ugly and do not carry an ounce of fat, but they are the most wonderful workers, and are obviously well used to collar work and big loads. Their 'pluck' is commented on by our drivers, and I heard one say – 'Them's not horses, them's engines!'

About the 16th, I was sent with the Coldstream company, to which I had reverted, to aid our engineers in constructing a new road in the woods near Suzanne. This village lay some three miles to the east of Bray, in a district occupied practically entirely by the French …

Second Lieutenant Geoffrey Fildes, 2nd Coldstream Guards

Already staked out by the RE, our road was fully prepared for our arrival. With a sublime faith in our powers for work, they had run it straight through a morass of mud, which lay stagnant beneath the shade of the wood. On inspecting the place, we found that, as a result of recent rains, we had to cope with a pond of mud having an average depth of eighteen inches. This ran down the bed of a disused road for about fifty yards. Accordingly we set to with ardour, for three days only had been granted us in which to complete this task. By cutting channels into a ditch, we were able to drain off most of the water before many hours; then the remaining mud was shovelled clear of the track, and the face of the old metal laid bare. On this we unloaded fresh stone chippings to bring the road to a level surface. Upon this again, the Engineers laid a wooden road as we completed each section of the way. But in spite of their repeated assertions as to the importance of this work, they seemed unable to provide us with much material. Except for what we could find in the locality, there was almost a complete lack of supplies; evidently the French had seized everything …

In the last week of June, came a spell of glorious weather, and with it a final burst of activity. All through the long summer days, banks of dust clouds hung across the wide countryside where endless columns of horse and motor traffic flowed along the high-roads. Guns were rolling up almost every night, batteries of guns, scores of guns; and in their train flowed streams of ammunition, ranking from the modest 18-pounder to the food destined for the heaviest pieces. Each morning, the tracks of caterpillar tractors on the roads revealed the night's activity.

And as our preparations behind the lines increased, so did the enemy's gunfire, seeking out the clouds raised by the Allies' transport columns. Long-range shrapnel fire became frequent, woods and hollows being favourite targets; but beyond an inevitable series of petty casualties among men and horses, no great loss was inflicted …

Throughout this week the Entrenching Battalion worked in desperate haste on such a new roadway. The nature of our task may be better estimated when I mention that in two days we prepared two miles of track, cutting through a coppice and a wood, and building along a hill-crest an embanked causeway. The most difficult part of our labours was the removal of roots of

Opposite: A Vickers machine-gun team well dug in on the Somme, probably in a reserve line.

trees, which in many places obstructed the way. Of course, a few days' rain would suffice to convert this 'X' road, as it was called, into the state of a quagmire, but so long as it was used for horse transport alone, it might be expected to render reliable service.

From our positions on the crest overlooking the Somme valley, a large expanse of open country lay visible to the eastward. There, wafted from the hazy horizon, the deep notes of our guns were clearly distinguishable as they flung back their reply to the enemy. Around us the atmosphere seemed charged with the myriad thoughts of an army. The crisis was at hand.

From mid-June until the eve of the bombardment, the weather was fine and warm with just the occasional evening shower. However, on 23 June there was a torrential thunderstorm. For the next week there was either heavy or intermittent rain, the skies remaining implacably overcast, hampering final preparations.

Second Lieutenant Geoffrey Fildes, 2nd Coldstream Guards

Work of the greatest importance remained to be done, and to the Guards Entrenching Battalion fell one more task of pioneering. Running north-east from the town of Bray toward the British ridge lay the Bronfay road, so

A tunneller of the 252nd Tunnelling Company, Royal Engineers, digging in the Somme chalk at Beaumont Hamel. The mine he helped prepare was blown just prior to the infantry advance, 1 July.

named on account of the farm that stood beside it on the sheltered side of the crest. Here, on the first day of our bombardment, I received orders to take a working party of Coldstream and Scots Guards.

By 8 a.m. we were ready to commence work. Our task was one of widening the roadway by several feet for a distance of three or four hundred yards. This route constituted the supply line of the local corps. Distant about three-quarters of a mile on our left front lay the Fricourt ridge, still veiled by a slight ground mist, while, in the valley behind it, lurked massed batteries awaiting their orders. Straight ahead, only a few hundred yards up the road, stood the farm buildings, now seething with orderlies and staff cars ...

It must have been about an hour later when the time arrived for our guns to open; thereupon, punctually to the minute, a sudden salvo broke the stillness of the early morning. But my expectation of a dramatic outburst was grievously disappointed. The noise seemed trifling in comparison with the gunfire which had opened the battle of Festubert. After watching the batteries for a while, some of us came to the conclusion that the stories we had heard concerning our ammunition supplies had been greatly exaggerated ...

For several hours our guns continued to thunder, firing in salvos of batteries; but so slow and deliberate was their shooting that for some considerable time it was hard for us to realise their activity was anything more than their usual daily routine. Many of us wondered when they were going to commence. However, as they continued with unabated precision hour after hour, one began to realise by and by the great quantity of shells they must have been consuming.

25 June: Attended two services and enjoyed good sermons. Our light gunfire continues unabated. 6.45: Whilst in church some of our largest guns opened out – up to six-inchers. The ground had begun to tremble now and the bombardment seems ever-increasing in intensity. Though our heavy batteries have not fired a shell, the crashing roar of some of the reports made me pray for the Germans.

Night. The whole heaven is lighted up by the glare of the gun flashes, one orderly was called out to fetch a wounded from Mesnil; he had a

Private Frank Williams, 88th Field Ambulance, Royal Army Medical Corps confused impression of a sort of hell let loose. The night sky was a mass of lurid light from the star shells and the incessant flash of guns, whilst the scream of aerial torpedoes and tear gas shells and the general booming artillery was punctuated by the explosion of mighty monsters of destruction, the whole combined coming to us behind with an ominous rumble, like the sea on a cavernous coast.

Lieutenant William Bloor, C Battery, 146 Brigade, Royal Field Artillery

26 June: Fired continuously till 1.30 p.m. (598) rounds. It was a sight to see the hostile trenches. The whole countryside was just one mass of flame, smoke and earth thrown up sky high. About 5,000 shells per diem are pitching on a front of about 500 yards. Whilst observing, I could not resist feeling sorry for the wretched atoms of humanity crouching behind their ruined parapets, and going through hell itself. Modern war is the most cruel thing I have ever heard of, and the awful ordeal of those poor devils, even though they are Boches, must be impossible to describe.

7 p.m. The Forward Observation Officer sent down 'Action' and I gave the order to fire from underground, where we control the guns. Was horrified to hear a shout that we had blown a man's arm off – ran out and found one of our signallers just returning from the OP [Observation Post] lying on the ground with his right arm lying on the grass beside him. He had run right in front of No. 1 gun, and the shell had hit him on the shoulder. Luckily the doctor was in the mess at the time; he came out and between us we got him bound up and sent away.

Captain Harold Bidder, 1st South Staffordshire Regiment

26 June: It was then dusk, and as it got darker the scene was very weird. There were heavy clouds, and under them a red band of sunset in the NW. The continuous flashes of the guns played on the clouds like summer lightning, while over the German trenches the shrapnel was bursting in white flares, the High Explosive in dull red glows. The Germans were sending up a few Very lights: these, in more than a semicircle round us, served to show the great curve in the line. Our shells whistled overhead, and, as it got darker still, showed as red shooting stars whizzing across. We opened with two machine guns. The noise of a stream of machine-gun bullets is like waves on a stony beach, a prolonged swish. The biggest noise was the earthquake crashing of the French trench mortars. I left in the early

morning and walked back here. You have to go carefully, for guns are everywhere, and (owing to the salient) pointing in all directions. A figure stepped out of the shadow of a little combe I was walking up. 'Ne passez pas au front des pieces,' it said – and I saw by my hand the muzzle of a .75.

It was too dark to see the reds, the yellows and the mauves of poppy, mustard and cornflower with which the last ridge is covered, where the fields were tilled not long since; but the birds were waking up, and the smell of the privet by the road and that almost pungent smell of earth in early morning grew stronger with the beginning of dawn.

28 June: Pouring with rain and knee-deep in mud everywhere. I went up to the trenches early in the morning and took six men with me, as I wanted to get a little job done – to wit – to make a splinter-proof roof for our Observation Post. The party carried sandbags and we relied on getting the necessary timber from the orchards in Maricourt. Every battery was bombarding, and the noise was perfectly hellish. We had to get out of the trenches to cut the timber and in about two minutes a shell hit the corner of the house we were in and blew it sky high. In the terrible noise that prevailed, I could not tell where it came from, or what it was. Several more came at intervals and 'prematures' from our batteries were splashing round us, too. Had the job not been urgent, we should have got back into the trenches and let it cool down a bit, but I simply couldn't as I had to get this finished. We went on working there until midday, and it was the most awful strain I have yet undergone … Just as we were finishing the job, Bombardier Greenwood got hit. It was a horrible wound in the stomach, and all the bleeding was inward. In ten seconds this fine big fellow, who was as strong as a lion and always had a beautiful ruddy colour, was writhing on the ground and his face was green in hue, and he was in awful agony. I knew there was no hope for him from the first, but told him the usual lies about it being nothing serious, etc. I got an old wire bed out of a deserted billet near and we carried him to the dressing station half a mile away. Finished the job about 4 p.m. and came back to the guns, very hungry. Passed a number of parties of infantry burying their dead. Today we have fired 272 rounds. The trenches are knee-deep in clay and the assault which was due tomorrow morning has been adjourned. 11 p.m. – Just had word that Greenwood has died of his wound.

Lieutenant William Bloor, C Battery, 146 Brigade, Royal Field Artillery

Private Frank
Hawkings, 1/9th
London Regiment
(Queen Victoria
Rifles)

28 June: A number of officers and men have been detailed to remain behind in 'battle surplus' at the transport lines. This is a new scheme to make sure of a nucleus on which to reform the battalion, in the event of the attacking troops being wiped out. The Regimental Sergeant Major wanted to send me back with the battle surplus, but I volunteered to go with my company, so I have been appointed to my old job of company runner … I am now beginning to think myself a bit of an ass, but anyhow it's no use worrying. The suspense is very trying and everyone is restless.

Lieutenant
Malcolm White,
Attd 1st Rifle
Brigade

June 28: Due to go up to the trenches tonight; but orders came round that we were to stay in bivouac, the attack being postponed a short time. Continuous rain.

29 June: I scribble my [diary] entry for the day, while my servant waits to pack up this little book in my valise. We go up this afternoon, and this book must not go too.

Captain Harold
Bidder, 1st South
Staffordshire
Regiment

30 June: The opening day was deferred owing to the weather. In the afternoon I rode up from the town following the gun teams, who had already started for the assembly trenches. The river and rose gardens looked very jolly. By way of a cheerful send-off, a gramophone in one of the houses I passed was playing the 'Dead March' in *Saul*!

I passed the night in the dugouts we had made on the ridge overlooking the Boche lines, by our night-firing position. We had three guns going a great part of the night. The three officers who were going forward with me slept there, too, when they had packed their men away ready for the start.

Word came round that the start was to be at 7.30 a.m. Soon after five I was out, looking round. The sky was clear, and so was our ridge, but the lower ground where the British and German trenches were was hidden in a sea of white mist. The sun was just topping the mist and catching the dew drops on the grass and thistles round us. The stakes of the barbed wire round our work threw long shadows towards us. The guns were blazing away; and great black mushrooms were shooting up out of the surface of the white sea in front as the big shells burst in the German trenches. It was a strange scene – we stood about on the grass round our positions, apparently alone in the world on this brilliant morning, only disturbed by the crashing of the guns behind and the weird upheavals in the mist surface.

30 June: Today is my [eighteenth] birthday, and anyone will concede that it is hardly an appropriate time to have one. We suddenly got order to move this afternoon. Our packs had been taken to Souastre and stored in some old barns, but we are well loaded all the same. Every man carries two hundred rounds of ammunition, three hand grenades, three sandbags, wire cutters, rockets, and flares, a sign board and forty-eight hours' rations. We marched via Souastre and Bayencourt and reached the plain between Sailly-au-Bois and Hébuterne at dusk. Here we were greeted by a salvo of 5.9s and made a slight detour to avoid the shelling. The roar of the artillery was deafening. Hébuterne, which was reached at about 8 p.m, was being shelled and we could see the village of Colincamps in flames to our right. Eventually we entered Yellow Street and proceeded in the direction of the fire-trench, but we were bombarded so much en route that it has taken us until 1 a.m. to get there. The bombardment has now died down and things are fairly quiet. Some men have been out to place iron pipes containing dynamite under the German wire. These are to be fired electrically tomorrow morning. Am feeling dreadfully tired, so I'm going to try and snatch a little sleep, though I don't expect to be very successful.

Private Frank Hawkings, 1/9th London Regiment (Queen Victoria Rifles)

There is a big attack coming off very shortly, and we are in it. And there is just a minute to scribble a line to you, with my love and greeting. We all hope it will be a success, though it will be a difficult business, I am sure. Our job will be to take the front system of trenches in this area. Man, I can't write a letter. There is much to think, but nothing to say really. I dare say this will not reach you, but I have asked a friend to send it for me when censorship does not apply any longer. We are taking part in a big attack, and I go up to the trenches this afternoon and shall not be able to write again between now and the beginning of it. All hope that this attack will bring us a little nearer the end of the war. There is little doubt that it will be a difficult business, but we hope for success after the bombardment that is going on. Our business is to take the front system of German trenches in

Lieutenant Malcolm White, Attd 1st Rifle Brigade

the area we are in. And now, I just want to say to you all, that, if I don't come through it, you must all be quite cheerful about it. I am quite happy about it, though of course I can't deny that I am very keen to come home again. I look at all this from a very personal point of view, almost a selfish point of view. It seems to me that, if I die in this action, it gives me a great, simple chance of making up for a lot of selfishness in the past. And when I want to reconcile myself to the idea of not coming back again, I just think of all those selfish mistakes I've made, and I am almost glad of the opportunity to put them right. That's my view of it. It is not priggish – I hope it doesn't sound like that. It is also a great comfort to think of you all going on, living the same happy lives that we have led together, and of the new generation coming into it all. I can't write more. My dearest love to you all.

Lance Corporal Arthur Cook, 1st Somerset Light Infantry

All private correspondence, cap badges, numerals and spare kit has to be left behind. We are fully charged with ammunition, grenades, water, emergency rations and all the paraphernalia needed for modern warfare. The men were in excellent spirits and full of hope for the morrow: it was going to be a welcome change from lying in a trench and taking everything without the opportunity of hitting back. Paraded at 9.45 p.m. and marched to the assembly trenches, and then told to get a couple of hours' sleep. We certainly rested our weary limbs, but sleep was out of the question.

Lieutenant William Bloor, C Battery, 146 Brigade, Royal Field Artillery

1 July: The Great Day! First of the great spring offensive – the 'Push' at last, long talked about, now definitely launched. Major has gone up to the OP with Gowland – he is to have the job offering chances of distinction! He goes forward with the infantry; I, as acting captain, have to stay at the guns and keep in touch with the horses and limbers, and to be ready to advance the battery which we are going to do as soon as the infantry have taken Montauban (and consolidated). 6.25 a.m. The bombardment commenced on the enemy front-line trenches. Watches were set with the greatest care, and at 7.30 a.m. exactly the guns were 'lifted' on to 'Dublin' trench, and at 7.36 into Glatz Alley. So far everything appeared to have gone well.

This extraordinary photograph was taken at 3.30 pm on 1st July 1916. Men of the 7th Queen's (Royal West Surrey Regiment) and 7th Buffs (East Kent Regiment) lie low on the Montauban Road before their advance to the German-held second line trench known as Montauban Alley. Two of the officers pictured are Lieutenant Christopher Haggard and Lieutenant David Heaton: both survived the day and the war.

A follow-up photograph taken when the men had reached Montauban Alley. The taking of the trench system and the village of Montauban was one of the few success stories that day, with British troops advancing well over a mile from their starting positions. Nevertheless, the 7th Queens suffered over 160 dead, who were either killed or subsequently died of wounds.

Lieutenant Cecil
Down, 1/4th
Gordon
Highlanders

Whenever there is a push people get too sanguine and think that we shall be in Brussels in a week and on the Rhine in two, but I very much doubt whether the object of this little show is really to break through. If we can kill and capture Huns galore and give them absolute Hades for several months it ought to give them a big shaking and at the same time give our army the experience which at least half of it hasn't got. Still, we shall see.

Opposite: An unidentified mine crater on the Somme, but certainly one of those blown on the first day of the battle.

Overleaf: Job done: Officers of the 183rd Tunnelling Company relax with souvenirs collected after the first day of the Somme battle.

One thing the Battle of the Somme was not was a 'little show', but in almost all other respects Down's words were sage. The casualties on 1 July were heinous. Around 3 per cent of all Britain's casualties suffered during the Great War were incurred on that single extraordinary day, including 20,000 dead. It was a terrible day for the British Army, but one from which tactical lessons were learnt, cold comfort, perhaps, for those who lost a brother, father or son. Lieutenant Evelyn Southwell lost his great, perhaps his best, friend Lieutenant Malcolm White. Both men were in their mid-twenties and masters at Shrewsbury School in Shropshire, having studied at Oxford and Cambridge universities respectively. Southwell was also a formidable rower and in youth rowed in the University boat races of 1907 and 1908, narrowly missing a place in the British Olympic team of 1908. The two men had met in 1910 and quickly became inseparable friends, sharing interests and a house together. In April 1915, after the death at the front of a close colleague, they left Shrewsbury and enlisted. 'I must go and take his place,' Southwell wrote to his father in March. Both men took a commission in the Rifle Brigade: Southwell was sent to join the 9th Battalion in France in October 1915 and White joined the 1st Battalion the following February. Southwell's fear for White was evident on the eve of the Somme offensive when in a further letter to his father he wrote, 'If ever you remembered anyone in your prayers in this world, I would like it to be my friend White … I know I do not ask in vain.'

Lieutenant Evelyn
Southwell, 9th Rifle
Brigade

4 July: I am in great anxiety about our Man [White]; though I can't say where he is or what he is doing. I had a letter from White two days ago … It was a short note, but very wonderful. Pray God all's well with our Man.

On 1 July the 1st Rifle Brigade advanced near the German fortified village of Beaumont Hamel. White was hit while leading his men across no-man's-land although he assured his servant that he was not badly hurt. At that moment a shell landed close by, wounding the servant and, it was believed, killing White. White's body was never found and his name is inscribed on the Somme's Thiepval Memorial to the Missing.

Lieutenant Evelyn Southwell, 9th Rifle Brigade

12 July: Mum, White is killed, I suppose. Anyhow, I've a letter saying from Bailey, 'You will have heard by now (I hadn't) that the thing … has happened.' He goes on to say he *may* be a prisoner; from which I infer he is reported missing, and do not hold any hopes of that kind, for we had heard that his battalion was very badly cut up. He was my greatest friend … I have faced the casualty list daily without a tremor for two years now, and now, when I am hard hit myself, I cry out! Mum, he was *such* a dear; he was so keen on everything, and the most true 'artist', in the full sense, that I have ever known.

This month, or whatever it is (no, it's a bare fortnight, isn't it?), has opened my eyes to the lot of those who sit and wait, as I have been doing since the 'Push' started. For goodness' sake, don't let his one case make you think you have *any* more reason than before to be anxious about my miserable safety … But I can sympathise with you, who are good enough(!) to be anxious about me, better now. Yet do please realise that one friend's death does not increase my risk or chances, any more than it diminishes it; you *must* not let it make you worry about it.

But I cannot be very happy … War is a terrible thing, especially lately, as all of us know …

Southwell's battalion was kept on the fringes of the Somme battle for several weeks. Throughout this time, he wrote letters home on a regular basis and updated his own private diary, extracts from which follow. What makes his story remarkable is that his life and that of his battalion was captured on the cameras of at least two fellow officers, including Lieutenant John Polgreen, who, despite regulations, took a large number of 'snaps' as the men rested behind the lines and while occupying the trenches. In mid-August, the battalion became heavily involved in the offensive.

7 August: There remains the high bank on which I lie behind the lines, and a perfectly idle afternoon, on which to watch from it that kind of motion which is notoriously the most exciting – the to and fro of heavy trains. One such has just gone by; sacred I think to the RFA, [Royal Field Artillery] for most of the uncountable trucks had one of those remarkable soldiers at least on board them, in various attitudes of repose.

Repose, certainly; though few but soldiers would find it so. In one there were men stretched gloriously asleep on the floor, seen through the half-open door; while over them, and nearly on them, stood their animals tethered and patient, with the kind of silent wonder on their faces which one is accustomed to find in pictures of the Nativity. Repose, certainly, in the General Service wagons, which, packed on the trucks, carried a gunner or two on the front seat, exalted very high, and serene in air with cigarette and magazine. Repose, too, I devoutly hope, for the animals as well; but eight horses to a wagon is a tight fit, I fear, and made no less so by the spurious label 'Moutons', which ridiculously stands on their carriage wall. There: that train is gone, with its endless rows of trucks, and its serene look of rest from the land of the 'Push'; and we are left without a train (a moving one, anyhow) to watch …

We are not at all perturbed by the delay; at least, I think not: I know one officer who (after his manner) is loving it. The rest of two battalions are stretched before me, about four deep among the rails, and I do not think they are in undue hurry. A Royal Flying Corps car dashes up beyond the rails, and a cyclist, or whatever he is, whizzes down the road behind my head. Aeroplanes, of course, come (with their kind of coquettish curtsying, peculiar to their kind when infantry are about), to see the trains and their loads; a Red Cross car flits in and out of the station; Frenchmen wander down the line in shirtsleeves and white trousers, or in a blue tunic and forage cap.

But nowhere is there much of a hurry, thank God. It is true the guns are pelting away somewhere or other; but nobody cares. The sun shines over our shoulders, and it is the infantryman's day out. Every moment sees him, indeed, a thought more comfortable; and as I write, he is already beginning to get his tea.

11 August: This morning I was alone; so I went along the river bank,

August 1916: The losses among the 9th Battalion's officers were very heavy. Top, left to right: Capt. McKinstry (survived), 2/Lt Heseltine (killed), Lt Purvis (wounded), 2/Lt Buckley (killed), Lt Heycock (wounded), Capt. Parsons (killed), 2/Lt Smith (killed), 2/Lt Elliot (killed). Bottom, left to right: Maj. Gull (killed), Lt Day (wounded), Lt Lynch (killed), Lt Hollins (survived), 2/Lt Buckley (killed), 2/Lt Elliott (killed), 2/Lt Kiek (wounded), 2/Lt Smith (killed), Lt Packenham (wounded), Lt Col. Morris (battalion commander) (killed). Of particular interest is Lt Herbert Purvis (wearing clothes, above). His son, Capt. John Purvis, commanded B Company and was killed in 1915. His father, aged fifty-five, came out to France not only to join his son's battalion but to command his company. Lt Purvis was badly wounded on 15 September.

and made a *highly important discovery*, which is that the Field Service Postcard makes a capital boat in skilful hands. I put one afloat this morning, within twenty yards of a huge artillery camp, but not in the least abashed by the watchful eyes of one of two inquisitive gunners at their ease on the bank. I put her well out, and with a poke from a stick off she went. All went well for quite a long time; it was necessary to throw one big stone into a shallow, to prevent her coming to rest much too soon. And there was a certain homesick look about her (perhaps she caught it from her designer), which was a little too apt to make her aim at unexpected little harbours on the way down. With this exception, however, she did well, and it was no fault of hers that she did go right down to join the _____. Oh dear, here's the censor again; one can't even run one's private navigation without being careful.

1 September: We are quite exhausted. After a terrible forty-eight hours' (on and off) bombardment of varying degrees in the trenches, we came out and marched to bivouac in reserve. I went off to sleep several times on the road, and bumped into the man ahead! Comic, that; but at the time I was not happy, because I was so done that it was a struggle to get in at all. This was one of the few times I've been so done that I had difficulty in keeping going, and it is, I suppose, rather a good thing for people who are as a rule *reasonably* strong, at any rate to be really 'done' occasionally – (not, of course, that I've been out here eleven months without finding out; but seldom, if ever, was I so tired as last night): it keeps them mindful of what sort of task is suitable for the smaller, and perhaps weaker, among the men.

6 September: Horrors? Well, yes, I suppose so; but there seems no useful purpose in recalling them. Even from the most lamentable remains of brave men, blown to every sort of bits, and accusingly unburied beneath the stars … There is some rather grim tale of a certain hand protruding through the parapet in some trenches, which a certain regiment grasped familiarly as they passed by. I am not at all sure whether this was a profane act at all, even though done in jest. Myself, as I said on hearing it, I do not feel humorous about the dead at all: I feel more inclined to salute them: in fact, when alone, I generally do. But it is not impossible, I think, to see something grimly sacramental in this curious greeting of

them; and I believe the shade of that warrior smiled to see it, and knowing the hands that grasped his for those of new comrades, he would not be troubled at all.

Oh dear, this is poor stuff. But what would you have?

7 September: There was a motor lorry going from Brigade HQ to Abbeville carrying quartermasters and mess corporals, in search of purchases of various kinds; and I was sent with our quartermaster (Paine) to get various odds and ends for anyone that wanted them. I dare say it was a kind of excuse for getting me a holiday, but anyway sundry officers are the richer by towels, shaving soap, slippers, wine, tobacco (oh no; I left that behind at the canteen, a bad business!) and so forth. Rather a good game, seeing all your money gradually fade away, and then remembering you'll get it all back next day.

You know there is a good deal to be said for riding of a morning through the wonderful country that is really France; real valleys and hills, and a real harvest waiting to be brought in, and real trees at which you look in surprise. To see if it is true that they really have their branches, and are not torn from their roots by shells.

Well, we reached the town … and after making a few purchases I went off to see the cathedral. It stands wonderfully well above the neighbouring houses, and though it is not like *the* Cathedral [Amiens], it was quite enough to make me catch my breath … As usual, I went into my own place to pray. I met tragedy, though on the way out. It was a black-clad woman sobbing into her handkerchief by a pillar near the west end, watched commiseratingly by a girl with two little children. It was a temptation, almost, to ambush her and murmur 'Du courage!', or something of the sort, but I thought not … This is the sort of thing that makes me feel the incarnation of selfishness, for really believing in my foolish moments that the war, taken as a whole, is not such bad fun …

9 September: We are, for the moment, miles upon miles upon miles behind the land of the 'Push', from which the division has come out: sufficient that we spent three weeks there, and the division is supposed to have made a great name. Our battalion was spoken very well of, I hear; we did not make any very organised attack, but were said to have held on to the captured trenches in a satisfactory manner: we had a longer go,

naturally, than anybody else in the brigade, as it was not the turn of the battalion to go over the top this time. I don't think I want to bother about this 'Push' just now, though. It is autumn, and there are good things about. And, between ourselves, that Wood [Delville Wood] is not one of the better places.

14 September [to his father]: You have, no doubt, by now got my letter explaining more or less. But in any case there is no need to add more, as I told Mum, except that I love you all very, very dearly, and that I believe, as I have said before, that it is good to be here.

Southwell's letter finished on the eve of the next phase in the Somme 'Push', the Battle of Flers-Courcelette. The attack, a concerted effort to be made by eleven infantry divisions, would see the deployment of tanks for the first time. These would spearhead the assault and although they were being used in small numbers, it was hoped that these vehicles, lumbering over shell-pitted land, traversing trenches and crushing machine-gun nests, would not only prove key in driving back the Germans, but significantly press the psychological advantage to the side with such a fearsome new weapon.

11 September: A quiet day in the trenches, we forage round to see what we can find. We are very interested in the large quantity of German gear & equipment of all kinds lying about. Rifles, bombs, packs, clothing, tools, bandoliers of rifle ammunition as well, a little too large for the British rifle so useless. Their bandoliers are an improvement on ours & keep the ammunition clean till it is wanted which is an important advantage. Their packs are rigid in form and like a suitcase and are covered with hide with hair still on (hair outside). A few dead Germans are lying about. Burying a man who has been killed in the open is usually done by shovelling a few shovels of earth over the body where it lays and the hands & feet are often left exposed. In the trenches the German dead are thrown down one of the numerous dugouts, as soon as our men get time and the entrance sealed with earth. There is no time or opportunity to do anything else in a place like the Somme.

Rifleman R. E. Harris, 3rd New Zealand Rifle Brigade

Overleaf: An exhausted Lieutenant Southwell (second right) after his battalion's torrid time in the front line.

Private Ernest Ford, 10th Queen's (Royal West Surrey Regiment)

We were bivouacking out in the open waiting for orders to proceed to the front and appropriate some of his [the enemy's] trenches. Well, at night we packed up – leaving behind our overcoats and all superfluous kit – and moved off in the direction of the ever-booming guns. It started to rain. We had a long march first through our heavy guns and then through the lighter ones – which were all firing incessantly – and eventually too to a communication trench. We followed this for what seemed miles and at length just as daylight was breaking we arrived in the front-line trenches and relieved a battalion there. It was perhaps fortunate that we did come by night for there were sights during the latter part of our journey which did not assist in giving us a good heart – to say the least of it! We found ourselves just in front of a large wood [Delville Wood] – at least, it was a wood once! But now it was a scanty collection of black scaffold poles set in a wilderness of churned-up earth, roots of trees and splintered wood. Our trench was merely a hastily dug ditch – far different from the elaborate structures we had been used to in another part of the line. In front of us was a stretch of land – a mass of shell holes terminated by a ridge about 250 yards away. It was along this ridge and behind it our shells were falling in a continuous stream and they kept it up all that day and the next night just as though it was being done automatically. The Germans shelled us a bit, but they didn't appear to know the exact position of our particular trench and didn't hit us at all; they were very severe on the poor old wood behind us. We caught a whiff from one or two of their tear shells – it makes your eyes sting and stream with tears.

Rifleman R. E. Harris, 3rd New Zealand Rifle Brigade

14 September: Rest all day. Roll overcoats in sections & examine the battalions' bombs to see if they are all right and no defective ones amongst them. Late in the afternoon we get issued with more ammunition so that each man has 2 Mills bombs, 200 rounds of ammunition and a large number of smoke bombs issued out amongst the men and our section (No. 8) being a bombing section, each of us has eight Mills bombs. A few men, several NCOs & several officers stayed behind to reorganise those who would be left when we came back. We started for the trenches about dusk, being played off by the brigade band playing 'Where are the Boys of the old Brigade?'

Captured German trenches occupied by 9th Rifle Brigade opposite Delville Wood, August 1916.

Lieutenant Southwell in the trenches shortly before going over the top on 15 September, when he was killed. His body was never identified.

We arrived at our destination about midnight, it was a narrow trench like a ditch called an assembly trench and was about 100 yards behind our own front line. Here we lay down in the trench or in shell holes to try to get a little sleep and awaited the dawn when we were to attack. It was too cold, however, to sleep as we had left our overcoats in the rear.

Private Ernest Ford, 10th Queens (Royal West Surrey Regiment)

At six o'clock next morning (15th) our artillery opened rapid fire, as only they can do it, putting a barrage or belt of fire along the German lines and twenty minutes later we were 'over the top and the best of luck', as the soldiers say. We simply walked over, keeping just out of range of our own barrage (fifty yards behind it) which slowly moved forward over the German positions. I was in the first 'wave' or line to go over and we hadn't gone far before the Boche opened fire with machine guns and shrapnel. It was like Hell with the lid off and the noise was deafening. I had gone about 150 yards when I had the impression that a horse had kicked me in the back. I got into a shell hole and investigated and was surprised to find it was a shrapnel bullet (one of our own bursting short!) had hit me. It had neatly perforated my clothes but on meeting my sinewy dorsal mussles(!) had to give them best. So on I went again over the German first line and had nearly reached their second line when there was a crash somewhere close in front and I collected six small pieces of shrapnel – (three in the hand and three in the chest) so I dived into a shell hole and tied myself up. Deciding that a chap with a damaged hand and a stiff back would not be much further use, I made my way back to our trenches (nearly blown up several times en route). There I had to stay for five hours, as it was impossible to get back owing to the heavy German shelling.

Rifleman R. E. Harris, 3rd New Zealand Rifle Brigade

15 September: As the dawn began to break our artillery fire began to get stronger & stronger till by 6.30 a.m., which was 'zero time', it was at its strongest. We were eagerly looking for the tanks and one could just be seen on our flank. Guns of all sizes by the hundred were now pounding away at the enemy's front line and the din was deafening. All along the enemy's front trench HE shells of all sizes were bursting and blowing his trench to atoms. It was one long line of smoke, flying earth and flame from bursting shells. Some light guns brought forward during the night were barking

away just behind us and their shells seemed to be going only a few feet above our heads. As yet the enemy's artillery was fairly quiet. About 6.30 we left our trench and went forward to the attack, some parties in extended order and some in artillery formation. We did not hurry but just walked steadily forward, picking our way between the shell holes. Everything looked so uncanny and unreal. Like a terrible dream.

Delville Wood as seen from the German perspective during the battle. A large shell explodes in the distance.

The sight of so many men strolling over the open ground, within a few yards of the German lines, as if they were going across a paddock in NZ, accompanied as it was by din and noise of the bombardment with its flame and smoke of bursting shells, was a sight so amazing as not to be easily forgotten. We had gone only about 100 yards when I got a bullet through the chest. It did not strike a bone and all I felt was a warm sting which I hardly felt at all.

By late 1916 a policy had been adopted that every battalion would leave a number of men, perhaps 100, to re-form the unit should it be badly mauled in action. Second Lieutenant Geoffrey Fildes would therefore wait behind with a small cadre of men as his battalion went over the top. From a distance he was able to observe the attack close to Flers and watch, with interest, the appearance of the tank.

Presently, heard fitfully between the lesser concussions of the battle, an unfamiliar sound stole on our ears. It seemed as if a vast aeroplane might be approaching at a low altitude. Looking about us, we could detect nothing out of the ordinary; but still the sound continued. Then, a couple of hundred yards or more down the road, we saw several figures running out of view down an embankment. Evidently, as it takes much to arouse such strenuous interest in the average British soldier, something out of the ordinary was afoot. We set off to investigate.

Second Lieutenant Geoffrey Fildes, 2nd Coldstream Guards

Louder and louder rose the noise from out of the concealed hollow. 'Some kind of engine,' we agreed. Reaching the crest of the hill, we discovered only a short distance away a crowd of men moving at a slow walk beside an incredible apparition. What a monstrosity! Its identity was evident at the first glance: this vast armour-plated insect could only be a Tank. Its wicked-looking guns protruding forward seemed like antennae, while a huge wheel trailing in its rear suggested a sort of tail … Our surprise was absolute. A four-horse chariot, with scythes complete, would have caused us no greater astonishment …

Roaring sullenly throughout the long autumn morning, the great howitzers in our vicinity maintained their steady fire and shook with their concussions the surrounding neighbourhood. Far in the distance played a ceaseless twinkle and stab of gun flashes, which alone revealed the situation of our countless batteries of field artillery. Once more the noise had swelled until it seemed to fill the entire world from one horizon to another.

Rifleman R. E. Harris, 3rd New Zealand Rifle Brigade

We were advancing in artillery formation at the time and I just turned aside and sat down in a shell hole and slipped my equipment off. I could not bandage myself as the wound where the bullet came out was in the back and it was this hole which was bleeding, not a drop of blood came out of the wound where the bullet went in, which was about an inch from the breastbone on a line with the left nipple and went between the ribs. It went just over the heart and fortunately did not cut an artery. About an hour later some engineers came along to deepen the trench just nearby and one of them bandaged me up as well as he could with my field dressing. About ten o'clock the enemy began to put over some shells just to the rear of where I was and as they began to get closer and dirt and pieces of shell were falling on and around me I got the engineers who were crouching in the bottom of the trench to give me a hand into it. Soon afterwards a Tommy officer was brought in and we lay there together for about two hours when several of his men whom he had sent for came and took him away on a stretcher. About two o'clock in the afternoon the engineers had to leave the work they were on and I should be alone and being in the bottom of the trench, out of sight and night coming on, there was no knowing when I would be found and picked up. One of the men called to some stretcher-bearers a little way off. They were Tommies and attached to the West Lancashire Regiment.

I didn't see much of our actual taking of our objective – but nowadays it is always the same. The Boche keeps up a good fire until you are on him – then up go his hands. His 'morale' is now entirely broken. This is of course due to our terrible artillery working in conjunction with our fine air service. All the while during the battle our aeroplanes – dozens of them – were flying to and fro, often descending within 100 feet of the ground – whereas there was not a Boche plane to be seen. Moreover we had nineteen observation balloons up, to the Huns three (and two of these were brought down during the day). We were also assisted by huge armed and armour-plated cars ('tanks', they are called) moving on 'cater-pillar' wheels; these will easily negotiate trenches and shell holes and will push down brick walls or trees. They are used in riding down machine-gun emplacements – but they have the disadvantage of moving at a very slow speed and the infantry get far ahead of them.

Private Ernest Ford, 10th Queens (Royal West Surrey Regiment)

As they were carrying me to the rear, we passed a battery which was not at that moment in action. One of the gun crew came running over to us with a bottle of brandy. I thought it was very good of him but not wanting any myself I thanked him and asked him to let the chaps who were carrying me have a nip as they were rather exhausted, having been working hard all day with no rest. He offered them the bottle and they did not need to be asked twice. On arrival at the advanced dressing station which was beside a road I was put on an ambulance and taken about a mile further back, to a stone quarry which was used as a dressing station and collecting station. Here were several hundred men lying on stretchers, there being a few Germans amongst them, one of whom had just died.

Rifleman R. E. Harris, 3rd New Zealand Rifle Brigade

Both Harris and Ford survived their injuries and the war. The 9th Rifle Brigade had attacked near the village of Flers and had suffered badly: 142 officers and men were killed and many more wounded. Lieutenant Evelyn Southwell was one who fell. His body was lost and his name, like that of his close friend Malcolm White, is engraved on the Thiepval Memorial.

The next day, Second Lieutenant Fildes heard definite news of his battalion and it was undoubtedly mixed. In the meantime every preparation would be made to welcome the survivors back into camp.

Second Lieutenant Geoffrey Fildes, 2nd Coldstream Guards

Tales of a great advance were coming through at last. The losses among the Guards had been severe, but their gains had created a new record for the war. This scanty information, coming after so many misgivings, nearly made us shout for joy. The attack had lost direction because, owing to the unexpected check on our right, the division had swerved considerably to its left, leaving its right flank exposed. But though officers had fallen in considerable numbers, the non-commissioned officers had risen grandly to the occasion; and when these became casualties in their turn, the rank and file had still gone forward.

Towards evening, crowning all, came the intelligence that the battalion would be relieved that night. Part of an encampment lying about a couple of miles from our transport lines was allotted to it, so shortly after dinner I set out in charge of a billeting party in order to make everything ready for its arrival. The business presented no great difficulties except the eternal problem of water supply, since the quarters reserved for our occupation would more than accommodate our slender needs.

It was near dawn on the following morning before our labour was completed and we were at liberty to seek a few hours' repose. By then, the battalion was almost due to make its appearance, but, according to a report, it could not be expected to arrive for another couple of hours; all ranks were exhausted.

Cyclist orderlies had already preceded towards the route along which the battalion was known to be approaching, and supplementary guides had been posted at all crossroads to deal with possible stragglers. We had endeavoured to anticipate all their needs, and had, in our humble sphere, spared no time or trouble on our comrades' behalf …

The early morning was somewhat squally; scudding clouds swept low overhead, veiling from time to time the struggling sunshine; and the air was fresh with the lingering chill of night. As we walked slowly up a slope in the neighbourhood of our lines, our ears were strained for the first sound of 'The Drums', for they had long since proceeded to Carnoy in order to play the survivors in.

Not many minutes had elapsed before the breeze wafted to our ears the intermittent throb of drums; the sound seemed under the circumstances intensely dramatic. Rising and falling on the wind, its mutterings at first grew no louder, and thus, rolling towards us from the invisible country beyond, it seemed almost ghostly. Soon its notes had reached the camp behind us, and men commenced to stream forth along the track in their desire to learn the fate of many a comrade. The breeze murmured to the lilt of fifes; the phantom battalion was nearing the brow. A great expectation seized us all.

Scanning the hilltop with eager eyes, we waited in suspense. Now we could hear the melodious tune of a familiar march – they must be very close at hand. Insensibly one's pulses stirred in response to the rattle of the drums. Over the skyline something flashed and whirled. Our gaze watched in eager fascination. Again the same object appeared, and we knew it for the sergeant drummer's stick. At last, his head and shoulders rose above the ridge, and behind him surged the emerging forms of the drummers.

Next, over the crest loomed the figure of our Colonel marching at the head of the devoted band. Rank after rank these poured over the skyline. Eagerly we counted their strength, wondering every instant how many remained to follow. All too soon a gap appeared, but we, still striving to disbelieve our fears, watched spellbound for the next body of men. But none came: the impossible was true. Before us marched all that remained of the old battalion …

Turning before their approach, we, with many a backward glance, retraced our steps towards the camp. Barely a word was spoken. Here amid our lines we took up our stand and awaited the arrival of the column. Along the side of the road stood many men, gazing in mute contemplation at the band of survivors. Now the drummers were almost upon us. Their music ended with a flourish, silence fell upon all. The moment was almost unbearable. Then, crashing forth with full volume of drum and fife, there rolled the opening notes of the Regimental March!

All eyes were turned to the lithe figure of our Commanding Officer, who now led in the glorious remnants. Haggard and drawn, but erect and admirable as ever, he strode past us acknowledging our salutes. Next, tramping forward in a supreme effort, followed the pathetic muster. They presented an amazing spectacle. A first impression was that of mud, mud everywhere, from the crown of their heads to their shapeless feet. Beneath many a helmet rim, bloodshot eyes stared brilliantly from swollen and dusty lids; moustaches seemed like clots of mud; complexions were grey, furrowed with dried streaks of sweat. Though much of their equipment was missing, here and there we caught sight of German souvenirs, a bayonet or a round service cap. In many cases their clothing was torn and stained with blood. Gazing wonderingly upon their ranks, we noted their sagging knees and their desperate efforts to pull themselves together: here a drooping figure propelled itself forward with the aid of a stick, there, another stumbled on with fixed and haggard expression. The music alone buoyed up these overwrought souls. And as one watched, one's heart went out to them, for their efforts were positively painful to witness. But now, at the word of command, every man sloped his rifle, every man picked up the step. So, lurching forward at its last gasp, smeared, tattered, but still tenacious, this vision of undaunted men staggered past.

Owing to the ill fortune that had overtaken the captain, I now found

Horse-drawn transport sloshing through winter mud. The horses suffered appallingly during the harshest winter of the war.

myself in command of 'Number 2', [B Company] so the day following the arrival of the survivors was for me a very busy one indeed. Complete reorganisation of the company was necessary, for out of the NCOs there remained but one sergeant and six corporals, and the total strength of the unit did not exceed fifty men. One could only be thankful for that wise foresight which had preserved the company sergeant major, for now that I was the only officer left his help became invaluable.

The battle ground on, the Germans being attacked remorselessly. The weather was gradually getting worse, and conditions began to militate against further large-scale attacks and instead smaller, piecemeal assaults were made with limited objectives. The conditions were becoming impossible.

18 October: Up at 3 a.m. Found to my horror that my bed was full of maggots which had worked through the ground from below where some men had been buried … I had a new hole dug to sleep in, but as I had no blankets, stayed up till 4 a.m. and then slept for a bit in my clothes on a chair. Poured with rain all day – mud up to the knees everywhere. In the afternoon I rode down to the wagon line to stay there for a few days and try and put things right a bit after the recent bucketing. Had an awful ride

Lieutenant William Bloor, C Battery, 146 Brigade, Royal Field Artillery

down – my horse floundering and often sinking to the girths in shell holes. Passed scores of dead horses and disabled wagons. In one case six horses in a water cart – the whole lying in their tracks, still harnessed.

20 October: The horses are in a lamentable condition – the fearful exertion and strain imposed on them by the heavy going up to the guns and back is leaving its mark on them all. An additional issue of 2lbs oats per horse has just been sanctioned.

23 October: Rode up to gun position with Moore. The horses were often over their hocks in mud, and my horses very frightened and plunging all over the place … A General Service wagon with six horses was hit this morning, and all the horses and three drivers killed just alongside the mess. I took the harness of this team as we are very short indeed (our harness tent being blown up), and then dragged the dead 'uns into a shell hole and covered them up. Stayed for lunch.

24 October: Poured with rain all day. Busy sending ammunition to A and B batteries for a 'stunt' which takes place tomorrow. Sent up 1,800 rounds. Much troubled for transport. We have no cooks' cart, no limbered cart, have just smashed another wheel of the water cart, and a GS wagon which we have salved, repaired and adopted, had just 'gone west' again. The weather has made it impossible to send vehicles up to the guns. The water cart has managed, with difficulty, to do the trip with an eight-horse team, but now water will have to be taken up in petrol cans. Sent eight horses away to hospital this afternoon – too worn out to be any further use … The truth is that they are always hungry, and the forage allowance is inadequate to maintain them in condition under these circumstances. I suppose it is entirely a matter of cost, and the authorities find it cheaper to lose so many horses than to find the additional oats and hay. Our old 'hairies' eat their hay nets, rugs, ropes and timber, and some of them even eat mud!

25 October: Heavy rain all day. Had to go to Mametz to water. This is four miles of an awful journey, and when one arrives there are about 1,000 horses round the troughs. The congestion and confusion is perfectly awful, and you cannot exercise any supervision over your horses, as it is a case of 'everyone for himself'. The same conditions obtain at the ammunition dump. The railway has been extended close up to our wagon

line, and all the ammunition for the corps comes up in one huge train. There is a perfect fight for it by everyone, and it is an amazing scene. There are hundreds of horses with packs waiting – about five divisional artilleries, several horse batteries and 60-pounders, and 8- and 12-inch guns by the dozen. The train no sooner stops than it is fairly raided, boxes are smashed open and as soon as a driver has his horses loaded he forces his way through the throng and gets off quite independently on his journey. The continual trampling has made a fine bath of mud about two feet deep all round the train for about 400 yards, and if you should be incautious enough to go there on foot you would stand a good chance of being knocked down and drowned!

30 October: The state of the country now beggars description, and the transport is having an awful time of it. The drivers get along by thrashing their horses every inch of the way, and when riding a good horse oneself it needs unsparing use of sharp rowels to get along through the mud. 'B' gun had to be withdrawn from the line yesterday for overhaul. I sent up a *ten*-horse team, but they came back about 8 p.m. without it. The horses were absolutely 'done in'. Reliefs congest the roads hopelessly, and blocks of two or three hours are common. A team left at 6 a.m. this morning to go to Becordel (five miles away) and did not arrive till 12.30 p.m.

This had become a war that tested men's endurance, physical and mental, to the absolute limit. For two years, boys, many ridiculously under age, had enlisted with the connivance of not just recruiting sergeants but sometimes of parents, who little thought their sons would see overseas service. Conscription in January 1916 had helped to stop the recruitment of under-age boys, but thousands were still overseas and, if they were not struggling with the physical conditions, they often were worn out mentally.

10 September [To Mrs Sorley] I am writing on behalf of a gallant youngster [Walter Young] in my company, and I believe known to you. His age is I suspect not more than seventeen now, and he has been out some while, and though he is an excellently sturdy youngster his nerves are obviously not strong enough for the racket of this existence, which is nowadays more violent than usual. The point therefore is that his parents or

Second Lieutenant Arthur Adam, 1/1st Cambridgeshire Regiment guardian can write and claim him back, by producing a copy of his birth certificate, only he himself is apparently entirely in the dark as to who his guardian is — he has of course no parents. So I wonder if you could make representations in the right quarter and collect a copy of his birth certificate, and get the thing done: he isn't a fellow I want to lose, but I feel it partakes rather of cruelty to animals to keep him out here just at present. I hope all may be going well with you and yours.

Second Lieutenant
Ernest Routley, 6th
The Buffs (East
Kent Regiment)

Dear Frank,

Just received your letter. No words of mine can express my absolute amazement at the news. In spite of all warning you go and volunteer to come out to France of all places. I really can't make you out.

If you only knew what you were asking for: you see you aren't a specialist in anything. You don't know trench mortars or machine guns. You are just an ordinary Tommy who can fire a rifle and perhaps throw a bomb. You don't know what you will be used for, do you? Well, I do. There have been thousands of casualties in the 'Push' and some regiments are hard put to it to make up their numbers, so they have asked for volunteers from Home Service Units, and you like a fool have volunteered.

I really can't see why you can't take advice. Surely you must admit that I know more about it than you. I have been in the 'Push' and have had three bayonet charges and by an extraordinary stroke of luck have come through, but I know full well my number will be up soon. One can't always escape.

You probably think it's a very fine thing to come out here and be killed. Well, just wait. It isn't being killed that worries you. It's the waiting for it. Just wait until you hear that you have got to attack, and then as you are waiting your turn to go over the top, you see your pals get cut down by MG fire, and then see if you think it's a glorious thing to die. It would be glorious if you could have a fair fight, but its absolute murder here and you don't get a sporting chance. If only I could get home out of it, I would give up my Military Cross and commission and all I possess, but I can't, and I am doomed to stick it. But you aren't.

Haven't you got the sense to see that Mother is nearly breaking her heart about me, because she realises one's life is not worth 2d. out here, and yet in spite of this you go and volunteer and just double her grief. I don't know what will happen to her – I know her heart isn't strong and the shock of this may finish her. If so, I hold you responsible … An infantryman's job is to die – if you miss one show, then you are in for the next. The only chance you have is a 'Blighty one', and even if you get that you will only remain in England until you are well, then you will come out again . . .

Please take this letter in the spirit it is meant. I appreciate your motives entirely as I had them myself. I know exactly how you felt as I felt the same way only I am paying for it now. Believe me to be,

Your loving brother, Ernest

Private Hunt, aged sixteen, 1/6th Gloucestershire Regiment, looks through a trench periscope while serving on the Somme in September 1916.

Private Walter Young died of wounds just a couple of weeks later, before any move could be taken to get him out of the front line. Lieutenant Ernest Routley was killed in October, aged twenty-four, a few weeks after writing to his brother. The Battle of the Somme had exhausted everyone but, crucially, it had taken much more out of the Germans and that was, in reality, its objective. On 19 November, the offensive was officially closed down.

18 November: The sun early, turned to sleet and general beastliness, so I decided to sally forth in search of Neville [a friend]. I had been informed that his battery was in action near High Wood which is North East of Bazentin-le-Grand and, being totally ignorant of the conditions prevailing quite near to the trenches, I thought it would be a simple matter to find him.

D'albiac, Wood, and I started off in the Lancia at 9 a.m. and proceeded to Albert. The roads were in an awful state and the sleet was persistent and there was any amount of traffic on the road. German prisoners were to be seen everywhere mending roads and generally doing odd jobs. Some of them are very smart fellows and, given a good Hun NCO to look after them,

Squadron Commander Geoffrey Bromet, 8 Naval Squadron, Royal Naval Air Service work very hard … Today they all looked horribly miserable but then so did every soul I saw. It was the sort of day that makes one miserable (unless one can sit indoors before a big fire) – cold and wet and mud calf-deep. We could hardly have chosen a better day on which to see 'the war,' in its most disagreeable form! Albert was most interesting and of course the thing of outstanding interest was the huge figure of the Virgin Mary holding the Baby out at arm's length which, instead of standing upright on top of the Cathedral spire, is bent over at an angle of about 120 degrees from the vertical. This cathedral is shelled considerably and is practically a ruin. The figure of the Virgin Mary has been secured in its present position by means of wire and rope and will, I suppose, be kept like that for the tourists of future years to see.

Today parts of Albert are quite untouched whilst other parts are absolutely wrecked. Few civilians remain but it is not by any means entirely evacuated. From Albert we went along the main Albert–Bapaume road until we got to La Boisselle. All the country to the left of the road is simply a huge brown waste dotted about with camps and horse lines etc. When one leaves Albert one leaves all sign of cultivation and (I was about to add civilisation) habitation behind one and the awful destruction and waste of modern warfare is brought poignantly before one. La Boisselle, once a pretty and thriving little village, I suppose, is no more. Not a brick or a piece of wood remain to convince me that a village ever existed. One passes along this dreary road, banked high on either side with mud and relieved here and there by dugouts, to Contalmaison. Nothing here to prove that there ever was such a place, and yet only quite a little while ago it was General von Kluck's headquarters and he lived in a fine chateau. We really begin to enter the actual war area here; the roadside has its heavy battery and ammunition dump at close and regular intervals, and the whole country round seems stiff with guns.

Up to this point the roads were not bad and our progress was not greatly interfered with by heavy traffic but as we drew close to the Bois de Mametz (on the map a fine wood; today a mass of old trenches, dugouts and stunted trees) things became pretty bad and got, later on, appalling. The traffic also grew and grew until, at Bazentin-le-Grand, we were simply one of a long and continuous stream of lorries, ammunition wagons, water

The danger of looking over the top is underlined by this photograph's caption: 'This was in full view of the Boche lines ... I was sniped at when taking this.'

carts, pack mules and infantry. All the roads were made up of pit props and some of the holes shook the poor old Lancia to hell – the mud more calf-deep everywhere. We eventually got as far as the turning off to High Wood where we left the car and started to foot it. I had asked dozens of men where the battery I was seeking was situated before I found somebody who knew. As I have said, the whole country round from Contalmaison to High Wood is stiff with batteries and to find any particular one is like looking for a halfpenny on a shingle beach. In the end, after going through the worst mud I have ever had to face and falling into a shell hole (this is excusable because one had to be a tightrope walker not to; so close are they to each other!) I found a dugout in which Neville should have been. He was not. I had been given the wrong address! This was an awkward plight in which I found myself. I had promised D'albiac and Wood a lunch at the end of their journey and here we were at last long past lunchtime and very cold and wet 'all dressed up and nowhere to go!'. However, the inhabitants of this dugout gave us a whisky and water and a warm up, and having drowned our annoyance we set off for home ...

From Albert we took the main road to Amiens and halted at the Golbert [restaurant] a little while after 6 p.m. Thoroughly cold and hungry

After the battle: a ghostly image of Delville Wood shattered almost beyond recognition. Thousands lay dead among the tree trunks.

and tired we were, but the thought of dinner and the long drive safely accomplished soon put us on excellent terms with ourselves, and only made us realise how much better off we were than all those hundreds of soldiers we met on our journey to and from the 'war'. The Golbert is an excellent restaurant; is always full and puts up an excellent feed. We had soup, oysters, a very nice piece of sole, an excellent egg à la something or other, roast duck, chocolate soufflé dessert and coffee. Everything was beautifully cooked, but the waiting was bad and the wine nothing to shout about. We took plenty of time over our first meal since breakfast and eventually arrived back at Vert Galant [aerodrome] about 10 p.m.

Overleaf: A tank going into action on Messines Ridge, June 1917.

1917

At times I love this life – at others I hate it; at present I am hating it, as I am on the verge of becoming a casualty – but that's another story.

Captain G. B. Manwaring (pseudonym)

———

There is quite a buzz of excitement in the air, for someone has mentioned the magic word 'Leave'. We are all imagining ourselves starting off home in a few days' time. Most of my time on guard last night was spent in discussing with my fellow sentry the manner of our arrival at home, what time we should get there, whether we should send word that we were coming or turn up unexpectedly; whether we should wash, shave and clean our clothes before arrival or walk in in all our glory of mud and dirt. I suppose we should get to London in the small hours of the morning, and I don't know what time the first train home is. I wonder if there are any clothes for me to wear – civilised clothes I mean, or civilian, rather, it's the same thing. Anyway I shall be quite happy so long as I have sheets and pyjamas, hot water in the bath and porridge for breakfast.

Gunner Cecil Longley, B Battery, 1st South Midland Brigade, Royal Field Artillery

First, leave actually began. Six men from the battalion went on leave every day. Names were taken in order of seniority, and every one was engaged in frantic calculations as to when his turn should come. Many cursed the day that they enlisted, in the sense that they wished it had been a day or two earlier. A day might well postpone their turn for leave for a month.

'Leave is a privilege, not a right,' quoted our regulation-bound adjutant in his most Service tones as, clicking my spurred heels together, I smartly saluted him and again asked if I were not nearly due for a 'drop o' Blighty'. The twinkle in his eye, however, aroused the suspicion in my mind that

Temporary Surgeon Geoffrey Sparrow, Royal Naval Division, Attd 2nd Field Ambulance

Officers of 3rd Worcestershire Regiment rest during the fighting on Messines Ridge, 9 June. The adjutant, Lieutenant Lawrence Piper (sitting, front), was killed the following day.

these stern words were mainly for the benefit of his orderly room sergeant, who was vainly trying to conceal the emotion which my humble request evoked in his well-disciplined mind. Nor was I mistaken, for a few days later a breathless runner dashed into my medical inspection room with the message – 'Please render to this office forthwith your address whilst on leave.'

Dinner that night was a joyous affair. The Colonel, with the prospect of rehearsing the normal formation of attack at an early hour on the following morning, shortly retired to woo that fickle jade Morpheus, and left the major, adjutant, quartermaster and transport officer – all of whom had promised to see me off for my train in the early hours of the morrow. We drew our chairs round the fire, each lit one of Wills's incomparable 'Trois Chateaux', filled our glasses to the brim, thanked God we were back in comfortable billets, and started to reminisce about home.

The transport officer told us of a delightful flapper he once met in the park and took to the movies, of the wonderful dinner they subsequently had in the Troc, and how, thanks to the excellent Cliquot, she had consented to adopt him as her 'lonely subaltern', and now sent him weekly boxes of luxuries from home; the major enthused over a 'typewriter' he used to know in his wild subaltern days; the adjutant, married, of course, expressed his disapprobation of the friends of his brother officers; whilst the rubicund quartermaster suggested that 'another little drink wouldn't do us any harm'. And so the hours passed until the mess cart which was to take me to the station was announced. The adjutant then read to me the dire penalties of attempting to smuggle home shells, 5.9s, Boche rifles, uncensored letters, or other property belonging to the government, and to the shouts of 'Goodbyee-ee, Goodbyee-ee', I set out on my journey.

The less said of that dreary drive to the station, of my interview with the sleepy and none too polite railway transport officer, and the apparently never-ending journey to the base, the better. The only item of interest was watching the small French boys, who, apparently with no great exertion, raced the train for miles, begging us for souvenirs, bully beef, and suchlike commodities dear to the heart of the gamin. Eventually we reached the coast and I made my way to the leave boat, where everything was bustle and full of interest. The MLO, resplendent in blue tabs, enormous spurs, an exquisite hunting stock, and carrying a murderous-looking trench stick heavily weighted with lead, scrutinised our leave warrants and marshalled us over the narrow gangway on board. The number of be-tabbed officers, red, blue, black and green, gave quite a tone to the somewhat dingy vessel, and caused the muddy, unkempt trench-worker to become very conscious of the many deficiencies in his sartorial equipment. At last we were off. A brigadier, setting his hat at the approved nautical angle, climbed up on the bridge beside the skipper, but unfortunately mal-de-mer claimed him for her own, and, with a haste rarely seen in one of his exalted rank, he rushed below.

Why, I dreamily wondered, do mechanical transport officers invariably wear spurs, why are ASC officials usually replete with revolvers and other warlike apparatus which they are so rarely called on to use, and why does every staff officer of field rank, as soon as he is in sight of England's shores, surreptitiously change his khaki headgear for a wondrous affair, resplendent with red and gold and patent leather peak?

The leave train majestically steamed into Victoria. A prehistoric porter of venerable appearance kindly consented to look after my scanty belongings, and I hastened up the platform to change my French money, cunningly avoiding en route an officious looking Military Policeman who was apparently chasing young officers who had carelessly left their gloves and walking sticks in the trenches, or whose putties and clothes had been somewhat torn on the German wire during the attack a few days previously. By dint of grossly overtipping numerous ragged urchins, I eventually obtained a taxi, and directing the driver to the hotel I sank luxuriously on to the cushions and wondered if dear old London had altered much since I last visited her.

Jealous though any man was of another's leave, second best, but nevertheless very important, was to receive a parcel from home. Home comforts, whether they included clothes or food, were warmly greeted and normally shared among close friends.

Pioneer George Dewdney, 72 Section, 'P' Special Company, Royal Engineers

I have done so well lately with parcels. On Tuesday I had two: – one from aunts and one from Albourne. They were both splendid and I have done quite a lot of entertaining since receiving them. Great excitement was caused by my aunt Polly's. It contained eight boiled eggs, a pot of fish paste, a packet of butterscotch and two rosebuds and a rabbit pie! The latter had travelled well, but the outside crust had a little mildew on it in places. So I proclaimed a meeting of the experts to decide the momentous question as to whether it was eatable or no. However, it looked so very tempting that good sense was overruled by appetite! Anyhow, twelve of us had a feed from it and thoroughly enjoyed it, then spent the rest of the evening (which was wet) watching for signs of ptomaine poisoning in each other. Bedtime came – no casualties; so some other bold spirits cleared it up for supper. I really don't know which was the better – the pie or the suspense. Now comes the awful task of writing to aunt, and while thanking her for the splendid pie, dropping a gentle hint that such things are rather explosive for a soldier's parcel.

The army's postal system was remarkably efficient and regular, soldiers receiving letters from home normally within three or four days. Harry Trounce was an American who had chosen to serve in the British Army. His mail came from California, 6,000 miles away.

Lieutenant Harry Trounce, 181st Company, Royal Engineers

The arrival of mail was always eagerly anticipated, and we were seldom disappointed. The British Postal Service, which is under the direction of the Royal Engineers, was particularly efficient. In all the time I was at the front, our mail was seldom delayed. We received the London newspapers the day after issue, and the *Continental Daily Mail* the day of issue. My own mail from way off in California was received regularly almost every day, reaching me nearly always three weeks after mailing. My friends in California sent me a plum pudding, candy, and other perishable stuff for the Christmas of 1916, and it arrived on time and in good condition. The number of parcels alone handled must have been enormous, many officers and men getting their supplies of tobacco, papers, magazines and other good things regularly through the mail. It has reached such a point that I understand many officers now send their laundry back to England each weekend.

But receiving letters from America paled when set against one small book that was lost, found, posted and reposted before finding its way back to its owner.

During the Gallipoli evacuation I happened to lose a small book in which I jotted down weekly reports regarding the sanitary condition of the trenches. Months later, sitting in a dugout on the Western Front, an envelope was handed to me by a breathless brigade orderly. It contained my long lost sanitary book, and also a pile of correspondence, showing that it had passed through the hands of twenty-six eminent staff officers, each of whom had added a short memo, as to what he considered the best method of finding the owner. To the civilian this may appear a cumbersome method of procedure, but in reality it is eminently businesslike, and answers its purpose admirably, in so far as the individual concerned is always reached.

Temporary Surgeon Geoffrey Sparrow, Royal Naval Division, Attd 2nd Field Ambulance

On 14 March the Germans began a careful withdrawal to the Hindenburg Line, a formidable defensive position prepared over several months. The Battles of Verdun and the Somme had cost the Germans dearly and it became imperative that they shorten their lines and withdraw. The new line was twenty-five miles shorter, releasing fourteen badly needed divisions from the role of merely holding the line. The retirement caused a logistical nightmare for the Allies, who followed cautiously for fear of booby traps, passing over ground which the Germans had destroyed in a carefully coordinated policy of scorched earth.

14 March: Today passed quietly enough … When I got down to Company Headquarters in the evening, I learned that the Hun was believed to be retiring this night from his positions opposite us: the old story again, but this time apparently the evidence was stronger; at any rate it proved to be more reliable, for as the night went on, we heard that the patrols, which the front companies were sending out, found the German line very lightly

Lieutenant Edward Shears, 1st Irish Guards

held, while our 2nd Battalion, in the 2nd Brigade on our right, was making the same discovery.

The battalion in our old line in St Pierre Vaast Wood was reported to have entered the German front and support lines. But, in spite of these excitements, there was nothing for us in the support line to do, but work at the trench or sleep.

15 March: We heard nothing definite about the happenings in front, until the middle of the morning, when MacMahon came round and told me that the companies in front were going to occupy the German front line. I accordingly sent forward two runners to bring me back news as soon as this took place. The Hun had evidently not retired his artillery, for he was shelling all in front with great intensity; and as, after waiting half an hour, we saw nothing of our runners, I sent forward two more. In half an hour these were back, with the news that our first runners had been killed by a shell which had burst on top of the right front of Company Headquarters, killing in all four or five men, and wounding Major Young and one man, both seriously. They did not seem to know whether or not the company had moved forward, but reported heavy shelling and apparent confusion in front. I saw that I should have to go forward myself to see how matters really stood, and having got a volunteer, a man called Dean, to accompany me, made my way up to No. 2 Company's Headquarters. There I found the casualties of an hour ago, and one or two live men who could give me no clear news of their company …

I returned to my platoon, and found that Sergeant Kane had been exploring a piece of German trench on the right front of our line. He had ventured into all the dugouts, and pronounced them safe from booby traps. I accordingly moved my platoon in there. It was a good deep trench (about eight feet down), with dugout accommodation for half a company, and the dugouts were clean and comfortable.

16 March: This morning there was a heavy mist, which entirely obscured the view, and the German artillery had ceased firing. Life was therefore much pleasanter … After breakfast, I had hardly started the men to work on improving the trench, when the Hun began shelling again with renewed vigour and extreme accuracy. I therefore got the men back into their dugouts, only keeping a sentry out. Not long after, the Hun dropped a

shell right into the trench, just where the sentry was standing, and killed him instantaneously. It was right at the mouth of my dugout, and shook us all up a bit. The poor man was quite an elderly married man, and much respected. I was very upset about him. The shelling went on without intermission until about seven in the evening, and after the hit at the mouth of my dugout, I felt extremely cowardly under it. I think a long stop in a deep dugout is most damaging to one's morale, for whether the shells are falling near your trench or some way off, they always sound as if they were practically on top of you. However, in the circumstances, dugouts were the best places to be in … I think that a retirement of the kind the Hun was executing is, under modern conditions, fairly easy. All he has to do is to withdraw his infantry by night, and hold up the

A shell-blasted tree: the German retreat to the Hindenburg Line allowed Allied troops to look around the relinquished battlefields.

pursuit by heavy artillery barrages at a long range, and machine-gun fire for about twenty-four hours, and then take back his guns.

17 March: It was hot and sunny today. The Hun appeared to have retreated off the map; and we were very happy. We basked on the parapet and enjoyed the war. There was one contretemps during the morning, and there might have been more, for some men digging in my trench, as a result of a disobedience to orders, exploded three German bombs, and two men were wounded – only slightly. Then, suddenly from the blue, three shells landed almost in our trench, and made us jump a bit. In the afternoon I went for a good walk through Saillisel, and on to the Beyreuth line. From there we were able to see all the villages round – Rocquigny, Mesnil, Bys, and Le Transloy – and nowhere a sign of the Hun. In fact he appeared to have retired on a very broad front, and we heard that our troops had entered Bapaume early this morning. It looked as though

the Germans were going straight back to the fabled Hindenburg Line.

We were tremendously exhilarated, and quite sorry to be relieved by the 2nd Grenadiers in the evening.

19 March: Until the retirement of the Huns had actually taken place, I never realised what a tremendous amount would have to be done on our side before we could follow them up effectively. There was a belt of country three or four miles wide with literally no communications, and the work of construction involved was colossal. This morning it started for us. We marched out to the Bapaume road, near Sailly-Saillisel, and started to clear the surface. The work cheered everybody tremendously; that we should now be working, packed as thick as flies, on a spot that had been one of the hottest on earth, made one positively laugh with joy. In places the road cleared easily. There were some six inches of mud and debris to scrape off, and then we came to the old surface unimpaired. Elsewhere shells had made large holes, and the job of filling these in was a longer one. However, some artillery was due to pass along this afternoon, and it was made clear enough for them. There was still a great deal of work to be done before it could take motor traffic.

The Royal Engineers helped prepare the ground for the advance. A huge logistical effort brought supplies forward in the dark, but this was made harder by an abrupt change in the weather, which became increasingly cold and wet. In the distance, demolition blasts could be heard as the Germans began to pull back, although troops picked for rearguard action kept up a constant fire. Over the Somme riverbed and adjoining marshland, close to Péronne, a major feat of engineering was undertaken as sappers built new bridges resting on floating pontoons, strong enough to carry infantry and light field guns, while other ranks were used as carrying parties, ferrying rubble from destroyed houses as ballast for the roadways.

Captain Victor Eberle, 475th Field Company, Royal Engineers

20 March: I rode with two of our officers across the river [Somme] and down the east side to Péronne to look for billets for the sappers. All the inhabitants had been removed. Churches, public and private buildings of all kinds, bridges and roadways had been blown up; water-supply sources

and communications destroyed. There were few signs of the town being shelled by the French and British. The almost complete ruination of the buildings in the principal streets has been brought about by the Germans blowing out the fronts or setting fire to them … Fires were still burning in many directions, with occasional explosions as booby traps and delayed-action mines exploded. We quickly learned that the most innocent looking object, such as an apparently discarded steel helmet on the ground, might cover a bomb arranged to explode if the helmet were picked up. Everywhere the debris of war and discarded equipment lay around. For any souvenir hunter the choice was unlimited. For my part, with my promised leave so far holding good, I watched my steps with the utmost circumspection and took no risks.

23 March: We were supposed not to show ourselves more than was necessary by day, so stuck pretty tight to our trenches. However, I got leave from MacMahon to explore a little of the surrounding country in the afternoon, and went forward with my orderly to a cavalry post ahead, and then up to the crest of the hill overlooking the next valley. From there, I could see a wide stretch of country, including the line of trenches, which from the direction from which Very lights had been thrown up last night, I believed the Huns to be holding lightly. However, there was hardly a sign of life, and I only saw two groups of about four men each in the whole country. Then I went on to look at the village of Etricourt. It had evidently been used by the Germans for billets up to their retirement, but before leaving it they had systematically burned every room in every house, so that now it presented a rather cheerless spectacle. Another demonstration of German thoroughness was provided in the valley, where a railway had once run: each rail had been severed by explosive at intervals of about five yards, so as to render it utterly useless to us.

Lieutenant Edward Shears, 1st Irish Guards

8 April: We are in most luxurious quarters more or less at the front, a farm stables practically uninjured by the retiring Boches. It has not been cleaned for ages, but the 'nures' [manures] are nice and soft, and I have just slept on a spring mattress gathered in from the adjoining ruins. We also have tables and chairs dotted among the nure-heaps, and a small artificial

Second Lieutenant Robert Vernede, 12th Rifle Brigade

Christmas tree, evidently left by the Boches. Our last shelter was not so good, being the ruins of the manse in another village. The snow and wind blew through it and the chimney beam caught fire and threatened to bring the chimney on top of us, so we had to go cold, which it was. There is no exaggeration about the state these villages are left in. The Boches cut out a brick or two at intervals in every house wall, insert explosives, and bring the whole thing down, so that often you can sit under the gables as they rest on the ground with the whole house and all the contents ground to dust below. The advantage to us of this destruction is that everywhere now there is fuel, broken beams and laths and doors and chairs with which one can mostly keep big fires going. The military advantage to them is less than nothing.

Opposite: Two Australians in Albert, on the Somme. Behind them, the town's basilica, and the famous figure of the Madonna holding the Christ Child leaning at 120 degrees.

To long-serving soldiers, it was extraordinary to see the land beyond the battlefields, the largely untainted woods and farmland beyond which the Germans had retreated. For those coming to the Somme for the first time, it was the former battlefields themselves that were astonishing. Second Lieutenant Geoffrey Fildes was returning to France after being wounded, with two officers who had not been to the Western Front before. They were all staggered by what they saw.

Setting forth once more, by a route that passed through the heart of the Somme country, we had been gradually confronted by a terrible panorama. From the open door of our goods van, we were able to realise more than ever before the magnitude and fury of the struggle of the previous autumn. In every direction as far as the horizon stretched a desert of brown shell-ploughed slopes and hollows, and scattered upon the face of this landscape, clumps of splintered poles, gaunt and blackened by fire, marked the sites of former woods and copses. Endless belts of wire entanglements, many feet in width, undulated into the distance, tracing rusty red lines across the vast expanse. Craters of every size pitted this land in countless thousands. Along the remains of abandoned trenches and gun emplacements they actually merged into one another, and so granulated by shellfire was the surface of the country, that it now resembled an extinct planet, its face

Second Lieutenant Geoffrey Fildes, 2nd Coldstream Guards

mottled with innumerable lifeless craters. Down by the river, which now invaded the low-lying ground beside it, zigzags of gleaming water revealed the position of former trenches. Scattered everywhere over the waste, clusters of wooden crosses leant at every angle, telling their tale of past assaults and counter-attacks, and it was still possible for us to trace in broad outline the story of those battles by the rotting accoutrements lying on every side. Here a British shrapnel helmet or a shattered Enfield rifle, there a dented French casque or shred of horizon-blue cloth, denoted the two armies' brotherhood in arms.

Ascending the gradient that wound up the valley ahead, our train pursued its way through this amazing scene. To sit and stare at what lay before us called for no effort on our part, as the country passed before our eyes like a cinematograph display. Thus we continued for an hour or more.

Neither of my companions accompanying the draft had served in France before, but, like most people, they had read newspaper accounts of the Western Front. Now, however, they were amazed. Seated beside them in our van, even I was enthralled by the passing spectacle, but it did not prevent me from noting their murmurs of astonishment. Their feelings were hardly to be wondered at, for, though familiar with the Somme, I, too, had not realised until now the degree and extent of its awful ruin. Life – human, animal and vegetable – had been engulfed; not a leaf, hardly a blade of grass, no sound of bird, greeted us; all was done and finished with. Here indeed was the end of the world.

Another mile or so brought us to the position of our recent support line, where quantities of supplies lay embedded in the hardened mud. Here sign boards indicated an old Brigade Headquarters, there, an RE dump. Long sections of weather-beaten parapet revealed the sites of our former trenches, these still guarded in front by endless belts of wire and stakes. Now the road was all but obliterated, so we were compelled to step carefully to avoid a fall.

It was a strange thing to be walking thus peacefully through this wilderness, for when last seen, enemy patrols had been advancing across it towards our position in the Blue Line. Then it had represented a wide expanse of no-man's-land, now it was part of France once more. As we made our way across this waste, parties of men belonging to Labour Battalions paused at their work to watch us go by, while motor lorries, revelling in apparent ownership of the road, choked us with their dust. In the distance, lines of horses out to water threaded their way placidly over the old battleground. Everywhere around were to be seen those miscellaneous bodies of men met with on lines of communication, left far behind by the advancing army. No doubt they cursed the country for its discomfort. In their eyes, it represented a region of 'rotten jobs' and endless 'fatigues', a desert justly spurned by the feet of the forces ahead of them, a world of salvage and of evil smells. Here a motor-transport driver lit a cigarette, turned his nose up at the air and slipped into top speed.

Then the weather had been fine; now it was atrocious. Snow and hailstorms swept over the sodden countryside. On 9 April, in a snowstorm, the British launched an offensive at Arras on German positions unaltered since their general withdrawal from the Somme. This was in fact a diversionary operation preceding the main event, a French assault on the Aisne. At Arras, fourteen infantry divisions attacked after a five-day bombardment. Then a week later the French attacked, but their assault failed dramatically and brought the already discontented French army close to outright mutiny.

At Arras significant gains had been made, including the storming of the strategic height of Vimy Ridge, captured by the Canadians. In large part to keep secret the French military problems on the Aisne, the British offensive was pressed for a further month. The casualties proved very high, the highest per day of any battle fought by the British forces on the Western Front but, as on the Somme, the Germans could afford far less the losses that they incurred.

Now let me tell you a bit about the largest battle in the world's history. You would gather from my letters that I was about to 'move' again, or in other words, go over the top. It did not come off as soon as we expected, so that was why I managed to drop you a line on Easter Saturday or was it Good Friday? No matter. On Saturday we moved to a deep dugout in 'battle' order, that is without our spare kit. Never shall I forget the roar of the guns, hundreds of them. On Easter Sunday we had nothing to do except load up

Corporal Thomas Belton, 5th King's Shropshire Light Infantry

Taking stock: British troops resting after battle.

with bombs, ammunition, rifle grenades, Very lights and other weapons of war. We stretcher-bearers packed our bags full of bandages and shell dressings. That done, we smoked and sang and *thought*. I was wondering what you were all doing, and I kept looking at my watch and guessing so and so was happening at the various times, six, seven and eight. I thought of the Holy Communion services being held, and of the prayers that were being offered on our behalf. At eleven, I fancied the choir singing 'Jesus Christ is risen today' and all the beautiful Easter hymns. Again at six, I wondered how many bells were being rung, and wished I could have made another. No use wishing, though. Night came, and I noticed more men saying their prayers than usual, and it was rumoured that the chaplain was coming round to hold a short service, but he did not turn up. I was very sorry, for the fellows would have responded.

However, we sang hymns and sometimes broke off into some old songs.

Midnight came, and the order ran down the dugout, 'Get your equipment on'. That done, we filed out and had a march over the ground we recently took, into some assembly trenches. Everything was done as quietly as possible, so that the enemy would not know we were there. We deepened the trench, and then we sat down, and talked about cold and rain! I was frozen to the marrow, and we could not stir because no movement was to be made. So the time rolled slowly by, and all the time our guns were pounding away, and it was very few who had not got a severe headache. I can vouch for mine being 'rocky'. 2, 3, 4, 5 and 6.30 a.m. came and went, and then we saw four tanks lumbering over the shell-swept ground. Then the fun began. Fritz began to shell us and up went our temperatures a few degrees. (Shelling always makes one warm.) Down came the metal, mingling with the rain and sleet. No casualties so far. Then there was such a crash, and I tried to look but it was dark. Am I blinded? I thought. No, only buried. Next I felt a shovel striking my arm, and I tried to move but couldn't. A few more digs from the shovel, and another heave and out comes my 'nut'. 'Are you hurt?' everyone near me was saying, but thank God I was right as rain, only for a shaking. My pal was in a like plight, but we both got 'normal' again after a while. We moved away from there, and bless me if the same thing did not occur again. I began to think Fritz had got us two 'taped'.

Ah well, nothing else happened, and the order came ringing down, 'Over the top, boys', and up we jumped, every man as one. A finer sight I never saw. Wave after wave in perfect order marching into the jaws of death. Down went many a good husband and son, but on we went, the remainder, without a flinch. We stretcher-bearers were soon busy putting dressings on the poor fellows who had been hit, and ever and anon the cries went up. Oh, it was awful. Our platoon officer and his servant got a leg blown off and I put a tourniquet on each and left them for the RAMC to carry back, but both of them were hit again and killed. Our orders were to carry on until we reached our objective, and bandage all, and then

Anxious but no doubt relieved to be alive: British prisoners captured during fighting in early 1917.

start to carry. Some of the poor fellows prayed for us to take them back, but we could not.

My pal was mortally wounded only a yard from me. I showed him his wife's photo, and read her last letter to him, and part of St John 17 and so passed away a real Christian soldier, and I could not but think of the Easter message as I saw the smile on his face as he died. 'Oh Death, where is thy sting?' It was with a heavy heart and wet eyes that I left him with the snow falling on his body. All around lay dead and wounded, and I did what I could for the latter, giving water to those wounded in the legs and arms, but flinging the water bottle away from those wounded in the stomach. You will gather how we suffered when I tell you that out of forty-two in our platoon who mounted the parapet, only eleven are left and I am one of them.

Your soldier boy, Tom

Men say that religion has failed. I think not, but rather just as life has been shorn of its falseness, its petty tyrannies – so religion is being stripped of its creeds and dogmas, and man is learning in all things to grasp essentials. Here one sees men up against the big things of life, and yet touched by a simple faith that would put many a so-called Christian to shame. One sees half-shy soldiers quietly slip into some church as though to look round, and yet if one watches them one finds more than that. I am not saying that this is universal, but probe deep enough below the surface of everyday life and it is there …

Captain G. B. Manwaring (pseudonym)

We had a service this morning, and after, some impulse moved me to attend Communion – why I know not; but as the atheist on the scaffold was moved to pray, 'Oh God, if there be a God, save my soul if I have a soul', so at times those very ones who can find no real belief in dogma, creed or ritual, outside that of nature, are moved to join the worshippers who can and do. The only officer present, the men looked to me for an example of ritual regarding standing, kneeling and responding, and so probing into the depths of memory I drew to the surface such as I could. As a matter of fact I believe I only made one mistake – and I am glad I went.

A drumhead service held for the troops out of the line.

Many a soldier, with or without faith, turned to army padres for help and guidance, and few were more responsive than Philip 'Tubby' Clayton, a thirty-one-year-old Anglican clergyman. In 1915 he had gone to France to serve as an army chaplain where, with another chaplain, Neville Talbot, he co-founded Talbot House in December 1915, named in memory of Neville's brother Gilbert who had been killed in July. The building they used was in Poperinghe, and it became a rest home and place of refuge for soldiers out of the line at Ypres. All were welcome, rank was irrelevant, an 'Everyman's Club' as it was styled. Entertainment was provided downstairs and a chapel upstairs, and during the course of the war tens of thousands of men walked through its doors. Tubby Clayton became widely loved and respected not just for his work, but for his effervescent and warm personality, and for the way he gave all he met the sincere impression that his time was their time. Throughout the war he never feared for his own safety, putting himself in grave danger on many occasions in order to visit soldiers and offer friendship and Communion.

Reverend Philip 'Tubby' Clayton, Army Chaplain

11 April: I have only a few minutes to spare, and cannot now write the account of our glorious Easter I wanted to – but I don't think the memory of it will fade with waiting. I had about 480 communicants, single-handed at Talbot House ... In the afternoon I started again, and had celebrations at battery positions and elsewhere, an evensong at a Kite Balloon Section, and evensong at Talbot House, and an evening celebration for some forty men who had been on duty in the morning. This made fourteen services during the day, which kept me from stagnation. Yesterday, I had another Easter with Major Shiner [Royal Garrison Artillery] and, except for the fact that an SOS went up just as I got there, and service was impossible till 10 p.m., all was excellent. A happy celebration in the morning, after which I walked across in an April snowstorm to arrange for two subalterns and a sergeant major (who are anxious to be confirmed) to come down today to Talbot House.

27 April: The Boche had a new balloon up and was shelling the road, so far as I could judge, by which I should normally go. So I trod delicately, and cut across the fields; when I rejoined the road, I could scarcely recognise it – just a chain of shell holes. The first people I came across were two gunners relaying the wires, who told me what had been happening all the afternoon. No casualties, fortunately, and no guns damaged, in spite of it all. But the place looked like the surface of the moon through a telescope. The gramophone in the officers' mess got a direct hit on it, and the place where I was going to sleep was simply one yawning gulf of wreckage. So we built a wigwam with canvas round the waterwheel of the farmhouse nearby, and camped there happily enough. My lantern, a communion box (which I had left there) were both smothered in brick dust but unhurt, and the grimmest thing was that the old farmer had died a natural death on Sunday (having refused to leave the farm in which he was born) and as he lay dead in bed, a shell blew in the side of the house and wounded the corpse. His poor old wife meanwhile refused to leave him, and just huddled up crouching and untouched against the further wall! We thought she would be almost maddened by it, but strangely enough she was thankful saying that she was so glad it had happened after his death, as the destruction of the farm would have broken his heart.

18 June: I had a rather rough journey with Pettifer on Friday and Saturday last. We reached our first objective – thanks to a lift in a RFC tender at about 10.30 a.m. After half an hour we wanted to leave, but the Boche was meanwhile dropping HE [High Explosive] of a heavy type on nothing in particular across the road … The next trouble was that after we had crossed a couple of fields he suddenly burst an air-crump high in front of us. So we got down hastily into an old trench for half an hour. Shrapnel is queer stuff. Long after the burst, just when you are tempted to peer round and say 'Where did that one go?' you suddenly become aware of twigs and branches from the trees above being lopped off by invisible knives, and you cuddle down again under the traverse of the trench, and wish the tin hat was ten times as big.

After some time wasted here, we proceeded (no one ever 'goes' anywhere in the army) … Imagine living in holes scooped out of the railway embankment. Here I had some lunch with the subalterns and then trotted along to the men. Sitting in the hedge with them, we were rudely disturbed by a heavy burst overhead, and tumbled helter-skelter into the nearest dugout – not a very capacious place. Half a dozen more separate bursts, and then a salvo of three (which was beastly). So I had some hymn sheets in my pocket, and passed them down inwards, the subaltern and myself sharing the entrance. Here we sang 'Hold the fort' rather appropriately, and had quite a jolly service, though I found preaching rather difficult, accompanied as it was by two menacing roars growing nearer and nearer, followed by terrific crashes, like an express train in a grand cinema collision. Meanwhile, I tried to tell the invisible audience what the words 'the Kingdom of God' really meant. The service and the shelling ended together, and when we went out of the doorway, the first thing we found was the body of a dear young signaller lying quite quietly half under a semicircle of corrugated iron, which formed his sleeping place. He was the major's clerk, a splendid fellow in every way, six months married. Apparently, he had been coming to lie down and sleep under cover, and the last burst of shrapnel must have caught him about five yards from the entrance to the dugout. He must have dropped without a cry, being hit twice through the head, and made some convulsive movement towards his little house by which he fell. This discovery was terrible; it was so utterly unexpected, for though they have had several casualties we thought no one had been caught this time. He was a most popular man, and the officer in charge quite broke down, for which I liked him all the better.

Captain G. B. Manwaring (pseudonym)

Evening – twilight darkens into night – one of those still summer nights when the inanimate appears to take on a life of its own, when one can almost picture elves and fairies stealing from their hiding places to frisk and frolic until sunrise calls the so-called living to life again. Outside, earth sleeps and sleeping earth wakes. War is far distant tonight, the dull boom of the guns is muffled and lost in a hundred and one murmurs of the night. Within, I sit alone in the farm; alone, and yet from the next room comes the laughter of young voices, finding cheerfulness now that the day's work is done – such is the eternal heritage of youth.

Boom – a distant gun breaks the silence and suddenly the meaning of it all is borne upon one. A 'runner' enters with countless orders, and sleeping men are wakened and despatched with messages to outlying billets. For here one's work is never done, by day or night. Such runners enter, breaking into meals or disturbing one's hard-earned sleep, until one prays just for a few hours to call one's own, to read or write or dream of the home life that seems so very far away. Those in England cannot realise what a Company Commander's life is like – even out of the line – its trials and worries and the awful responsibility of it all. Some two hundred men, most of whose education consists in the ploughman's daily round, looking to him for every little thing. Grievances to be settled, justice to be weighed out, financial matters to be adjusted and the great responsibility of life and death, for on his orders men go to meet certain death or wait in comparative safety. When life is cheap it isn't one's own that counts, it's those lives that are dependent on you, and behind them the lives at home in England.

I had two pathetic letters today, one from the fiancée of a man to whom I had to break the news of her loved one's death, thanking me – oh, so piteously! – for my kindness, and asking if I could tell her how she could get some souvenir to take with her down the empty years that lie ahead. The other more pathetic still, and yet more touching than any I have ever received.

Let me quote a little of it to you. The writer had lost both husband and brother. This is what she wrote: 'Please don't laugh at me, but I am a lonely woman now, and if there is in your Company a lonely soldier who would be glad of letters and cigarettes, do me a kindness and let me have his name.' Somehow I found tears in my eyes as I read it, it was so infinitely sad and yet so beautiful.

Oh, the many sides of life that lie in these soldiers' letters! The pathos of the men whose dear ones are lying ill at home; messages to children they have never seen and may never see; words of comfort and hope to mothers, fathers, sisters, brothers, wives and sweethearts. Now upbraiding, now consoling. Now joking, full of humour and cheerfulness and never a real complaint against it all, only a devout wish that it may be finished soon. Truly one dips below the surface of life, and we who have seen all this can never be the same careless pleasure-seekers again.

A barking dog heralds the approach of a plane. Night after night we hear their drone as they pass to and fro, sometimes lonely wanderers of the air, sometimes in flights or squadrons. At times the anti-aircraft guns bark defiance, at others they pass peacefully away, and all is quiet once again …

Lieutenant Algernon Hyde Villiers, 121st Machine-Gun Company, Machine-Gun Corps

I wish I could tell you how happy and well I feel, what a different man, for the change from subterranean gropings to the light of heaven. The nights, I think, make the greatest difference – or rather, I should say, the hours devoted to sleep. In a deep dugout one wakes up like an underdone bun, and though I did not sleep heavily, this morning I feel thoroughly refreshed. The air was free to come in six inches from my nose, and there is a draught clean through the shelter.

Then a bath in a half-tub filled with rainwater and a thorough inspec-tion of my clothes was greatly cheering … Now, instead of a chilly, stuffy, one-candle-lighted den, I am at ease in a sandbag and steel shelter, with bright sunshine pouring into it. The lack of air, and the unnecessarily bad messing of my late hosts, had quite upset my interior economy … but all that has gone and I have enjoyed an excellent luncheon, with salad and stewed plums and delicious biscuits. In the dugout we had tea and coffee – mixed one day, and on another occasion the tea was made in a tin half full of disinfectant. In a deep dugout the dark makes it very hard for the cooks, and nothing tastes right in that stale atmosphere. It is curious, too, how chilly it gets down there in the small hours. It must be horrible in winter. I did my level best not to think of these things when I was there, and insisted with myself that I must be glad to share, in a trifling measure, the discomforts of which thousands had had months, and even years, to put up with. Having managed to get through my first such spell I expect subsequent descents will be much easier.

We carried on with four guns from 11.30 to 2.30 last night, supporting an operation of a minor character, which turned out quite well. During the night there were some glorious big bombardments to either side of us, splendid to watch, and really prodigious to think of in relation to our position of two years ago, in the matter of artillery.

Destruction everywhere, but a destruction that was grand while it was Captain G. B. Manwaring (pseudonym) dreadful. And so to dugouts, and the night-time 'hate' and gas – a doze, and the wonderful dawn of a perfect daybreak. Exploration of trenches, broken by pauses to look at aerial combats far up in the blue, where planes looked like bits of silver dust whirled about by the breeze. Interest covered and crushed every other emotion, and though many of the things that lie about seem loathsome in cold-blooded language, I found nothing of loathing there …

Crash! bang! boom! and like rabbits to earth once more; we have been spotted, and whizz-bangs fall – a dozen wasted German shells. Packed like sardines we lie and try to snatch some moments' sleep; shave in our breakfast tea, and clean our teeth in our lunchtime coffee, and wash not at all. With revolvers by our sides, and respirators on our chests, we live in the perpetual night of underground, coming to the surface to work or see a little of God's sunshine, or explore as shells permit and the spirit moves us. Time as a measure has ceased to be and our watches serve just as checks on our movements. I love the life, and oh, how I hate it too!

Let me describe our dugout: a window frame some three feet square in the chalk in the side of the trench, a steep dark flight of steps, and one reaches the outer tunnel; at the end of which a distant candle reveals my sergeant major, clerk, and gas NCO. From this open little rooms about five feet square where officers' orderlies sleep; from this a lower tunnel of the same dimensions, reached by a similar window and shorter flight of steps, and one comes to our living room; a six by two shelf serves as a table, at which, if one is sitting at it, no other can pass. At the end, the telephone and signallers; an emergency exit, in case the first is blown in, leads to another part of the trench. From our living room a lower tunnel runs forward into a little sand-bagged pit at the top of a flight of stairs; this passage serves as our store, kitchen, larder and everything else we want. Our furniture is crude in the extreme; from nails in the walls hang packs, coats, spare pieces of equipment, postcards, timetables, orders, fly-papers and tin hats. On the shelf or table is an oil lamp, some bottles, glasses, tinned milk, butter and jam, yesterday's newspapers and all one's possessions that go for a trip into the line. Scattered about the floor are closed stretchers, which, balanced from stairs to table or from petrol tins to pack, form our beds. With Burberry for pillow, or an air-pillow sometimes, and fleece lining for covering, we snatch an hour or two's sleep by night or day, until our turn for duty comes. Often as I sit reading in the lonely night vigils I look up suddenly and wonder if this can be real, or whether I am not asleep and dreaming some strangely impossible dream. Reality is seldom with me these days, and all is lost in vagueness in this life, where hour after hour drags by; where a day may seem a year from dullness, or a lifetime's excitement may be crammed into a matter of seconds. We are not ashamed of being afraid, as we often are – not afraid of any definite thing, but just afraid of being afraid; when the time for action comes there is little time for fear.

The German army on the Western Front was battered mercilessly in 1917. The Battle of Arras came and went, and then, on 7 June, there was the short-lived Battle of Messines, the most successful assault to date in which the Germans were literally blown off the Messines Ridge by the almost simultaneous explosion of nineteen mines buried under their lines. Six weeks later, the British launched their summer offensive at Ypres, a three-month battle followed at the end of November by a further strike at Cambrai. By the end of 1917, the Allies had been on an offensive footing for almost half the year.

It was the battle launched on 31 July, the Third Battle of Ypres, for which the year is remembered, not for any strategic results but for an attritional battle that was fought in nigh-impossible conditions. Unseasonable high rainfall, combined with a high water table, and the destruction through shellfire of ditches, flooded the ground over which soldiers dragged themselves week after week. The first day of the offensive was, in the main, a success for the British, but that afternoon it began to drizzle, then it rained, and rained, and rained.

Private Robert Cude, 7th The Buffs (East Kent Regiment)

We are moving up into the line again soon in preparation for the 'Do'. West Kents are attached to 54th Brigade as 'Moppers Up', Queen's are on 53rd Brigade strength for consolidation purposes, East Surreys are on road fatigue: and Buffs are 'Stretcher-Bearing' to whole of division: so whole of brigade is allotted to their various tasks. One very good plan of the staff, and one that is put into execution here, has more of wisdom about

it than we believed the said staff possessed, that is, two ground plans of actual ground which the attack covers are laid out in scale, showing all Jerry's trenches and fortifications, wire, etc., in fact, everything necessary for officer and man. It is laid out like a large allotment, and each battalion is taken in turn, and has the attack, also peculiarities of the ground, explained to them. This is something extremely brainy, yet so vitally necessary, that one wonders why it was not tried before. Every contour is shown, and his machine-gun posts, also likely places to expect them, on the whole it is very realistic, and the officers are very frequently viewing it and marking their maps accordingly. They know what part of the line they will be interested in, and so, each to his own degree of intelligence, marks his map where he thinks he will meet trouble, etc. What a smash this will be? For we have Tanks, Cavalry and Royal Horse Artillery waiting for the breakthrough. Fritz is assured of a warm time soon, all is in readiness.

An extraordinary image: Signaller Sidney Banyard, 215 Siege Battery, Royal Garrison Artillery, captures the opening moments of the British bombardment, 3.45 a.m., 31 July 1917. The night sky is lit up by the fire from massed artillery.

Private Sydney Fuller, 8th Suffolk Regiment

30 July: Our packs arrived at 1 a.m., and we turned in until 8.30 a.m. The day was spent in preparing for the 'stunt', which we had been told was to be 'the biggest of the war'. Not feeling very optimistic, I made my will on the small leaf provided for that purpose in the pay book … Saw several air scraps over the lines towards evening. Orders were issued for us to move at 9.45 p.m. Started off 10 p.m. across country, keeping to the left of Dickebusch for some distance, then crossing the road near 'Café Belge' and going past Chateau Segard. Here we began to get some shells. Crossed a canal by means of a steel bridge (Shrapnel Corner), and did not loiter as there were too many 'bits' flying about. The track for our division was marked by small direction posts and at intervals were small iron rods on top of which were small iron discs, painted white, with the divisional sign painted in black. The battalion's scouts had been posted at intervals along the track as a further precaution against our going astray in the darkness. Our guns, especially the 'heavies', were very active. So were the enemy's, and the shells were flying all over the place, many being 'gas' shells.

Second Lieutenant Thomas Floyd, 2/5th Lancashire Fusiliers

Zero was fixed for 3.50 in the morning. As the moment drew near, how eagerly we awaited it! At 3.50 a.m. exactly I heard a mine go up, felt a slight vibration, and, as I rushed out of the little dugout in which I had been resting, every gun for miles burst forth. What a sight! What a row! The early morning darkness was lit up by the flashes of thousands of guns, the air whistling and echoing with shells, the calm atmosphere shaken by a racket such as nobody who has not heard it could imagine! The weird ruins of Ypres towered fantastically amongst the flashes behind us. In every direction one looked guns were firing. In front of us the 166th and 165th Brigade were dashing across no-man's-land, sweeping into the enemy trenches, the barrage creeping before them. I stood on the parados of Liverpool Trench and watched with amazement. It was a dramatic scene such as no artist could paint.

Lieutenant Jack Walthew, 4 Squadron, Royal Flying Corps

At 3.15 a.m. we were all called to stand by our machines. I managed to get a couple of boiled eggs and some tea. The weather was most hopelessly dud. The clouds were at 800 [feet] so we had to fly at 700. This was almost suicidal as a machine is a very big and easy target. However, as we were the contact patrol flight we had to go up and try and do something. The other flights have been on the ground all day. I left the aerodrome at 5.30 a.m. and scraped over houses and trees etc. until I got to our guns. Here the fun started as there was, so experts tell me, the worst barrage that has ever been known, and I had to fly through it.

I could hear and occasionally see the shells and every minute I was expecting to see one of my wings vanish. However, nothing hit us until we got over the lines (which had been pushed forward considerably) and here in eight minutes we got thirty holes through the machine from machine guns. Ten of them passed within a few inches of Woodcock. The wireless transmitter, valued at £200, disappeared. Three spars on the wing were broken and lastly a bullet went through the petrol tank. I smelt a smell of petrol and in a few minutes it all came rushing over my feet and legs.

31 July: Reached the ruins of Zillebeke about 12.30 a.m. A good deal of gas in the air, smelling something like mustard, but it did not appear to do much harm. We had some difficulty in finding our signalling apparatus, which had been brought up to the village by limber. Saw one of our tanks burning fiercely near the village and behind some bushes, lighting up the ground for some distance around. Two other tanks could be seen nearby. Found our telephones etc. at last, also a heliograph belonging to some other regiment. We were led wrongly in the trenches, and were wandering about like lost sheep, amongst the mud and shells, until just before the barrage started, when we stumbled, more by luck than judgement, on a trench called 'Wellington Crescent', which was our proper position. The barrage started at 3.50 a.m. It was just beginning to get light and the tanks looked very queer as they crawled from their clumps of bushes and other hiding places and went forward. From the top of our trench we could see the country behind our lines for miles, and every bush seemed to be hiding a gun – the flashes were to be seen everywhere. The noise was so great that we could only shout in each other's ears to be heard at all. The enemy shelled our trench intermittently with 5.9s so we had to keep our heads down most of the time. I saw some of the Norfolks killed and wounded by a shell immediately in front of us. A tank which came forward

Private Sydney Fuller, 8th Suffolk Regiment

on our right ran right over some of the men in front, who were lying on the ground either dead or wounded. We shouted ourselves hoarse, but it was of no use – the men in the tank could not hear us and the tank was over the men in a minute.

One of our men was wounded beside me in a rather unusual manner. He suddenly complained that something had 'stung' him on the left shoulder, and on removing his tunic etc., found that a bullet had entered at the top of the shoulder, and had passed down in the front of his chest, under the skin, coming out near the centre of his chest. He was standing upright when he received the wound.

Second Lieutenant Thomas Floyd, 2/5th Lancashire Fusiliers

Before the battle had been raging half an hour, German prisoners were streaming down, only too glad to get out of range of their own guns! I saw half a dozen at the corner of Liverpool Trench and Garden Street. They seemed very happy trying to converse with us. One of them – a boy about twenty – asked me the nearest way to the station; he wanted to get to England as soon as possible.

The tanks went over. As daylight came on the battle raged furiously. Our troops were still advancing. Messages soon came through that St Julien had been taken.

Our time was drawing near. At 8.30 we were to go over. At 8 we were all 'standing to' behind the parapet. Colonel Best-Dunkley came walking along the line, his face lit up by smiles more pleasant than I have ever seen before. 'Good morning, Floyd; best of luck!' was the greeting he accorded me as he passed; and I, of course, returned the good wishes. At about 8.20 Captain Andrews went past me and wished me good luck; and he then climbed over the parapet to reconnoitre. The minutes passed by. Everybody was wishing everybody else good luck, and many were the hopes of 'Blighty' entertained – not all to be realised. It is a wonderful

Opposite: Sidney Banyard's friend, Joe Batty, stands in part of an abandoned and collapsing trench in the Ypres Salient. He is wearing a small box respirator.

sensation – counting the minutes on one's wristwatch as the moment to go over draws nigh. The fingers on my watch pointed to 8.30, but the first wave of D Company had not gone over. I do not know what caused the delay. Anyhow, they were climbing over. Eventually, at 8.40, I got a signal from Dickinson to go on. So forward we went. Could you possibly imagine what it was like? Shells were bursting everywhere. It was useless to take

any notice where they were falling, because they were falling all round; they could not be dodged; one had to take one's chance: merely go forward and leave one's fate to destiny …

The field was strewn with wreckage, with the mangled remains of men and horses lying all over in a most ghastly fashion. Many brave Scottish soldiers were to be seen dead in kneeling positions, killed just as they were firing on the enemy. Some German trenches were lined with German dead in that position. It was hell and slaughter. On we went. About a hundred yards on my right, slightly in front, I saw Colonel Best-Dunkley complacently advancing, with a walking stick in his hand, as calmly as if he were walking on a parade ground.

Private Sydney
Fuller, 8th Suffolk
Regiment

About 3½ hours after the barrage started (zero) the battalion, according to plan, formed up in an 'artillery formation' and began to advance, to take up the advance from where the division in front had halted. As soon as we began to move we were horribly shelled by the enemy, 4.2s and whizz-bangs and many of our men were killed and wounded. It was evident from the way that the shelling was done that we could be seen by the enemy – it was the troops out in the open, to the left of Sanctuary Wood, which were shelled worst, and as they continued to advance the enemy's shelling followed them … the division in front of us should by now have captured the whole of the first ridge in front and the enemy should therefore have been unable to see the ground we were advancing over. However, we pressed on and soon reached the German front line of a few hours before. This was not a 'trench' in the ordinary use of the word, being 'banked up' instead of 'dug in', owing to the marshy nature of the ground. Here we came under heavy rifle fire and machine-gun fire, the air seeming full of bullets. This also was not as it should have been, if the division in front had 'done its bit'. We spread out in 'open order' and went on. The going was very heavy owing to the mud and we soon had to stop for a short rest. The enemy's trenches were almost obliterated by the heavy fire of our guns. Trunks of trees were lying across them, anyhow, and the whole of the ground had been pulverised by shells. One badly wounded German lay writhing in agony on the ground near where we stopped. He was evidently past help. One of the signallers who had managed to get a little more than his share of rum issue, was desirous of shooting the dying German. 'Bastard', he called him but we put a stop to that business. I saw two bullets strike the wounded German immediately afterwards and he ceased to move so evidently someone had no scruples about it. Possibly (but not probably) someone shot him to 'put him out of his misery'. However, there were many men who shot down any of the enemy, regardless of circumstances – wounded or prisoners it made no difference – and it was noticeable that the men who did that sort of thing were loudest in condemning the German 'atrocities'. Two wrongs evidently made a right with them.

During the morning news, although meagre, is very disquieting, and at night the news is confirmed. In front of us the 30th Division make a hash of things, and the sum total is no appreciable advance has been made, still 53rd Bde is now in action, so things may be a little brighter soon! Although news is bad, it is solely confined to this sector, elsewhere we are completely successful. The French achieve more than they set out to do … 'Tanks' are soon in action in large numbers, but very little headway was made … The battle develops into a seesaw; first one side takes ground only to lose a little elsewhere. Jerry is extremely tenacious hereabouts.

Private Robert Cude, 7th The Buffs (East Kent Regiment)

British tanks either knocked out or bogged down behind the Menin Road, 31 July 1917.

Lieutenant Jack
Walthew, 4
Squadron, Royal
Flying Corps

How we got back, I don't know, it seemed the longest journey I have ever made but eventually we landed safely. I had to write out a report on the flight and then had a shave and was just going in to have some breakfast when I got orders to take up another machine to try and find the 30th Division who had got lost. So, off I went again and tootled over our lines for an hour. The first thing that happened was that the wireless transmitter again disappeared, leaving only a big hole in the fuselage. After this we weren't hit quite so much as before. Meanwhile we called to the infantry to light flares for us, but as they wouldn't do this we had to draw the fire of the Huns on to ourselves so as to discover where the enemy line was and deduct ours from it. We managed to do this fairly successfully and came back unhurt.

*Below: Two officers'
servants, 11th West
Yorkshire Regiment,
stand outside a
captured German
pillbox at Stirling
Castle, Ypres.*

Second Lieutenant
Thomas Floyd,
2/5th Lancashire
Fusiliers

Suddenly we were rained with bullets from rifles and machine guns. We extended. Men were being hit everywhere. My servant Critchley was the first in my platoon to be hit. We lay down flat for a while, as it was impossible for anyone to survive standing up. Then I determined to go forward. It was no use sticking here forever, and we would be wanted further on: so we might as well try and dash through it. 'Come along – advance!' I shouted and leapt forward. I was just stepping over some barbed wire defence

when the inevitable happened. I felt a sharp sting through my leg. I was hit by a bullet. So I dashed to the nearest shell hole which, fortunately was a very large one, and got my first field dressing on. Someone helped me with it. Then they went on, as they were, to their great regret, not hit!

… When I had been there about half an hour the enemy put down a barrage just on the line which contained my shell hole! It was horrible. I thought I was lost this time. Shells were bursting all around me, making a horrible row … I was covered with the fumes from one or two of them and also sniffed some gas. I put on my box respirator. One piece of shrapnel hit me on the head but, fortunately, I had my steel helmet on my head; so I was all right. I decided that I might just as well be blown to bits in the open, trying to get back to safety, as lying in this shell hole; so I made a dash for it and got out of the nearest barrage. I inquired the way to the nearest aid post, and was told that it was a long way off. But I proceeded in the direction indicated. Before long I met Corporal Livesy returning from his bombing stunt with about half a dozen prisoners and a shrapnel wound … We were joined by more prisoners as we went down. German prisoners have only to be told which way to go and they go. They are quite sociable people, too – many of them bright-eyed boys of seventeen and eighteen. They are only too glad to carry our wounded men back; they need no escort. We got on very well with them. I suppose that in a sense we were comrades in distress, or, rather, comrades in good fortune, in that we were all leaving the field of horrors behind us. Yet they were the very Boches who, an hour before, had been peppering us with those bullets. One would never have imagined that we had so recently been enemies.

After a short rest to get our 'wind' again, we went on, still through a storm of bullets to Stirling Castle, which was more sheltered from the enemy fire. Another short rest and we again went on, stopping finally on 'our' side of a bank, on top of which was the Menin Road. We then discovered that we were at the limit of our advance – the first division (the 30th) had not captured anything like the amount of ground allotted to them, hence the reason why the enemy shelling and machine-gun fire had been so deadly when we advanced. I saw only a few men of that division – goodness knows where they had got to. I only saw four dead Germans and a few prisoners. Nearly all were 'Iron Cross' men. One man of the 30th Div. was sitting

Private Sydney Fuller, 8th Suffolk Regiment

Stretcher-bearers removing a wounded man from the battlefield. Atrocious weather made casualty evacuation from the Ypres Salient extremely difficult.

Above: What the soldier sees: September 1917, a shell burst over Inverness Copse near Passchendaele. Note the rolled-up stretcher in the foreground.

Right: What the airman sees: an official German aerial photograph taken at 1,600 feet of the pockmarked ground at the end of the battle in November. British dead litter the ground.

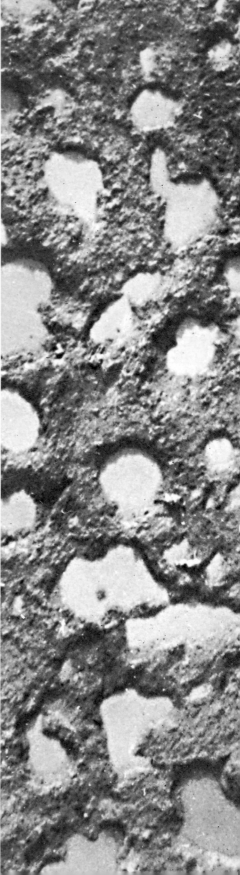

bolt upright on the side of the bank near us – dead. He had evidently bled to death. Shortly after we had reached the bank the enemy dropped a heavy 5.9-inch barrage about 100 yards behind us. He was still heavily shelling Sanctuary Wood and I saw two of the remaining trees brought down. Six of our tanks got stuck in the boggy ground immediately behind us. Four of them managed to struggle out again, but two sank so deeply in the mud that they were left … When the tanks had gone a little way up the road towards Inverness Copse, they were one after the other knocked out by small shells – probably from an anti-tank gun.

Three enemy planes were flying about at a height of about a hundred feet, and the enemy's infantry continually fired white Verey lights, presumably from their front line to indicate their position. We took no notice of these planes at first, believing them to be our own planes – they were very similar in appearance to our 'Nieuport' biplanes. Happening to be watching when one flew over us, I was astonished to see a black cross on each lower plane. I waited until one came over again to make certain and then did what I could with my rifle. I was yelled at for firing 'at one of ours' – no one else seemed to have noticed the black crosses. However, when next they came over and their nationality became plain to everyone we gave them what we would have presumed to be an unpleasant time, considering the low altitude at which they were flying. We fired scores of shots at them, but did not, apparently, touch either of them. They continued to fly around, dropping small bombs on the RFA and even on our infantry, the foremost of which was now in front of us.

Saw one C Coy man who had been wounded in the hand and had had a hole drilled through the side of his tin hat by one bullet. He said that his tin hat was blown almost off his head by the explosion of the shell, and as he put up his hand to pull the hat straight again, the bullet smashed his fingers and passed through the tin hat without, however, injuring his head …

A very big enemy howitzer – probably one of the famous sixteen-inch, was dropping occasional shells about half a mile or more to our left, and even at that distance I could not help wanting to 'duck' when one of these shells came roaring over. Late in the afternoon we moved with Battalion Headquarters to the left, where the road was not on such a high bank.

Here, we found a tunnel running under the centre of the road – evidently an enemy communication trench. The tunnel had been broken or blown in at intervals by our heavy shells. The parts left intact had already been examined by the RE and marked 'Safe'. In the tunnel were many enemy telephone lines – all kinds of wire. It had been supplied with electric light too, many of the bulbs remaining. We remained in a portion of the tunnel until 9 p.m., when we were ordered to move. The enemy was shelling the road as we got out of our hole, so we 'got a move on'. We went down the road towards Ypres for about 250 yards, stumbling over dead bodies, barbed wire, 'pavé', etc., falling into shell holes every few steps. Our padre was with us, and he said to one man (referring to the shelling), 'Warm, isn't it?' The man replied (not noticing who he was speaking to, in the darkness and confusion), 'Huh, it's ____ hot'.

This afternoon it's been raining so we've had nothing to do. It's an awful shame the weather is so bad, as given fine weather we could have done some much better work and chased the Huns for miles. Our only casualties are two missing. I shall not tell you anything about how we are getting on with the 'Push' as I am not certain myself; but I think they are getting on better further north. We have not done at all badly, but we've had a lot of opposition.

Lieutenant Jack Walthew, 4 Squadron, Royal Flying Corps

The primary function of the Royal Flying Corps in the Great War was to be the eyes of the army in the air, undertaking ground observation and photographic reconnaissance, supplying as up-to-date information of enemy dispositions as possible. Reconnaissance aircraft were slower and more cumbersome and had to be protected by squadrons of fighter aircraft.

Leaps in technology afforded aerial superiority to one side then the other, and at Arras, in 1917, it was the Germans who were in the ascendancy. The RFC deployed over 350 aircraft in support of the infantry offensive, but losses were terrible among the young, skilled RFC pilots whose planes were outperformed by the enemy's. This imbalance was corrected that summer with the arrival of improved aircraft such as the SE5 and Sopwith Camel, helping to swing the pendulum in the Allies' favour, an advantage never again relinquished. By mid-1917, the Royal Flying Corps was providing close support to infantry attacks, dropping bombs and strafing the enemy, and co-operating closely with tanks and artillery.

In 1915 Lieutenant George Miall-Smith had been serving with the 8th Norfolk Regiment in the trenches, but by 1917 he was with No. 11 Squadron, a unit that could already boast two holders of the Victoria Cross and a number of other aces. That summer, as the fighting raged around Ypres, George Miall-Smith described to his parents, in great detail, what it was like to undertake a sortie over enemy lines. Shortly afterwards, on 25 September, aged twenty-two, he was killed in action.

Lieutenant George Miall-Smith, 11 Squadron, Royal Flying Corps

My slumbers are interrupted by a rough prod in the ribs from my servant, who informs me that it is 6.30 a.m. I turn over with a discontented grunt, to see him disappearing through the door.

'What is the weather like?' I hastily shout before he is out of earshot. I have already taken an eager look out of the window at an early morning bright with sunshine, but still cling to desperate hopes of ground-mists, storms on the horizon, etc. etc.

'It's a lovely morning, sir,' replied my servant, probably thinking of the bed he is just going back to while I am over the lines. His head disappears behind the door before I can reach for a boot to hasten it.

After telling one another to get up for about ten minutes or a quarter of an hour, my room companion and I find ourselves shivering over our basins, conjecturing on the possibilities of the finest morning ever seen turning 'dud' within the next half-hour.

'Hello!' my companion shouts to a fellow outside as he adjusts his collar in a glass in front of the window, 'any chance of it coming up dud?'

'Not the faintest hope, and a good thing too,' jokingly. 'I feel like strafing Huns this morning.'

'Oh, I've no use for these confounded patriots,' my friend replies in disgust. 'I prefer my bed.'

I join him in hearty agreement. We then face two hard-boiled eggs and some tasteless tea until victory is obtained amidst conversation such as, 'Which formation are you on?', 'How far over are we going, do you know?' and cheap jokes.

After a hasty return to my room for my flying gear, I stroll down towards the sheds with a few others, cleaning my goggles on the way. On reaching the aerodrome I see the machines set out in neat lines of fours opposite the hangars, the mechanics standing round in groups, or here and there a mechanic giving some final adjustment to a machine. The wind indicator shows a gentle breeze from the east, and the rising sun shines from a clear sky. I join a group of officers struggling over maps to hear the latest information about our course. One fellow, after getting his map entangled round his head, spreads it on the grass and we all lean over.

This is going to be 'photographic distant patrol' consisting of eight machines in two formations of four machines each. One formation has the camera machines while the other escorting it flies above it.

'Do you know where we are going?' one of the group remarks.

'Yes, to take four aerodromes, my boy.'

At this moment the flight commander who is leading the formation arrives from the squadron office where he has been receiving final instructions about the 'pin points' we are to photograph. All attention is now occupied finding the 'pin points' on the maps and discussing what route should be taken.

'We'd better get on the ground now,' eventually remarks the leader, folding up his map. 'We get off before the other formation and rendezvous over the aerodrome at 3,000 feet.'

The group breaks up and we walk over to our machines, buttoning up our coats and fixing on our helmets. I find that my observer has already got into his 'office' and is having a look at his gun and his ammunition drums. As I approach the machine I take one affectionate look up and down its sturdy length and according to an acquired habit of mine, I thank fate for giving me such a fine war horse.

As I clamber into my seat, two mechanics approach the propeller and one goes round to the tail. There then ensues a mysterious conversation between myself and the mechanics at the front of the machine, punctuated with the turning of the 'prop' and the moving of different gadgets. Such remarks are heard as, 'Switch off, clean out, petrol on, suck in' and eventually 'contact'. After this has gone on for a few minutes, the engine with a kick and a roar suddenly starts and the propeller in front whirrs round, throwing back a strong draught on my face. I sigh with relief and begin to settle myself comfortably in my seat. While my engine is running and warming up, I have time to look about me. It is a very busy scene. On either side of me are machines in my row with the heads and shoulders of the pilots bobbing down to their instruments or leaning out, shouting to the mechanics. The pilot next to me has not yet managed to start his engine and the mechanics are struggling frantically with the propeller. The observers just behind the pilots are in different attitudes. Some are fixing their guns on the mounting, others, having satisfied themselves that everything is ready, are sitting down facing the tail of their machines, their brown leather helmets only being visible. In front of me a similar line of machines stand like a row of hawks awaiting battle. As I look, one of the centre machines rocks and sways and glides from the ranks, a mechanic at each wingtip clutching on and steadying its lurching movements and keeping the machine straight. When the machine has gone some distance she is followed by another and yet another until all four machines are crawling along in a line like a flock of crazy geese. The leading machine on reaching the further end of the aerodrome sluggishly turns towards us, then hesitates. Slowly her pace increases until she is coming at us quite fast, then she gracefully rises off the ground and roars right over our heads.

I turn to my instrument and see that the temperature is now up high enough to 'run up' the engine. With my right hand I gradually open the throttle until the engine is roaring away at full revolutions. By this time the machine on my left is just moving forward to follow the other four who are chasing one another off the ground. I shut my throttle and wave to the mechanics that all is well and I want to get along. I shout at my observer who leans over to me. The roar of the engine does its best to drown my voice but my observer and I are used to talking to one another under these conditions and his ear is close to my mouth. 'You are ready?' I shout. He replies with a nod of his head.

'Has the leader got streamers on the tail?' comes next from me. Another nod.

Opposite: Two unknown Royal Flying Corps pilots dressed for the cold of high altitude.

'Keep a sharp lookout for him and keep a red light in your "Verey" pistol.' With that I gently open the throttle, my observer sinks down into his seat behind me, and the machine glides forward along the ground

after my left-hand companion, who is now some 150 yards ahead. Keeping fifty yards behind him I follow him across the aerodrome, rocking and swaying until we turn into the wind at the further end. When my companion's machine is clear of the ground I have one hasty look round my instruments, then gradually open the throttle. The machine, moving slowly at first, bounds along the uneven surface of the aerodrome until with a movement of the control lever she rises from the ground and we pass over the top of the hangar. I listen very attentively to the throb of my engine, as it is very uncomfortable to have an engine failure when below 1,000 feet. But all is well, and as my aneroid reaches over 1,000 feet I sigh with relief and feel that I can now settle myself down comfortably. I load my gun and look round for the leader. At first I cannot see any other machines in the sky except a straggling formation some 2,000 feet over my head. But the horizon is still high and machines below my level have the dark background of the earth. My observer in the end comes to my rescue by touching me on the shoulder and pointing out a machine under our tail. I quickly turn the machine round and come in behind the leader, checking our pace when I can see the movements and brown coat of the leading observer, who exchanges greetings with me by a wave of the hand.

Now follows a long period of steady climbing in a wide circle round the aerodrome while I stick to my position above and on the right rear of the leader. As the pointer of the aneroid gradually moves round to 5,000, 6,000, 7,000 and 8,000 feet, the horizon slowly sinks below the level of our eyes, giving us in our spherical field of vision a larger proportion of sky and a smaller proportion of earth. The country is mapped out before our eyes, but it is a living map, exquisitely coloured. Neat little red houses peep out between a mossy cluster of rich green trees, the blue smoke from their chimneys curling and twisting lazily in a tired breeze. My eye travels up the long straight stretch of a road; it is one of the French main roads and is as straight as a ray of the sun.

How lazy and how contented it all looks. But no. I speak too soon. What colour is the ground beyond that town? The green of the field thins out to the ugly brown of the shell-torn battlefield. The peaceful fields, intersected with roads, give place to the rough brown patches crossed by a labyrinth of aimless paths. My eye ventures still further towards the east, crosses this irregular brown belt and rests with relief once more on the green belt. This, then, is the line, and beyond is the enemy territory. On the near edge of the brown belt, the roads are clearly visible. No longer do they lead to our bright, red-roofed villages but to cruel black patches of upturned earth and bricks, villages only in name. From some of these tumbled masses near the centre of the brown belt clouds of smoke rise and are carried away by the breeze.

While I have been looking about me and musing in this manner, we have been steadily climbing. The atmosphere is quite cold and an icy wind beats on my cheeks, leaving them numb. My aneroid tells me that we are 12,000 feet up, and as we are heading straight for the lines, I realise that the leader is now going over. I therefore banish all idle thoughts of ruined villages, tennis, or unpaid mess bills. I glance round our formation to see if all our machines are in place. I see M on my left, silhouetted against the sky, and on turning my head over my left shoulder, I see B quite close above and behind me. I feel jolly glad we have such a stout flight. Still higher, behind us, is the other formation, almost amongst our own. We are now over the lines and the brown belt beneath us is seen to be dotted with puffs of white and bluish smoke. Thousands of infantrymen are down there,

A picture taken in an RE8 by the observer sitting behind Lieutenant Hubert Wrinch, 'C' Flight, No. 5 Squadron, Royal Flying Corps, during a sortie over the Western Front in August 1917.

I suppose, but we are too high to see anything further. I take a keen look all around the sky above, on a level and below me. At first I can see nothing except our own artillery at regular intervals below us all along the lines. However, on a second look I see a small speck of microscopic size about our level but far north, soon multiplied by three, then four, on closer inspection. A nudge of the elbow soon brings my observer's head over my right shoulder, and according to our custom, I point out this discovered formation. 'I see,' he nods with his head and continues to keep them under his observation.

They are much too far away to tell whether they are of the sausage-eating or roast-beef type, but after watching their hovering tactics for a while, I feel sure their names are 'Fritz' and I do a harmless 'hate' at them for a while. Several other wandering formations my observer points out to me but all of them that approach near enough to tell turn out to be British.

'Whoof! Whoof!' I glance to my right from where the sound comes and see two ugly, distorted balls of curling black smoke drifting away from me; lower down and further away still, I see quite a collection of similar puffs of smoke. Archie must have been firing at us for quite a while without

The seemingly innocuous 'puffs' of anti-aircraft fire around a Vickers FB5 'Gunbus' of No. 18 Squadron.

my knowing it. I look back again at my leader who is doing a turn to the right, and have to hold up in order not to overtake him. As I am looking at him, two more venomous puffs of black smoke appear from nowhere between us. I know I shall do no good charging about so I fly on straight. Then 'Whoof!' a very loud bang, so close I can feel his blast. I am watching the leader now and have no time to attend to the last burst. He is increasing his pace and turning. As soon as I am settled again, I look over my machine and see a jagged split in the bottom panel of about six inches long. It is quite harmless and will give the mechanics something to do. I point it out to my observer, who laughs and signals the 'wash-out' with his hands. 'Close enough all the same,' he shouts in my ear.

All this while our attention has been taken up by this unpleasant gentleman and we have had no time to look about us. As we strike out again to our prospective 'sittings' for photographs, I see a formation of six machines coming diagonally towards us. They are a good distance away and I cannot make out who they are. My observer has also seen them, as he is looking at them over my shoulder. They approach us in a determined manner, and I notice our leader edges towards them so that we shall meet them 'nose to nose'. Both parties are now approaching at top speed. I glance hastily at my instruments and make sure my gun is ready. At the same time I see my observer out of the corner of my eye moving his gun into a more comfortable position. The other formation has now changed direction and is moving to get round to our south side a bit more. I take practice aim through my telescopic sight at one of the leading machines which is much too far off yet to fire at. Dead straight at them we approach, and they are growing bigger every second, but I can still only see their dark lines as they appear end on. They are pretty close now and I feel for my trigger, at the same time picking out a machine to attack. At this moment, their leader, followed by the rest of the formation, swings round at right angles across our front. The sun shines on their forms, illuminating a clean-cut rudder with red, white, and blue bands. I take a deep sigh of relief as I recognise a well-known scout machine of ours. My observer, also relaxed from the tension, shouts 'Nieuports' in my ear.

'I thought they were being rather brave for Huns,' I replied; 'they didn't know who we were, either.'

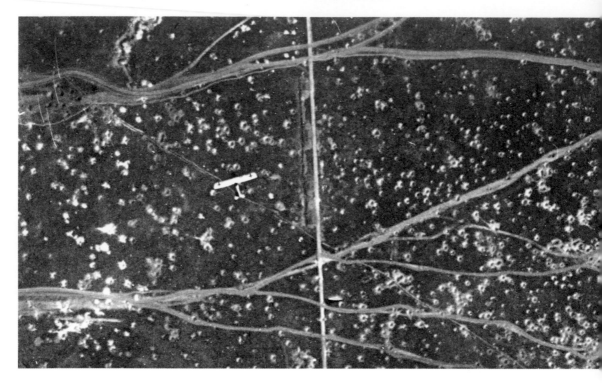

A photograph taken by a British observer of the pockmarked ground in June 1917. Flying below is a German aircraft with the tell-tale black crosses on the wings.

We are now nearly over a large French town held by the Huns, and the light is so clear that we can see into the streets and can distinguish small dark objects – probably vehicles. A river coils away below us and near to that a canal, the ripples on the blue water lazily moving down its length. I look keenly along the roads to see if any activity is afoot; but I look in vain. The Germans do all their movements by night.

I realise that we are nearly over one of the aerodromes to be photographed, and after referring to my map and my observer, I can pick it out below us. It looks just the same as any of our aerodromes, with its rectangular sheds close up to a hedge. But what are those little white objects on the grass? Why, they are Hun machines; what would I not give for some bombs to drop on them!

My observer roughly draws my attention away from this interesting sight by a prod in my back. I see him pointing low down on our right rear. My eyes follow, and I soon spot against the dark green of the fields an almost black object hovering and swaying like some poisonous fly. He is obviously a Hun, but is a few thousand feet below us and at quite a safe distance away. I search for his pal whom I know I am certain to find near him, and sure enough there he is, just behind, swaying about.

We are a good way over the lines now, but we do not turn home yet as we have still two more aerodromes to 'leave our cards at'. I notice that we are up at 14,500 feet now, and reflect that Archie, even if he had a go at us, would be very inaccurate at this height.

Those two Huns are climbing steadily up to us now, and I look back periodically to see how they are getting on. I can see their forms much better now and can distinguish their repulsive fish tail and swept back wings. They appear to be both of a dark green colour spotted with lighter greens and very hard to see from above at any distance. One is rather bolder than his brother, and can only be about 1,000 feet below us, but away to a flank. He is bravely flying parallel with us, but is still climbing, and as he lifts up one wing a little, I can see a broad yellow band round his fusilage. I take the precaution, nevertheless, to get a little closer to my leader and to search the sky for more Huns.

We are now beginning to turn towards home and have apparently taken all our photos. Mr Yellow Fritz is sidling up very boldly towards us, so I shout at my observer to fire a few rounds at him.

Rat-tat-tat-tat-tat-tat-tat.

The tracers from his gun fly out in luminous streaks towards the nose of the Hun, who, not appreciating our generosity, lifts up his wingtip and dives away from us, turning again when at a safe distance. Where has his brother gone? I see him! He is trying to creep up under our tail and I point him out to my observer, who has already seen him. As I watch him I see his nose rise slowly and point at us until I can see straight down his length. At the same time puffs of blue smoke appear from the front of his machine and flashes of flame. He is trying to fire at us. I turn my machine a bit so that my observer can fire, and very soon Mr Brother Fritz is diving away also. This sort of 'peep-bo' goes on for a while, Fritz creeping up near in hopes of catching a straggler until he is fired at, then diving intrepidly out of range. However, we are not at liberty to engage them yet as we have not taken all our photos, and have to be content with driving them off. While I am watching the Brothers Fritz over my right shoulder I suddenly hear my observer firing over the other side. After committing the usual 'nudgery' on him very hard with my elbow, I ask him what he is firing at.

'Two more have come up,' he replies. And sure enough, on making a thorough search there seem to be at least four more below us. I scan the skies anxiously above us and see to the north of us a suspicious looking formation of five machines about 1,500 feet above us. There is obviously going to be trouble, and the signal for battle will come from the leader. I therefore watch him very closely. Sure enough, in a few minutes a red flare is fired, and I tighten up every muscle in readiness. He is turning slightly now from east towards the north and is increasing his speed. Down goes his nose and he swings swiftly round underneath my machine. For a moment I lose him out of sight below me, but a steep dive and quick turn reveal him to me again going down, down, fast in front of me. My speed increases. Faster and faster we go. The wind pressure is terrific and presses my head back with a vicious force every time I look out. At first I see nothing but my leader and make every effort to keep with him, but soon I see what he is after. Three Huns are in front attempting to dive away from us; their dark forms are swaying about as though panic-stricken. The leader is making for the left-hand Hun, so I pick out the middle one, and with every nerve braced to my utmost, I point the nose of my machine at him. For what seems an age, but in reality is only a few seconds, my whole attention is concentrated on getting near. Nothing else in the world exists for me save this Hun and myself. I anxiously watch for the moment to fire when he will be near enough. Down, down I go; stronger and stronger becomes the gale of wind in my face until I am almost intoxicated with the speed and the excitement. Now I am near enough. I grasp the trigger, and with a pop-pop-pop-pop the tracers fly out like sparks in front of me. At first they are going wide, but I steer my course until they go right at his nose and then hold my fire there hard.

For a brief second or two I seem to be right on my nose and my tracers are going right into the Hun. But I cannot get down quick enough. He is turning and diving under my machine and I shall lose him. A second later he disappears underneath me. I immediately pull my machine in and the force on the control lever is terrific. I endeavour to turn round on him again but now I have lost him. My first thoughts are for my own safety, so I look round quickly to see if I am being attacked, but am intensely relieved to see only our own machines circling above me, our upper formation whose duty it is to prevent our being attacked from above. It appears that I am one of the lowest in the formation and the Huns are hanging back east of us. So I circle round a bit to get some more height underneath our own machines, meanwhile watching for another good chance to dive again should the leader dive. This opportunity is not long in coming. I am just going to dive on a suitable Hun when one of our own machines streaks across my front after him. I hold off to see what he is going to do and to watch the result of his attack. But apparently from nowhere two more Huns dash after our machine and approach his tail. In a flash I am down on them and after one short burst they turn up on end and disappear into some small clouds which have collected. For the next ten minutes we alternately dive on Huns and climb again, circling round one another until we get so low that it is unsafe to go lower. The Huns are now a good way below us and are edging further east. It is obviously no use continuing the scrap under those conditions.

We are down to 6,000 feet, so we begin a steady climb towards our lines and make an attempt to get into a correct formation once more. I look at the clock in my machine for the first time since we saw the Huns, and find that we have now been up for two hours and only have a short time more to go.

The Huns have disappeared, the clouds are thickening below us so that the ground can only be seen through a few irregular patches between them. Our excitement is obviously over for this trip, and I smile under my goggles at the thought of another safe journey home. The finishing of a game of tennis is transformed from a speculation to a certainty. And so is the paying of that wretched mess bill.

'Did you see any of them go down?' my observer bawls in my ear.

'Not for a certainty,' I reply. 'Did you?'

'I'm pretty sure of one. I saw something fly off him.'

'Good! I wonder who got him.'

A monotonous fifteen minutes follows in which we continue to climb and move up and down the line 'killing time'. My attention is divided

Overleaf: A nurse anaesthetises a wounded soldier about to undergo an operation.

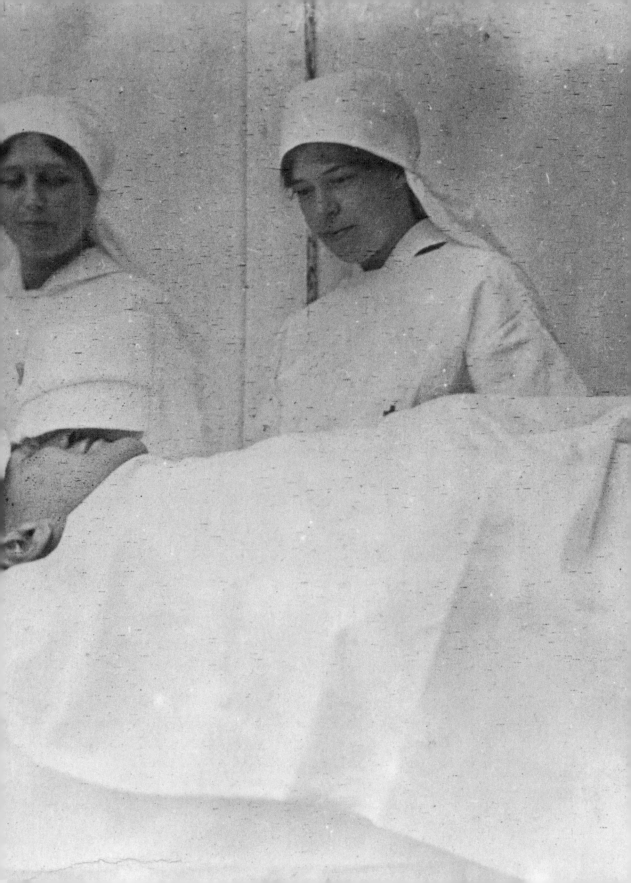

between watching my clock and trying to persuade myself that the leader is turning west and home every time he makes the slightest movement.

The signal to go home soon follows and we sink through the clouds, emerging underneath in a mad race home.

Full throttle, nose down, voices singing all the joyful song in creation at once – that is how we come home. When about 300 feet up, almost over the aerodrome, I see another machine below and on my left attempting to get in in front of me. Ha! I shout, with a sly look at my prospective victim, noticing at the same time that it is M___, to whom I owe a few debts of this kind. So down goes my nose and I cut across him. At the same time I hear the roar of his engine as he is compelled to go round the aerodrome again.

'The best bit of work I have done today,' I proudly observe to my colleague as we taxi in. 'By jove! He will be mad.'

Captain G. B. Manwaring (pseudonym)

It's not always easy in this life to look on the bright side; still one must do one's best to keep not only oneself cheerful, but to be an example to all those under one. To know that they can do things so much better than you can, and yet to pretend always that you can do everything better than they, for to let those who look to you for leadership imagine that you are wavering is to court disaster for yourself and those around you.

Life here, in spite of all, has its humour, and to see others laugh and join in their laughter, although shells are bursting within a hundred yards and often within twenty, and bullets are whizzing round one's ears or splashing at one's feet, seems strangely natural. I would like to go to sleep, and for a while at least forget, but two of my platoons are out, and I am not going till they get back. Things are a little quieter now, though not much. From tomorrow for five days or so I shall be in command of my position, shut off as it were from the outside world. I expect the time will pass quickly. It's a great responsibility, and it's that that tells. It isn't as though I'd worked up to the position and had experience behind me, I plunge straight into it, walking before I can crawl. Still, I hope and expect to come through all right. Imagination on these occasions is rather a handicap. Don't think that I am depressed, I'm not, but these letters are more or less pictures of the moods I am in, and my time for writing is during the lonely vigils of the night, when depression holds its strongest grip on the tired mind and body; this and the never-changing scene of desolation around one, the waste, wreckage and carnage of war, must tinge one's mind towards gloom.

Fritz gave us the devil of a time last night; things were fairly quiet till 11 p.m., then he gave us twenty minutes in his best style, whizz-bangs and aerial darts fell thickly around us. At 11.20 p.m. gas shells came for five minutes, and at 11.30 p.m. for ten minutes. Living as we do at the bottom of a quarry, the place was full of poison, a dark night, men coughing and groping in their respirators, some got the wind up properly. Men came clamouring for the SOS call to be given, and so I resolved to go and find out what was happening. I went out through the barrage, a man clutched at me and loosened my mask. Three shells burst simultaneously round me, fragments pattering on my hat and round my feet. Up to the top to find one post 'na poo' [destroyed] then along to the next. I remember getting up to run across, and then next thing finding myself at the bottom of the quarry, bruised, shaken and slightly gassed. I conclude that I was blown up.

Manwaring had not been wounded but hurt in the fall, an injury that caused him severe pain in the shoulder for days until, after seeing the regimental doctor, he was advised to go down the line at the next opportunity for further treatment. In a letter to his sister, a nurse, he described a new, half-forgotten world of comfort and above all, peace.

I've not been able to write before, hence the gap in my letters. Since writing I have been given a chance of learning, first hand, of the wonders of the Medical Services out here. I was lucky to go through while able to see and note and wonder at its organisation, without my faculties marred by excessive pain, or the handicap of shattered limb; just a dull ache with occasional shooting pains, which may lead me anywhere or may be right again soon. Anyway a rest that already is freshening tired mind and aching body; and peace. How thankful I am, none but those who have been through it can realise.

After waiting at the transport lines, I at last received orders to report at the advanced dressing station, and wait for a car, as I was not bad enough to be 'an urgent case'. I took my turn and eventually left about 4 p.m. on Thursday afternoon. A ride along a now familiar road, to a now familiar town, viewed this time through the square opening of the back of a motor ambulance, and so to a field ambulance. An hour's rest, tea and toast, and on again by car to a casualty clearing station situated in a chateau amid a wooded park. A quiet, peaceful evening, and a moonlight walk about the grounds, and so to bed. I am not going to describe in detail what a hospital ward is like, for you are more qualified to do that than I. Just a night picture, and the acknowledgement that no praise, however great, can be too great for the kindness, the care, the consideration that is shown by doctors, nurses and orderlies for all committed to their charge.

A long wooden hut filled with its row of beds on either side – a silence so great that one can all but hear it – marred at times by the thud of a falling chestnut on the wooden roof, or soothed by the gentle whisper of trees without. A subdued light which to tired eyes is perhaps more restful than darkness. A sudden sound without and the muffled tread of stretcher-bearers' feet, as they carry in the unconscious form of a nineteen-year-old boy. A boy, who from a night-bombing raid has crashed to earth with dislocated hip, bashed-in head and face cut to pieces in his fall. A light at the far end of the ward as surgeons, nurses and comrades gather round or wait for news. For in each fresh case one loses for a time a little of one's own pain. A half-smothered groan that no will on earth can keep behind the clenched teeth, as the surgeon's fingers, be they never so gentle, feel about the wound. A whispered consultation – good news, and the stretcher-bearers withdraw.

Next day – yesterday, in fact – a thirteen-hour journey in a Red Cross train brought me to a well-remembered base. A drive in a car (driven by one of those girls who are doing such good work out here) and I am at rest in a delightful place in the heart of that forest I wrote about some months ago …

A happy, idle, pleasant life, this hospital existence – though one that would tend to boredom after a while. At 7.30 we get up and have a bath, at 8.30 we breakfast, and read the paper in the grounds. Dress leisurely and wait for the MO's morning visit. Free till lunch we wander, doze in the sunlight, read or play games; at 12.30 we lunch, and then, unless treatment hours clash, are free till 7 p.m., when we dine. Golf, tennis, croquet are at our disposal; many parties of walking patients, VADs and nurses go off to the sea for an afternoon bathe, for the water is still delightfully warm – and tea – tea with all its luxuries of fresh bread and fancy cakes! Generally, I wander to the sandhills on the shore, that are so like home, and just lie in the sunlight, dozing and listening to the murmur of the waves and watch the French and English girls walking on the front.

My injury is getting much better, I am pleased to say – though, I fear me, many of the old games and sports have gone for ever. Never again shall I be able to tramp with a pack on my back, nor row in an eight or four, never to play football; perhaps never to ride or golf. However, time alone will show, and I am not grumbling. So much – so very much – that before I took for granted is left to me, and how I shall value it. A new scale of valuation for the little pleasures of life, and for life itself, has come, and I feel has come to stay, and surely this must last throughout the lives of those that have seen the price mankind has had to pay.

And so, apparently, at any rate, my fighting days are over, and I am to become a unit in that vast machine that works night and day behind the lines. Of course, I should never really have come out, but seeing the chance I took it, and shall always be thankful that I did. For in these months I have had years of educational value, and have gained experience that will be useful to me throughout my life. To have learnt at first hand of war from which all romance has been stripped is indeed a gain, apart from the knowledge that danger brings and, greatest gift perhaps of all, the knowledge of human character. Well, no knowledge comes without payment, and I shall pay, for years to come, by a fractured dislocation of the shoulder and the constant ache of synovitis and rheumatism which such an injury will bring – yet it has been worth it.

A young English patient in hospital at Neuilly, Paris. His wounded leg was amputated after gangrene set in.

Overleaf: Stretcher bearer enjoying a game of draughts at the entrance to a dugout.

There was a slightly wounded German officer there who could speak English. I pointed to the row of stretchers, each with its burden of battered humanity ... and asked him 'Well, Fritz, do you think it's worth it all?'

Sergeant James Duncan, 143rd Siege Battery, Royal Garrison Artillery

---

G ot to Folkestone at 9 a.m. and spent the morning chiefly in fruitless efforts to obtain a pass into the town. I was to set sail in the afternoon, I was told. However, there were not enough boats for us all and I was left here: got a pass at 3.15 with no instruction about time of return or anything else. Out I toddled and met J ... who was bringing his wife to see me off. I turned back with them and they showed me all the glories of Folkestone and then took me home to tea, after which we three went to the theatre to see *The Priest's Secretary*. It was awfully good – and the luxury of it all when I expected to be passing the time in some dirty old rest camp somewhere! The first army meal – a chunk of bread and meat to be eaten as best one could – nearly broke my heart! – I hadn't realised how rough the army life was before – but coming at the end of fourteen days' return to civilisation!!

Well, I didn't see the point of upsetting the good Military Police at the gates of the camp here by rolling in at that time of night so I accepted J's cordial invite to spend the night with them. I was called from dreamland yesterday morning at 8 a.m. and after a huge breakfast came back here at 9.45. Of course I felt guilty and approached the fearsome MP at the gate (especially as I had seen men from another camp already marching down to the morning boat). However, I gave J a very superior 'au revoir' and strolled by the MP with a grand air and not as much as a glance. Not a word from him! I slunk round to the billet to see if the others had gone but was just in time for the 'fall in'.

Pioneer George Dewdney, 72 Section, 'P' Special Company, Royal Engineers

A chalk-drawn caricature of the Kaiser: a soldier presents his artwork for the camera.

We sailed at 4.45 p.m. However, it clouded over and the sea which had been beautifully calm became choppy. My vessel was scarcely a luxurious affair – an old paddle tub dug out from the bed of a dried-up lake I should imagine. Moreover she was in frolicsome mood and any old lady in that temper is to be avoided. This one liked a big roll and then half buried herself and us in every big wave she met. I was cold, too, and thought of the cabin. Then I looked round and saw what some of the men were doing and decided that a cool head was more to be desired than a warm body just then. I sat down – got wet and cold – and vowed that after all I would <u>not</u> be a sailor in the next war.

Lieutenant Colonel Rowland Fielding, 1/15th London Regiment (Civil Service Rifles)

Unknown British and ANZAC troops disembarking in France just prior to the start of the German Spring offensive.

Once more I have vowed that never again if I can help it will I travel by the 'leave' train. I had forgotten to bring a candle, so, the cold being bitter and the windows broken, I shivered in the darkness.

It is beyond my powers adequately to describe the horrors of the 'leave' train. The scandal of which still continues after 3½ years of war. Though timed to arrive at the divisional railhead in the early morning we did not do so till the afternoon, and, after fifteen hours on the train, I reached my transport lines near Villers-Faucon at 2 p.m. in a blizzard, having had nothing to eat since last evening.

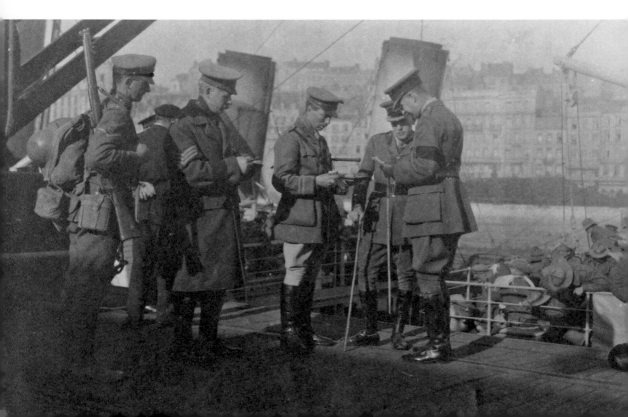

At the transport lines I found officers and men still under canvas, and as the ground was deep in snow the appearance of everything was very uninviting and conducive to nostalgia:- I believe that is the word.

The battalion is in new trenches in the front line, and after getting some food I walked to my headquarters, which are in a sunken road beyond Lempire, calling in at the headquarters of the 48th and my own brigade on the way up.

The line is very quiet.

Lieutenant Colonel Fielding was returning from two weeks' leave and, as normal during the winter, offensive operations had been largely suspended. Yet, unlike any previous year, this was an unnerving period of calm for it was known that the Germans were planning to unleash an offensive of their own, forcing the Allies to begin preparations to contain the expected onslaught.

Since the October Revolution in Russia, the new Bolshevik government had sought peace with Germany, being no longer willing or able to prosecute the war. In December a ceasefire was announced, permitting Germany to begin transferring one million battle-hardened troops from the Eastern to the Western Front. To end the war in one great strike was for the Germans an imperative. The USA had joined the war on the Allied side in 1917 and it was only a matter of time before American troops arrived in France in numbers enough to tip the balance of war irretrievably against Germany. Germany's war economy was faltering and the civilian population was suffering greatly from a dearth of energy supplies and a lack of food. The war had to be concluded quickly.

27 January: Today is the Kaiser's birthday, and we half expected that things might happen, but there has been a thick fog, and all has been as silent as can be. I am afraid the troops are not so sorry as they ought to be.

'Am I offensive enough?' is one of the questions laid down in a pamphlet that reaches us from an army school some thirty miles behind the line. It is for the subaltern to ask himself each morning as he rises from his bed.

Most laudable! But, as the Lewis gun officer remarked today, it is one of the paradoxes of war that the further you get from the battle line the more 'offensive' are the people you meet!

Lieutenant Colonel Rowland Fielding, 1/15th London Regiment (Civil Service Rifles)

Captain George
Nichols, C Battery,
82nd Brigade,
Royal Field Artillery

The Colonel, the adjutant, and myself had a seven miles' ride before us. The Germans had not attacked, but the general move-up of fresh divisions was continuing, and our brigade had to take over the part of the line we were told off to defend by 5 p.m. All the talk on the way up was of the beautiful quietude of the area we were riding through: no weed-choked houses with the windows all blown in; no sound of guns, no line of filled-up ambulances; few lorries on the main thoroughfares; only the khaki-clad road repairers and the 'Gas Alert' notice boards to remind us we were in a British area … The way from Brigade HQ, past the batteries and up to the front line, was over a wide rolling country of ploughed and fallow lands, of the first wild flowers, of budding hedgerows, of woods in which birds lilted their spring songs. The atmosphere was fresh and redolent of clean earth; odd shell holes you came across were, miracle of miracles, grass-grown – a sight for eyes tired with the drab stinking desolation of Flanders. A more than spring warmth quickened growing things. White tendrils of fluff floated strangely in the air, and spread thousands of soft clinging threads over telephone wires, tree tops, and across miles of growing fields – the curious output of myriad spinning-spiders. There were quaintly restful visits to the front line. The Boche was a mile away at least; and when you were weary of staring through binoculars, trying to spot enemy movement, you could sit and lounge, and hum the ragtime 'Wait and See the Ducks Go By', with a new and very thorough meaning. The signal officer was away doing a course, and I took on his duties: plenty of long walks and a good deal of labelling to do, but the task was not onerous. 'We've only had one wire down through shell fire since we've been here,' the signalling officer of the outgoing brigade had told me.

Whether the Boche would attack in force on our part of the front was argued upon and considered from every point of view. There were certain natural features that made such an attempt exceedingly improbable. Nevertheless infantry and artillery kept hard at it, strengthening our means of defence. One day I did a tour with the machine-gun commander in order to know the exact whereabouts of the machine-gun posts. They were superlatively well hidden, and the major general himself had to laugh when one battalion commander, saying, 'There's one just about here, sir', was startled by a corporal's voice near his very boot toes calling out, 'Yes, sir, it's here, sir … '

Camouflaging is now, of course, a studied science, and our Colonel, who issued special guiding notes to his batteries, had a few sharp words to say one afternoon. The British soldier, old and new, is always happy when he is demolishing something; and a sergeant sent to prepare a pit for a forward gun had collected wood and corrugated iron for it by pulling to pieces a nearby dummy gun, placed specially to draw enemy fire. 'Bad as some Pioneers I noticed yesterday,' said the Colonel tersely. 'They shifted a couple of trees to a place where there had been no trees before and thought that that was camouflage.'

The German proposal was to attack at the point of the line where the British and French forces met, driving the French south towards the capital and the British north-west back on to the ports. The Allies did not know when the Germans would strike, but there was another problem: a shortage of manpower. Since the Third Battle of Ypres, relations between the British Commander-in-Chief and senior politicians back home in Britain had reached a nadir. The Prime Minister, Lloyd George, was determined to withhold reinforcements to ensure that Sir Douglas Haig would not be able to conduct offensive operations of his own. At the very moment that the Germans intended to strike, the BEF was seriously undermanned.

16 March: I was up this morning at three o'clock and marched forward with the battalion to man trenches again, as yesterday. At 6.25 one of our SOS rockets went up, and was followed by many others along the front. Immediately, the artillery and machine guns opened uproariously all along the line.

Today (as have others which have passed) had been officially mentioned as the likely date for the great German effort, and all naturally thought for a short while that at last the expected had arrived.

However, after half to three-quarters of an hour of deafening din, all became silent, and it was evident that it was a false alarm. Such are the 'jumpy' times through which we are passing.

Lieutenant Colonel Rowland Fielding, 1/15th London Regiment (Civil Service Rifles)

Sapper Albert
Martin, 122nd
Signal Company,
41st Division, Royal
Engineers

17 March: The German attack is expected very shortly; consequently a 'nervy' atmosphere is commencing to make itself felt. To stir up our brutal instincts and passions we have been treated to a morally disgusting harangue by a major of the physical jerks department. The whole brigade was marched out to a field a few kilometres away where we squatted down in a hollow while the blood-red major (straight up from the base) delivered his oration in a strikingly melodramatic manner. He endeavoured to make us 'see red' and it is a matter for sad reflection that civilisation should come to such a sorry pass. The authorities apparently think that the civilian-soldier is too soft-hearted and gentle so it is necessary to raise the spirit of Cain in him. The whole speech was utterly disgusting and I am sorry to think that England should consider such a thing necessary. It was revolting and I believe I could better have withstood a dose of the abject platitudinous piffle that deals with the 'nobility and righteousness of our cause', 'the honour of dying for England' and 'remember Belgium'.

19 March: There is little to think or talk about except the imminence of the German attack. Gradually we have been making the preparations necessary for our part, and as a final touch we were treated to a false alarm this afternoon for the purpose of seeing how quickly we could turn out with wagons packed and everything ready for the march. As it was we were packed up and all in line in a remarkable short time, and the Brigadier was very pleased. But we didn't tell him that we knew what was coming, four or five hours before the alarm was sounded. I am on night duty tonight and, judging from the tone of one or two telegrams that have passed, it is pretty certain that the attack will commence on the 21st.

Captain George
Nichols, C Battery,
82nd Brigade,
Royal Field Artillery

At 5.10 p.m. on 20 March I was in the mess. The day had been hot and peaceful, the only sound of gunfire a six-inch howitzer registering, and, during a morning tour with the second lieutenant who had come from one of the batteries to act as temporary signalling officer, I remembered noting again a weather-beaten civilian boot and a decayed bowler hat that for weeks had lain neglected and undisturbed in one of the rough tracks leading to the front line – typical of the unchanging restfulness of this part of the front.

Suddenly the door opened, to admit Colonel, CO of the Infantry

Battalion who were our near neighbours in the quarry. 'Have you had the "Prepare for Attack"?' he asked abruptly as we held ourselves to attention. 'No, sir,' I replied, and moved to the telephone to ring up Divisional Artillery Headquarters …

Midnight: I had sent out the night-firing orders to our four batteries, checked watches over the telephone … The doctor and signalling officer had slipped away to bed, and the Colonel was writing his nightly letter home. I smoked a final cigarette and turned in at 12.30 a.m.

3.30 a.m.: The telephone bell above my head was tinkling. It was the brigade major's voice that spoke. 'Will you put your batteries on some extra bursts of fire between 3.45 and 4.10 – at places where the enemy, if they are going to attack, are likely to be forming up? Right! – that gives you a quarter of an hour to arrange with the batteries. Goodnight!'

My marked map with registered targets for the various batteries was by the bedside, and I was able, without getting up, to carry out the brigade major's instructions. One battery was slow in answering, and as time began to press I complained with some force, when the captain – his battery commander was away on a course – at last got on the telephone. Poor Dawson. He was very apologetic. I never spoke to him again. He was a dead man within nine hours.

I suppose I had been asleep again about twenty minutes when a rolling boom, the scream of approaching shells and regular cracking bursts to right and left woke me up. Now and again one heard the swish and the 'plop' of gas shells. A hostile bombardment, without a doubt. I looked at my watch – 4.33 a.m.

I am still Battalion Bombing Officer & am billeted with the left reserve company – 'C' – when the attack starts – At 5 a.m. on 21 March the Germans start a gas bombardment of great strength on our front, support & reserve lines – by 7 a.m. all communication with the front line was ceased, wire from buried cables being knocked out of action – I report to the adjutant at HQ dugout, and am told to stand by and await orders.

The last message from the front line is 0820 stating the Germans are now attacking, by the time this bombardment has lifted and we can see the hillside in front of us covered with advancing Germans. By 10 a.m. we

Second Lieutenant Hubert McBain, 2nd Durham Light Infantry

This photograph was taken by a German storm trooper moments after entering a British front-line trench, on the morning of 21 March 1918. Both British soldiers have just been killed. Blood appears to be seeping from the head of the man on the right. Behind is the thick morning fog that helped screen the German advance.

On the left, at the forefront of the photograph, is a Mauser AZ carbine. Built for use by the cavalry, this rifle was shorter than that used by German infantry. However, it was popular with German storm troopers as its shorter length made it easier to handle in narrow trench conditions. Interestingly, the rifle has a round jammed in the breech. This suggests it did not belong to the photographer but to another man who probably abandoned the rifle in the heat of battle in order to grab anything else he could use.

Next to the Mauser are two British ammunition boxes: both have been ripped open. Presumably the bottom box is empty and the second box opened and then stacked on top. As each box carried 1,000 rounds, this would be indicative of a stout defence before the position was finally overrun. On the right is an open crate holding grenades, while on the floor is a bundle of abandoned webbing. Webbing was generally removed from a wounded man by stretcher-bearers in order to lighten their load.

The rifle on the right has a taut leather sling indicating that it was probably one of several spare rifles placed at intervals along the trench. Attached to the top of the barrel is a number 31 or 32 grenade parachute signal. Fired from the rifle, the grenade exploded in the air before gliding down by parachute. A bright light was emitted alerting supporting artillery to an emergency in the front line. The thick fog that morning rendered the grenade useless.

On the floor on the right is an empty bag for a PH gas hood. This hood was officially replaced by the small box respirator in early 1917. However, many men chose to keep the PH hood as a back-up in case of emergencies.

On the leg of the dead man on the left is a clip of .303 bullets. This suggests that he was pulling the clip out of his ammunition pouch to reload when he was shot and killed, the clip falling on to his leg.

The dead man to the left is still wearing an army greatcoat. The army had an official winter and summer time. On 1 April, all greatcoats were due to be handed in. The army preferred not to have greatcoats in the front line for longer than necessary as their bulk restricted movement when a man was in action.

can see the Germans going through on both flanks but our front line has held out so well that we in the reserve line have not yet been attacked – at 10.20 the Germans advance towards our reserve line in extended order but are mown down by our rifle & Lewis gun fire – after two of these attempts they give it up. At 10.45 a bombing party of Germans work down the communication trench & attack our Battalion HQ which causes a momentary panic – but we soon counter-attack with bombs & kill and wound them all and establish a block in the communication trench and fire rifle bombs with great effect at the next party of Germans who are thinking of attacking up – fortunately they do not – We hang on till dusk when Breton sends for me, and I am given orders to take a few men out and form a defensive flank should the Germans, who are now well in rear of us, decide to attack us.

British wounded making their way back for treatment. This picture was taken during the opening hours of the battle.

11 a.m.: The Colonel had spoken more than once about the latest situation to the brigade major of the Infantry Brigade we were covering, and to our own brigade major. The staff captain had rung me up about the return of dirty underclothing of men visiting the divisional baths; there was a base paymaster's query regarding the Imprest Account which I had answered; a batch of corps and divisional routine orders had come in, notifying the next visits of the field cashier, emphasising the need for saving dripping, and demanding information as to the alleged damage done to the bark of certain trees by our more frolicsome horses. Another official envelope I opened showed that Records were worrying whether a particular regimental sergeant major was an acting or a temporary sergeant major.

The doctor and the signalling officer had gone forward to visit the batteries. Hostile shelling seemed to have died out. The mist was denser

Captain George Nichols, C Battery, 82nd Brigade, Royal Field Artillery

than ever – a weather phenomenon that continued to puzzle. The telephone bell tinkled again; the Colonel turned from the big map board on the wall and took up the receiver. 'Col. speaking! – Yes! – Have they? Sorry to hear that! – Umph! – No! no signs of an attack on our front. Let me know any further developments – Goodbye!'

He looked towards me and said briefly, 'The Boche infantry have got over on our left! Came through the mist! I'm afraid the –rd (our companion Field Artillery Brigade) have caught it badly. Two of their batteries have lost all their guns. Get me the brigade major of the brigade' – turning to the telephone again. He told the brigade major of the Infantry we were covering the news of the break on the left. No, our infantry had not yet been attacked; but up in the front it was difficult to see anything in the mist. The Colonel studied his wall map with intentness, and put a forefinger on the –rd Brigade gun positions. 'If he's through there we can expect him in (naming a village of great strategical importance) in a couple of hours.'

Second Lieutenant Hubert McBain, 2nd Durham Light Infantry

As soon as we dash out of the trench to take up a position we come under heavy MG fire – Lt Osborne & Sergeant Allen are both knocked out – as soon as I got to the ground overlooking the rear of our trench I am sniped at by a German from eighty yards away in a bit of ground where our Aid Post is – I dash for a shell hole in order to take cover & am wounded in the left thigh by the same man – as it is nearly dark now I crawl for about 300 yards towards the rear, being unable to bind up my wound. I lose a lot of blood – I reach a sunken road where I see one of our machine-gun teams ready & waiting for the Germans – they inform me that there are stretcher-bearers only a few yards away. I am carried back on a stretcher for six miles being most of the time under shellfire – I arrive at Beugny at half past nine at night – where I am laid out on the grass with hundreds of other stretcher cases and am attended to and ticketed – then put in a Ford ambulance and taken back to the casualty clearing station.

Lieutenant Colonel Rowland Fielding, 1/15th London Regiment (Civil Service Rifles)

As things began to look more and more serious Father McShane, the young chaplain, went round the battalion, and gave absolution to all … We were on the move by 12.30. The enemy was still shelling heavily, and we had several casualties as we went forward through the barrage. We passed two huge twelve-inch howitzers on the broad-gauge railway, already abandoned, and the adverse trend of the fighting became still more apparent, as we passed the 18-pounder positions, from the vigorous efforts that were being made to get away the guns and howitzers. With their usual dash the field gunners were struggling to move these guns, but, though they had been pulled out of the pits, they were in many instances destined to go no further, there being no horses left alive to draw them.

As we reached the firing line the trench was being heavily and effectively shelled. A few hours before it had been a reserve trench – almost our rearmost line of defence; so far behind, in fact, that it was only partly dug. There were considerable gaps; and, as there was no communication trench leading up to it, the only approach was across the open.

We found it occupied by a few living stragglers – remnants of the garrisons of the forward positions, and strewed with the bodies of the dead who had already fallen to the enemy's shellfire. As the companies assembled for the counter-attack the hostile shelling seemed to increase, and, more than once, there was a direct hit upon a bay, killing or wounding every man in it. A whizz-bang skimmed the parapet, splashing my face with earth with such a smack that for a moment I thought my cheek was shot away. I felt and found only a drop of blood. With my usual luck a graze was all there was to show, once the dirt was brushed away.

12.40 p.m.: The Colonel was again speaking to the Infantry brigade major. Still no signs of the German infantry in our front line. Then in one swift moment the whole situation changed. A sweating, staggering gunner blundered into the doorway. He made no pretence at saluting, but called out with all his strength: 'The Boche is through.'

'Who is that man?' demanded the Colonel, whipping round like lightning, and frowning. 'Bring him here! Who do you belong to?'

The man had calmed; but before he could reply there was another interruption. A strained voice outside shouted, 'Is the Colonel there? Is the adjutant there?'

Hurrying through the doorway, I saw a tall, perspiring, hatless young subaltern, cursing because he had got entangled in the guy ropes of some camouflage netting posts. It was Hetherton of C Battery.

Captain George Nichols, C Battery, 82nd Brigade, Royal Field Artillery

The Colonel came outside. 'The Huns came on us in the mist, sir,' panted Hetherton, 'out of the wood. They've killed Dawson, sir.' His voice broke – 'and some of the others. There were only four of us got away. I came on to tell you.' He stopped and breathed hard. The Colonel looked stern, but his voice was smooth and collected. 'That's all right,' he said, almost soothingly. 'You cut off with your party and report to the retiring position.'

The young man looked dazed, but saluted, and was moving off when the Colonel caught him by the arm. 'Come and have a drink, Hetherton, before going on,' he said; 'it'll do you good.'

Sapper Albert Martin, 122nd Signal Company, 41st Division, Royal Engineers

21 March: Although we were well behind the lines, the sudden and terrible thunder of innumerable guns woke me at dawn. The long-expected German advance had commenced … We are in the soup and we've got to get out of it. Gaiety and mirth have been dwindling of late, and what merriment there was as we rose this morning had little spontaneity about it. But the British soldier in the mass never gets downhearted. So when late in the afternoon we were formed up and marched away, we kept our spirits up with singing and laughing … At nightfall we entrained and understood that our immediate destination was Mericourt on the Somme, a few miles behind Albert and a place that we had known in 1916. We were uncomfortably crowded in the trucks and could only squat down with our knees up under our chins. Of course all leave was stopped.

22 March: Horribly cramped, I only doze fitfully all night yet it is surprising how soundly some men can sleep in any position. One by one they woke up and stretched, kicking and pushing all the other fellows around them. It was broad daylight when we opened the doors and found that already we were beyond Mericourt and were actually passing through Albert. We crawled along until we reached Achiet-le-Grand where we detrained at 8.30 am … The whole signal section and Brigade Headquarters staff were lined up and inspected by General Townsey who carefully noted that each man had his full supply of ammunition and iron rations. It was a rather impressive inspection with shells bursting less than a mile away and all the multitudinous sounds of warfare rattling in our ears. There was no particular ceremony about the business; it seemed more like a fatherly

interview and there is no doubt that General Townsey felt considerable anxiety for our welfare.

23 March: Up soon after daybreak as we knew not what was before us. The cooks were preparing breakfast, bacon was frying and tea was brewing, when we received orders to retire immediately as the Germans had resumed their alarming advance. Tea and bacon were thrown overboard …

First of all the major called the roll and went through other necessary routine business. Then the Colonel came forward and addressed the men. He was visibly affected and had difficulty in delivering his little speech, for emotion was half choking him and tears were rolling down his cheeks. He was tall and big, with a square jaw and a hard-cut face that had probably never felt a tear before. His words had a simple nobility and directness about them and I shall remember his speech as one of the most considerable that I have ever heard. We were not surprised afterwards to hear him spoken of as a brave and splendid man. I do not know who he was but I shall not forget him.

24 March: We were met by a continuous stream of retiring troops, fatigued almost to the point of absolute exhaustion, staggering along hardly knowing where they were going. Hot, tired horses pulling guns of all calibres while on the gun limbers, artillerymen, who had been firing their guns for three whole days and nights, slept a precarious slumber in the continual danger of being jolted into the road and being trampled by the team immediately behind …

Along the road a little way, we passed a big howitzer that had just been got into position, and was beginning to open fire again. The roads were so congested with traffic at this point that we had to make tracks across some fields only to get our feet entangled with telephone wires. These were dangerous for the horses but we had no mishap and eventually turned into a large field on the left of the road. It was 10 p.m. before we got the transport ready and looked round for some shelter for ourselves. But there was none. QMS Cass doled us out with two blankets each. Wrapping these round us, we lay down on the grass against a long, low mound …

26 March: There was a tense feeling in the air this morning and strange rumours were flying about. At 8.30 a.m. orders were received that every available man was to be sent to some unnamed spot. Only NCOs and the

actual drivers were to remain with the transport. Captain Reiner decreed that all Signals must go, so we were issued out with iron rations and a double quantity of ammunition, and under Lieutenant Edgar we passed back through the village and up the road leading to Sailly-au-Bois. There was an alarming stir at Div HQ in Souastre – staff officers were dashing about furiously and gallant NCOs who had never been in the firing line looked livid and scared as if they did not know what to do. We were not left long in doubt as to the cause of the commotion, for we had barely got clear of the village when we met men hurrying from the opposite direction. Lorries, horse transport and men on foot all seemed anxious to get past us. Then we met some who called out as they hurried by, 'Don't go up there, you bally fools – Fritz is in the next village!' Mr Edgar halted us, ordered us to load rifles and fix bayonets, and was surprised to find that RE Signals do not carry bayonets. Then we were lined across the field on the right of the road and quickly the word was passed round that the German cavalry had broken through and might be upon us at any moment. Except for a few yards of trench there was no shelter for us at all and only one of our party had an entrenching tool. We borrowed it in turn and scraped grave-shaped holes to lie in, building the earth up in front of us to form some slight protection. Other men were doing the same thing in front of us and behind us and within half an hour there were fourteen lines of resistance drawn right across the country. We kept our eyes on the horizon and waited. It was a most horrible wait. Some there were in our line who were faint-hearted and crept back to the security of a little sunken lane behind us.

The ground fell away slightly in front of us and then rose to a long line of low hills on the horizon. For three hours we lay and watched the skyline but nothing German made any appearance. A number of horsemen came over but they were British and soon we were talking to a sergeant of artillery who told us definitely that the rumour was false. We got up and stretched ourselves, and breathed freely once more. It is positively extraordinary how this rumour spread over such a vast expanse of country in such an incredibly short time – just like a big puff of wind.

The full weight of the German offensive had been thrown against one army in one part of the line, and while the entire BEF appeared imperilled, by no means could it be said that every member felt or appreciated the seriousness of it at that time.

27 March: Many thanks for the parcel – especially the dates, which I suddenly remembered I was carrying, as I stood on the bridge at midnight. I was on a night fatigue. It was a grand night judged by a pre-war standard, but I thought that the folks of London may not be thinking it so in these days. Fritz pays occasional visits to places round about here, but as he doesn't come in relays, I don't mind a handful of bombs now and then.

I expect you are wondering how Jerry's attack has affected me. Very little really. I have been on one trip to a place amongst our guns for a twenty-four-hours' fatigue, but we were well away from danger although the noise of the guns after having been so long away from it quite put the wind up me for an hour or so. However, I soon got accustomed to the 'faint sweet music'. I quite enjoyed the trip. The roads, of course, were very dusty and I had missed a bath parade through being on that job. I decided on my way back

Pioneer George Dewdney, 72 Section, 'P' Special Company, Royal Engineers

The German offensive on the Lys: the 4th Worcestershire Regiment holding on after a successful counter-attack. 'Germans attacking at this moment', the contemporary caption notes.

that my first concern should be a journey to 'our wood' and the stream there. I went into it, muck up to my eyes, and three days beard, and mighty tired: I came out frisky and fresh – clean all over, clean change, face shaved, hair 'shampooed' – thanks to the little stream with the flowery banks and my small parcel of necessities. We do queer things out here though, and I must admit that the idea of discovery during such a wild exploit was rather disquieting. A few days later there was really an alarming rumour about the attack. I wish I might describe all the scenes – the excitement, the very humorous side and the note of real pathos that occurred – all to subside to the usual conditions and routine a few hours later. Once during the scare, when walking along about the village, I was sure that I was soon to be well away for Berlin. I thought that German farm work might be enjoyable at this time of the year. But no, the Jerries along the road were prisoners after all! So here we are still, carrying on as before, hearing all kinds of rumours of gains and losses, but knowing nothing definite about what is really going on comparatively near by. Newspapers are all brought up in three days – I am looking forward to the *Mirror*, that I may see whether we are fighting round Paris or Berlin, or both at once.

    4 April: I am afraid that like most folk in England, the great German

March 1918: two Germans lean on a British tank knocked out during the Somme battle of September 1916.

offensive has made you all rather alarmed on our behalf. But trust me to be well out of everything. I think that you may consider his [the German] effort exhausted for the present – not but that he had taken a good run for his money, although dear at the price, I think. And now it is all over we arrive on the scene. It was but yesterday that we moved 'up the line'. However, this front is quite undisturbed and very quiet judging at what can be gathered at our billet a few miles behind the lines [Bully Grenay, 20 kilometres north of Arras]. Our new home is not too bad. First impressions are often rather glum and usually prove to be wide of the mark, but after the shock of seeing a few battered houses following on our months 'beyond the war' I have come to the above conclusion. I think the signs of war are old ones, too. Everything has been most quiet since we came, and the fact that civilians still carry on with an absolute lack of concern suggests that there is little doing at the front in these parts. The village is of a fair size and the shops seem able to supply all essentials.

George Dewdney was exceptionally fortunate. He was billeted in the one short section of the British line near Loos that would not be attacked at all during 1918. The German March assault had been to the south of where Dewdney's unit was serving, and had taken a great swathe of land, but ultimately, by early April, had failed to separate the Allies or drive the British back on to the Channel ports. The German assault ran out of momentum, and key objectives, such as the critically important rail junction of Amiens, remained in Allied hands. Then, in April, the Germans launched a second assault, this time in Flanders, with a view to capturing three commanding heights and forcing the British evacuation of Ypres and the Salient as a preliminary to pushing the British back on the ports. The attack commenced on 9 April and met with initial success. In Poperinghe, Talbot House remained open, for now.

12 April: Very momentous issues, but by the grace of God we shall not fail. Fortunately, thank God, I'm in splendid health and good spirits, and everyone is open-hearted and good. Toc H stands up till now, and its doors are open. I am naturally anxious, but it is good to hold fast by God. The time is historic, and another Waterloo may come, in God's providence.

Reverend Philip 'Tubby' Clayton, Army Chaplain

On 16 April the Germans captured Meteren, a few miles south-west of Poperinghe. Owing to the delicate position, Poperinghe was largely evacuated of troops. Worse was to come when, on 25 April, the Germans captured Kemmel Hill, a strategically important position that dominated the area, leaving Talbot House as one of the few doors still open in the town.

17 April: The end of an eventful day; but I can't explain all the events, – no near shaves, though a certain amount of shelling round about. Yesterday the House was closed down by order, today the APM [assistant provost marshal] intervened and lodged a purple protest against my being moved away to other work, my transfer having come through. He was splendid, and I hope has saved me from being shifted, for I should be very sorry to leave yet awhile at least. We have two vans of furniture on the railway, so I can flit at a moment's notice. But I don't think the time has yet come, as the House is quite useful still, and more brotherly than ever.

Although the battle lasted less than three weeks, the Germans inched forward but failed to get within five miles of the vital railway junction at Hazebrouck. Nevertheless, for a second time in a month the situation appeared critical for the BEF, and would remain so for many weeks.

15 May: Corps has just ordered the House to be closed temporarily to troops from today and we can't resist. Probably, indeed, it is wise, but it's hard luck on the wayfarers … It is very hard to close the door, but it's better to avoid a concentration at present, not that the town is bad, but it might suddenly take a turn for the worse … Anyhow, we've kept the door open longer than anyone else, and it is not the Boche that closes it now.

20 May: The authorities are determined (quite kindly) that the House should be evacuated now. For a fortnight it has been the only House open in the town; and as the town is now altogether out of bounds, it seems only folly to remain. We have cleared everything worth having, even the electric light fittings; and all the valuables, chapel furniture, etc., are safely on the train in a truck all to themselves … It is in one way heartrending to leave the House. On the other hand, there is nothing for it to do now.

Arriving in the Salient was a young Royal Engineers officer, Second Lieutenant George Atkinson. He was astonished at the overall strategic position and how Ypres had remained in British hands.

16 May: The Ypres Salient on an ordinary lively night is a sight to be remembered. The rise and fall of the Verey lights makes a circle of fire all round us, and except just where the Poperinghe road connects us with the rest of France we appear to be completely surrounded. It is more than a marvel to me how they have failed to cut us off in that little bottleneck. On this particular night Fritz was raining shrapnel into Dickebusch and our people were giving him a warm time in reply. The 4.5 howitzers were firing hammer and tongs, and as I watched the angry shell bursts on the ridge in front I began to feel quite sorry for the Boche infantry. However,

Second Lieutenant George Atkinson, 2nd Army, Royal Engineers

German prisoners carry in the wounded after a failed attack during their Lys offensive in April.

his field guns sent some high explosive over just to the left of my barricade, and my sympathy rapidly vanished. Cycling back in the grey of the morning we saw a 9.2-inch howitzer being tugged into position by a tractor, and a cottage in Brandhoek just set on fire by a direct hit. We didn't linger!

19 May: Rode round with the Skipper, taking over all the demolitions from him as he goes to the gunners tomorrow as liaison officer. I am now responsible for the explosive charges under all the bridges behind Ypres, and in case of evacuation of the Salient I've got to be the last man to leave, blowing up everything before I go. It's a regular suicide club, as I know that fully half the charges won't go off unless I fire my revolver into them – disadvantages of belonging to a corps with high ideals – 'blow yourself up rather than fail to blow the bridge'.

21 May: Vlamertinghe very heavily shelled with HE and shrapnel just as I was going in, Boche got another direct hit on the old church tower and brought more masonry down into the road. Cycling along the Switch Road behind a lorry when a shell dropped into the swamp about fifteen yards on my right. Tore some big holes in the lorry cover and splashed me with mud. Lucky the ground was so soft or else I should have had a little more than wind up! At night had 260 PBI working for me on the Green Line. They are the best workers we've had yet, and only came out of the line last night …

At five minutes to twelve the moon was shining on a peaceful but desolate scene; the frogs were croaking in the shell holes, and the only signs of war were an occasional Verey light beyond Ypres and the lazy droning of a night bomber overhead. At midnight there was a crash behind us and instantly our guns let out together, surrounding us with a wall of noise and leaping, white-hot flame. The SOS [signal] began to rise from the German lines and shortly afterwards the steady crashing of his shrapnel barrage was added to the din. This went on steadily for three-quarters of an hour, while we grovelled on our stomachs in the mud, and punctually at 12.45 settled down to the usual desultory shelling. Had only one casualty in my party, but he was a nasty sight – chewed to pieces by a direct hit. On the way back Mellor and I cycled into some gas and swallowed a bit before we got our bags on, coughing and sneezing all night and had devilish headache. Just outside Vlamertinghe we ran into a smashed ambulance

and four limber mules and two drivers literally splashed about the road –
our wheels were wet with warm blood. Later on we found a saddle horse
blown in two but could not see any signs of the rider.

By the middle of May, 'P' Special Company, Royal Engineers, had been moved
north-west of Poperinghe, much to the interest of George Dewdney, one man
among many who had become greatly taken not only with the caring work
of Tubby Clayton, but with the man himself.

22 May: I am on the track of an old friend – Reverend Clayton of Talbot
House. He had to give up that place   it must have nearly broken his
heart – and has come some distance away to run three or four YMCAs.
One could not contain his energetic spirit I expect. So if there is not 'line'
tonight, I hope to attend one of his services. I look forward to seeing him as
one only does the best of friends. We tried to go to a service this morning
but were unlucky – an old noticeboard misled us. So we went in search
of Clayton and found one of his huts in a wood along a country lane, and
there was the same comforts and some of the effects even as at TH.

Pioneer George
Dewdney, 72
Section, 'P' Special
Company, Royal
Engineers

25 May: It says something for the influence of that man that he was able
to draw from the company which had been paid that day, about twenty-five
men of whom not more than ten at the very outside, would have gone
to a service in the ordinary way. It was quite possible, too, that that was
our last free evening for some time, and therefore the opportunity for
spending money hardly to be risked. Anyway, it was a grand service as
everyone agreed. I think Clayton's services appeal so because he seems
to run them on the assumption that that is <u>not</u> the first time one has
been to church, as so many preachers imagine it to be. He does not choose
'Fight the Good Fight' and 'Onward Christian Soldiers' every time and
his sermons – though preaching is not his forte – are sufficiently intellectual
to keep one thoughtful and interested. He saw us among the congregation
and at the end he gathered the whole band of us around him, and then
gave us such a welcome as only he could. I never knew such a smile as his
is. It is just the outward visible sign of the inward and spiritual grace
underlined with the greatness of his human nature. 'Well, this <u>is</u> a surprise!

P Coy: came back again! Dear old things, dear old things.' And he has such wonderful humour and unconscious optimism. It was a tonic to meet him again. He said that if we were 'off' last evening we were to go and search him out at 'Dingley Dell' and have tea.

Dingley Dell was a meadow and orchard beside a deserted aerodrome, north-west of Poperinghe, where Clayton had four Armstrong huts and from which he proposed to run 'Talbot Park'.

7 July: This morning we had a communion service in Camp Clayton. Our man. Do you know, he loved P Company so much, that he is arranging for a Talbot House in camp! He has managed to get a hut and now he wants us to help him arrange 'The House' on the lines of a quiet reading room – for writing, lectures, etc. He wants a 'fatigue party' of painters, and a genius to devise a means of hanging pictures on corrugated iron. Someone has to be constantly in attendance; he wants us to run it on our own. It'll be great fun if we can manage it without causing friction: the trouble will be to keep it from becoming exclusive to the men who know Clayton better … We must make it a go, if only that Clayton may not be disappointed.

15 July: There has been a great dearth of literature in camp of late, but our own little Talbot House is progressing and that, amongst other things, will help to make circulation more complete. Clayton has been made chaplain for this area:- thus he will have wider scope for his work and more facilities for carrying it out. He is forbidden to have anything in the villages in the shape of Talbot House, where troops might congregate, lest Jerry start shelling … However, he hopes to get a spacious billet for himself where friends may 'just drop in'. He is the <u>limit</u> for 'getting round' orders, in the interests of the troops.

Our war of late has been away from the trenches so we have been able to shelter from the heavy, frequent thunderstorms we have been having. Your fear that I might be transferred to the infantry, though not impossible in these stirring times, is most unlikely.

The Yanks are amply rushing along now in support of our infantry. The past fortnight had seen wonderful changes in that respect – in which time the general opinion of them has changed from something approaching contempt, to real admiration. They're splendid fellows. We're all right now and every day brings improvements for us. There is a fellow in our camp at present visiting his brother, who is one of our section sergeants. He looks the same as any ordinary man about twenty-two – perhaps more than usually unassuming. He has a Victoria Cross and has just won the Distinguished Conduct Medal. He was offered a safe job behind the lines, but he wouldn't have it and wants the Military Medal to complete the list, he says! He looks so serenely harmless, too!

The most likely candidate for this description is Sergeant Arnold Loosemore. He won the Victoria Cross in 1917, subsequently winning the Distinguished Conduct Medal in June 1918 when aged twenty-two. He also had a brother, Sergeant John Loosemore, serving with the Royal Engineers. On 18 October 1918, Arnold Loosemore was badly wounded in both legs by machine-gun fire, his left leg being amputated. He died of tuberculosis in April 1924, aged just twenty-seven.

We have had terrific rainstorms of late. I shall never forget a sight I saw on Saturday. One of our own observation balloons was up, when a thunderstorm burst right overhead and there was a terrific flash of lightning which must have struck the connecting cable of the balloon. Before it reached the balloon, the men seemed to have taken to their parachutes:- the tragic thing was that they did not get clear. The parachutes came down in two tails of smoke below the mass of flames and smoke that had been the balloon. It was one of the most awful things I have ever witnessed.

The Yanks were coming in ever greater numbers and already they were appreciated on the battlefield. By July, the Germans were almost finished as an attacking force and for most of June and July both sides paused for breath after the great exertion of the spring. The lines held, which ensured that Talbot House remained closed for the time being. Tubby Clayton eventually reopened it on 27 September, and without proper authority to do so as his self-proclaimed habit of 'acting for the best without order in writing' ensured.

The ground around Kemmel Hill, so recently a relatively unspoilt backwater, was as mangled and mutilated as much of the Ypres Salient just a few miles away. The ground was testament to the bitterness of the fighting and the courageous rearguard efforts of the Allies in withstanding German attacks.

Second Lieutenant George Atkinson, 2nd Army, Royal Engineers

30 June: The whole of Kemmel Hill and the valley and the ravines in front are one solid mass of shell holes. The earth has been turned and turned again by shellfire, and the holes lie so close together that they are not distinguishable as such. The ground in many places is paved with shrapnel balls and jagged lumps of steel – in ten square yards you could pick up several hundredweight. There was a magnificent view of all the Boche forward lines, but of course he has a much better view of ours and also of our back areas. They say it is death to move a finger in front of the hill and all our work will have to be done at night.

On our way back we came across an old French battery position which had apparently been defended to the end in the great struggle. The guns were right in the open and must have caught the full blast of the German fire, for the limbers were all shattered to pieces and many of them were turned over into the shell holes. The gunners were killed to a man round their pieces, and could have no finer monument than their pile of empty shell cases. Their bodies still lay there unburied, mixed up with the carcasses of the horses with which they had tried to get the guns away at the last moment – some were headless, limbless, and with their entrails strewn around them – most had had the clothing blown from their bodies, and some had been half eaten by the rats.

The pressure on young subalterns such as Atkinson was tremendous as casualties threw extra workloads on the men who were left. The exhaustion felt by so many that summer was almost tangible.

5 July: Got back to billets to find that Derry had gone sick. More work for the rest of us, and we are nearly tired out now. In the evening Blacker crocked up and went sick too – pure undiluted funk on his part. Three officers left now to do the work of ten and the major will go soon. He hasn't been to bed for a week, and must have walked at least twenty-five miles

every day. I had a talk with him and persuaded him to order the transport officer up from the horse lines, so that will make four of us. I have got two brigades to look after now. Forward again about 7 p.m. and nearly completed wire across the valley in spite of usual machine-gun fire – two men hit in my party. Heavy shellfire all night.

6 July: Coming home about 4 a.m. I met the major alone, and although nearly finished, I went back to help him to lay out a new line. Poor old major is nearly done, but he will drop before he gives in. I hope we can last until some more officers come, but my eyes are jumping and my head sings like a tornado – how few people must know what it is like to be really exhausted in the body and yet to have a mind which drives you on.

8 July: Had three hours' sleep and went up again at night after a heavy afternoon's work. Very heavy thunderstorms all night made it almost impossible to move about. Was so exhausted with falling into shell holes that I started to crawl about on my hands and knees in the mud – once I almost cried with sheer weakness. On the way home I fell off my bike and was so weak I had to leave it in a shell hole. Once or twice I touched my revolver – there is always that. It is a terrible thought, and even now,

1914: 'Above me rose the massive hill of Kemmel … I went up the steep, moss-grown path which led through a wood of beech, oak, and fir.' Captain Cecil Brownlow, RFA. 1918: Kemmel Hill now smashed to pieces.

half an hour afterwards, I can't understand it – how much less can people at home! … Could sleep for ever and would dearly love to die.

17 July: Was coming home this morning about 5 a.m. very weary, when Jerry put down still another barrage. There were no trenches handy and I spent a nasty half-hour in a ditch on the side of the track. When you have once been strong it is awful to lie in a ditch and quiver like a jelly when shells are falling fifty yards away. I am going all to pieces and my imagination is killing me. Last night I was alone inspecting the wire when for some hellish reason I saw a picture of myself disabled by a bullet and lying for hours until I bled to death, in days it would have been, for my vitality is tremendous. For several minutes I couldn't move, covered with a clammy sweat and paralysed with fear. Great wind-up today – the Huns are expected to make their last effort for Calais tomorrow. Every available man working on battle positions, and all guns fired a counter-preparation on German roads. If they do attack seriously it will be the end of my diary.

18 July: Worked like devils all last night and then spent an awful hour before dawn, standing to and waiting for the attack. Every time an odd shell came over we held our breath and waited for the crash of the general bombardment. The strain was terrific and my stomach felt as if I had eaten a whole live jellyfish. The attack didn't come.

During July, British and Empire troops probed the Germans lines in preparation for a major assault on 8 August. That day, Allied troops breached enemy positions to a depth hitherto only dreamt about. Suddenly German resistance cracked, vast tracts of land were retaken but perhaps more significantly thousands of prisoners were captured, far more than ever before. Success that day showed Allied predominance on the battlefield and was symptomatic of a great tactical achievement.

The tipping point had been reached and the Germans would no longer be able to hang on to the land they had taken at such cost in the spring and early summer. Soon they were forced into a series of tactical retreats, giving up strategic positions no longer deemed tenable. They were not a spent force; their fighting retreat throughout September, October and November was to prove that, but confronted with overwhelming Allied firepower, in a war where artillery was king, the Germans had no option but to fall back. The Allied army began what was in effect a rolling offensive, very costly in lives, yet gaining a momentum unheard of on the Western Front. By the end of September the Germans had been thrown back onto their last prepared defensive position, the Hindenburg Line. Once this was breached, open warfare resumed. There was an undercurrent of 1914 again but so much had changed. The British Army was a far more effective fighting force; four years had honed their tactics while the adoption of new technology allowed troops to fight in a combined all-arms offensive in which cavalry, artillery, infantry and aircraft together delivered blow after blow on an increasingly demoralised enemy.

7 August

Dearest Mother

This is the evening before the attack and my thoughts are with you all at home. But my backward glance is wistful only because of memories and because of the sorrow which would further darken your lives tomorrow.

Lieutenant Hedley Goodyear, 102nd Battalion, Canadian Expeditionary Force

With hope for mankind and with visions of a new world a blow will be struck tomorrow which will definitely mark the turn of the tide. It will be one of a grand series of victories which will humble the selfish and barbarous foeman and will exalt the hearts that are suffering for freedom.

I have no misgivings for myself in tomorrow's encounter. It does not matter whether I survive or fall. A great triumph is certain and I shall take part in it. I shall strike a blow for freedom along with thousands of others who count personal safety as nothing when freedom is at stake. In a few moments I shall make the final address to my men and shall strengthen their hearts, if they need strengthening, with the language of men of war! We shall strive only to achieve victory. We shall not hold our own lives dear …

I do not think for a moment that I shall not return from the field of honour but in case I should not, give my last blessing to Father and my greatest thanks for all he did for me … I should not choose to change places with anyone on the world … I shall be my father's and mother's son tomorrow again. God bless you all.

Lieutenant Hedley Goodyear was killed the next morning but the victory he predicted was won, and emphatically so. The offensive was well planned, well executed and, because preparations had been made in great secrecy, the Germans were taken almost entirely by surprise. The British Army had amassed over 340 tanks, 800 aircraft and over 2,000 artillery pieces to support an infantry attack against a depleted German defence. The Australian and Canadian Corps advanced over seven miles by the afternoon and although the offensive slowed almost to a halt as the Germans rushed reinforcements to the line, the halt was temporary. As the Germans retreated, so French farmers returned with little hesitation.

Sapper Albert Martin, 122nd Signal Company, 41st Division, Royal Engineers

17 August: The civilians are cutting the corn – two women and a man are engaged in the business all day long. Where they go at night is a mystery. All day long they are in full view of Fritz but he has left them alone – yet they are in the midst of Fritz's legitimate objectives – and shells are no respecters of persons. One of their carts, loaded high with wheat, broke my [telephone] line where it was carried on high poles across a roadway. It was useless to try and erect the poles again so I came back for a pickaxe and then buried the cable under the roadway. This comic air-line requires some attention. On average I have to go out and mend a break about four times a week; only about half of them are due to shellfire.

Major Seabury Ashmead-Bartlett, 173 Infantry Brigade, Royal Field Artillery

21 August: The victory which the British have gained north and south of the Somme is entirely due to the moral superiority of our men, as we have never been able to make good the losses we suffered in the spring.

There are only about a dozen inhabitants left in Fréchencourt, but I suppose more will return now that the Boche is being driven back. The unfortunate people will have only the husks of their homes to return to, for all the furniture and fittings have been removed for use in dugouts or for firewood, and as the villages in this part of the Somme valley are very badly built – of timber and plaster for the most part – a single bomb generally shakes a great number of houses to pieces. What peasants remain are performing prodigies of labour in harvesting the corn, most of which will never be gathered. Every inch of soil is cultivated, but the methods and appliances are most antiquated. Up to the spring of the year, this part of the country was forty or fifty miles behind the front line, and the inhabitants lived undisturbed by war, but when the Boche swept forward in his great offensive they suddenly found themselves in the battle zone, and had to abandon their homes and all that they had worked so hard for.

22 August: Heilly had been badly knocked about by shellfire, but is now quiet. We established our headquarters in a little house close to the Halte. Two months ago it was a happy bourgeois home, now though but slightly damaged it has been stripped of all its contents. Books of the classical variety were scattered about the house and garden. I started to read Alexandre Dumas Junior's *La Dame aux Camélias*, but found it hard to arouse any interest in the life of that unfortunate courtesan. After lunch the General and I rode up to reconnoitre

A signaller climbs a pole to secure a telephone wire.

the front from the high ground north of Morlancourt. To the north was the valley of the Ancre and ruined villages. In the far distance lay Albert, or, rather, the distorted ruin which marks the site of that once prosperous little town …

27 August: At 5 a.m. our barrage came down and the troops began their advance. German prisoners soon commenced to arrive at the advanced report centre … I interviewed about twenty prisoners in all. Most of them were of poor physique and worse morale. When they learned that they were to be well treated, they expressed delight at being captured and offered to do any work that might be required of them.

At 7 a.m. I moved the advanced report centre forward to where we established ourselves in some old elephant shelters erected by the British in 1917, captured and used by the Germans in 1918, and now retaken by us. During the morning, between the intervals of receiving and passing on reports, I collected a good many stragglers. All save one were genuine cases; men who had become separated from their units by shellfire which had driven them to earth. Poor fellows – all of them were tired, most of them badly shaken. One or two asked to be allowed to remain behind, but war is an inexorable master and demands the ultimate sacrifice from all, so I had to harden my heart …

The brigade does not number more than 900 bayonets. We have been fighting for three days and the men are very tired, nevertheless we have to attack again at dawn tomorrow. I am sorry for our poor fellows, but it must be done, for if we can harass the Boche sufficiently we may be able to inflict a decisive defeat on him this year. His men are as tired as ours, and badly discouraged in addition.

28 August: We attacked again this morning at 5 a.m. and captured our objective … The Germans offered little resistance to our attack, but afterwards put down a pretty heavy bombardment on the front-line trenches. I'm afraid that in this type of rearguard action they inflict heavier casualties upon us than they suffer themselves. On the other hand, they lose prisoners and material and suffer progressive demoralisation.

29 August: In the afternoon W. and I rode to see if we could find out anything about the enemy, who was reported to be retiring. We passed through Maricourt, yesterday the scene of heavy fighting, today crowded with troops and transport … Beyond is the old Somme battlefield, and we had to thread our way through a maze of grass-grown, dilapidated trenches with tangled rusty wire in front of them, relics of 1916. The Péronne road runs through the midst of the battlefields, bordered by the skeletons of what were once magnificent Lombardy poplars. Now they are stumps stripped of leaves and branches; even the bark has been blasted from the trunks; yet from their roots young shoots are springing – a symbol of the future. We were on a high, flat-topped plateau with steep valleys running down to the Somme. The chalky soil is seared and pitted with shell holes, so numerous that they are practically contiguous. No buildings or vegetation other than rank, unwholesome grass remain, and only a few shattered stumps mark the site of woods.

Captain George Nichols, C Battery, 82nd Brigade, Royal Field Artillery

One of the main aspirations among officers and men was to continue the advance in such a way as to make sure of decent quarters o' nights, and to drive the Germans so hard that when winter set in we should be clear of the foul mud tracts and the rat-infested trenches that had formed the battlefields of 1915, '16, and '17. Major Mallaby-Kelby was a keen pushful officer, immensely eager to maintain the well-known efficiency of the brigade while the Colonel was away; but he took me into his confidence on another matter. 'Look here!' he began, jocularly and with a sweeping gesture. 'I'm going to ask you to make sure that the mess never runs out of white wine. It's most important. Unless I get white wine my efficiency will be impaired.' I replied with due solemnity, and said that in this important matter our interpreter should be specially commissioned to scour the countryside.

By 1 p.m. it became so certain that the enemy had inaugurated a retreat that the major issued orders for the brigade to move forward three miles. We marched steadily down the valley, and halted for further instructions west of a deserted colony of battered Nissen huts, gaping holes and broken bricks shovelled into piles, still entered on the maps as the [Somme] village of Guillemont … Along the valley we had passed were row after row of solidly built stables left uncleaned and smelly by the fleeing Hun; rotting horses smothered with flies; abandoned trucks marooned on the few stretches of the narrow-gauge railway left whole by our shellfire. In the wood stood numerous Boche-built huts, most of them put up since the March onslaught. The Boche, dirty cur that he is, had deliberately fouled them before departing. The undulating waste east of Trones Wood, hallowed by memories of fierce battles in 1916, had remained untroubled until the last few weeks; and the hundreds of shell holes, relics of 1916, had become grass-grown. The hummocky greenness reminded one of nothing so much as a seaside golf course …

The side spectacle that struck me most when [a day later] I walked by myself through Combles was that of a solitary Royal Engineer playing a grand piano in the open street, with not a soul to listen to him. The house from which the instrument had been dragged was smashed beyond repair; save for some scrapes on the varnish the piano had suffered no harm, and its tone was agreeable to the ear. The pianist possessed technique and played with feeling and earnestness, and it seemed weirdly strange to hear Schumann's 'Slumber Song' in such surroundings. But the war has produced more impressive incongruities than that …

The problem of the last few days had been the water supply for the horses. Although the sappers were hard at work in Combles, there was as

Overleaf: A barrage balloon rises into the air: the Allies increasingly acquired not only air but observation superiority over the Germans.

yet no water within five miles of the batteries. The Boche by smashing all the power-pumps had seen to that; and the wagon lines were too far in the rear for moving warfare. 'We shall be all right when we get to the canal' had been everybody's consolatory pronouncement. 'The horses won't be so hard worked then.'

The Germans were fighting on foreign soil, and with the widespread realisation that they were beaten. They were also hungry and painfully aware of how much better British troops were equipped and supplied. At home in Germany, the civil population was sick of war; it is no wonder that new drafts to the front were unwilling to fight and forced onto trains under armed guard, and occasionally at gunpoint. Now they were fighting Allied forces who were reinvigorated by the signs of German defeat and the knowledge that an almost inexhaustible and motivated supply of American troops was strengthening Allied numbers in the field. It is a miracle that the Germans fought on as long as they did. Nevertheless, the facts do not lie. The British took 329,000 German prisoners on the Western Front during the Great War, 201,600 of whom were taken in 1918. Of these, fewer than 15,000 were taken in the first seven months, as opposed to nearly 187,000 captured from August to the Armistice.

Captain William Wilson, 1/6th Cameronians (Scottish Rifles)

I think, to pass the time, I'll write you a little sketch of one day in the great stunt. At two o'clock in the afternoon a chit comes round, as we are in a sunken roadway in fairly good dugouts and huts. 'Company will move to sunken roads leading south from cross-roads at U25, 6.45' (or some such thing) 'in support of the ___ brigade. Move to be completed by 5.45 p.m., and notified by code word "Bananas". Company Commanders will reconnoiter the roads forthwith ...'

Up I get, rather ill natured, and walk with a perspiring runner down the trench, and have a look at the place – no dugouts, no anything. Two platoons put in road to cut niches for themselves, and put a sheet of corrugated iron on top. Two platoons in trenches, Company HQ in field behind. I, as a man of luxurious habits and somewhat refined tastes, take a disused and partly roofless stable as my spot. Go around and see all okay, arrange as to rations and water, and exchange reports with HQ as to my place.

Back come the wounded of the ___ Brigade through my lines, walking cases first, some cheerful, some wind up, and later stretcher cases, some also cheerful, some fed up, some ominously quiet. Then we try to cook a little tea, dinner, and supper combined but have to put out our fire four times, because a bombing Taube, with its ominous drone, comes over, looking for a place to lay its eggs.

A barge takes the wounded down the River Scarpe, September 1918.

A walk round to see all is quiet, then back to my stable, too cold to sleep, so huddle up, smoke a cigarette or two, then at midnight, just as I am beginning to doze off, up comes a runner. 'Company Commanders will report at Battalion Headquarters immediately, with maps.' Turn to my subaltern and say, 'Well, we're for it tomorrow morning; it is a case of "over you go and the best of luck".'

Off to Battalion HQ I go. 'Come in. Have a coffee? Are we all here?' And so to detail, objective, routes, and the task. Zero hour is confirmed, and watches checked. Nothing to be done till the word 'Move' comes and then all companies to be at jumping-off trench before 4.30 a.m. Back, and go over position with my platoon commanders, and, just as we are finished, in comes order, 'Move'. Send runner round platoons, etc., all to be at sunken road facing north at 3.13 a.m. Then we have a cup of tea, and don't stop for Taubes. After all, if you go over the top at 5.30 an aeroplane at three doesn't matter a cuss.

At 3.30 the road is full of struggling figures, and up you go to the head of the column. 'Everybody here, Sergeant Major?' No. 13 Platoon not yet up. Fussing and annoyance. At last reported all up, and we march off. Half a mile, and we get to what the map calls a village, but no signs of anything except long grass and desolation. Then we come to four crossroads, and down to a corner where with a match I look at the map. Yes, it should be the centre one. Then on below camouflage strips and behind trees. The road gets worse and worse, and shell holes thicker. The place gets more desolate till we are quite sure we have lost our way. However, up pops the head of the battalion scout officer, who says, 'What company is that?' 'D Company.' 'Oh, have you seen A and C?' 'No.' 'Well lead on five hundred yards, and to the right, and you'll get your trench.'

At six o'clock just as a pale yellow and blue, or what poets call saffron, was showing in the east, there is a dead silence, and at three minutes past there is a sudden crash as our guns open; 2,000 yards away is the enemy line, and we watch the bursts, half shrapnel, half high explosive, and one in six of the latter, smoke …

Opposite above: In an attempt to slow down the pursuing Allies, the Germans felled trees to block the road.

Opposite below: A heavy howitzer about to fire. Towards the end of the war, German artillery was incapable of replying in kind to the heavy barrages delivered by the Allies.

The BEF possessed just over 1,500 field guns and howitzers of all types in France and Flanders on 1 July 1915. This almost tripled in number just prior to the Battle of the Somme to over 4,000, and by July 1918 that gross figure had risen to over 6,700. But the number of guns was not as important as their increasing calibre, and size was critical to Allied success. Heavier guns, such as the six-inch Howitzer, grew in number from 40 in July 1915 to over 1,000 three years later, while the number of the 9.2-inch howitzers rose from just 14 to 228 over the same period and there were other similar examples. The weight of shells fired during the great preliminary bombardment of the Battle of the Somme and in the week afterwards (fourteen days) was 5,350 tons. In 1918, during the rolling British

offensive, the daily weight was 7,585 tons maintained over seventy days. Finally, the heaviest bombardment of the entire war came in the week when the enemy's Hindenburg Line was broken. The Germans simply could not withstand such a maelstrom in which not just the power but the way in which a bombardment was delivered was so formidable.

Major Seabury Ashmead-Bartlett, 173 Infantry Brigade, Royal Field Artillery

31 August: At 2.30 p.m. came a message that we should have to attack at dawn, but it was not until 5.30 p.m. that we received definite orders. The battalions had to march in the dark [but] formed up on the starting line by zero hour, a very fine piece of work as they were moving over unknown country. At 5.30 a.m. the assault was launched. It met with complete success, our troops going straight to their final objective with comparatively light losses … overcoming all resistance in an incredibly short time.

Major T., commanding the 4th Battalion, London Regiment, took us round the front line. Incidentally, he lost his way and took us down the slopes of the valley traversed by the Canal du Nord to a position about 500 yards in front of our outposts. We were made aware of our indiscretion by a German sniper firing from the direction of St Pierre Vaast Wood. We jumped into a shell hole, and after waiting a while, ran one by one, from shell hole to shell hole back to our own lines. A 5.9-inch shell nearly got T. as he was doing his last sprint. I was twenty yards from there, in a trench when I heard it coming and as I threw myself flat, had a vision of flame, smoke and earth going up into the air where a second before he had been. When the smoke cleared away I saw him lying flat and for a moment thought he was dead; but, jumping to his feet, he ran into the trench cheerful and unmoved.

The full list of our captures is 325 unwounded prisoners, eight field guns, many machine guns and one motor ambulance complete with driver. Not bad for a tired brigade which only numbered around 900 bayonets when the action began.

Not bad at all! Over-running field guns and a motor ambulance highlighted the depth and speed of penetration into the German lines when guns were not normally within 2,000 yards of the trenches and, when threatened, were limbered up and taken away with all haste.

3 September: Today we heard that the Canadians are well across the Hindenburg Line east of Arras, and if the Germans cannot hold the Hindenburg Line their retreat will only be limited by our powers of endurance. There are no signs at present of it becoming disorderly, but they have only fifteen fresh divisions in reserve; so if we can continue our pressure for another two months I do not see how they can hope to resist the force that America will have fit for battle by then …

Exploring the old trenches of 1916, one comes across many strange and sad mementos of past battles. In grass-grown trenches and shell holes are rusty French and German steel helmets, or rifles with the bayonets fixed, dropped there two years ago. Close by perhaps a wooden cross wreathed with metal flowers commemorates the spot where their owners lie. Twice had the tide of battle swept over their heads since then, but now at last they have rest; for the storm is dying down and the tide is ebbing never to return …

Opposite: The dry bed of the Canal du Nord, captured on 27 September. This picture (and the previous three) was taken by Acting Major Oswald Riley, 79 Brigade, RFA. Very few officers still owned a camera in the last months of the war.

Second Lieutenant George Atkinson, 2nd Army, Royal Engineers

9 September: My home consists of three battered sheets of corrugated iron, a wagon cover and the back of a hen shed, reared miraculously against a bank of earth which is the mainstay of the edifice. Light comes from a candle in a port bottle. It is cold, damp, miserable, and the headquarters of two sections, Royal Engineers. Yet you wouldn't offer it to a tramp at home and a pig would scorn it – great are the blessings of civilisation!

I decided to keep one section in reserve, so took No. 3 up the line for night work. Arrived very late as all the tracks were knee-deep in slush and it was dark, dark as the inside of an infidel. We floundered around for several hours, but it was quite impossible to do anything in the nature of serious work – the line was new to us, and the difficulty of finding the posts was increased by persistent machine-gun fire and the most devilish weather imaginable. The ground was in an awful state, and it often took us twenty minutes to move a hundred yards – the men swore sublimely and their humour was the only dryness in the night …

Opposite: A gas attack in the Salient dated 29 September. In the foreground the ruined town of Ypres with an observation balloon overhead.

The men had a drop of rum when we got back, and it was about 4 a.m. when I crawled into my flea bag. A family of beetles played, 'Come and sit on my chair' across my toes, and an old brown rat wanted to keep me company. I turned him out three times, but the poor devil was so persistent and so pathetic that finally I let him stop. Immediately I fell asleep he came and stroked my hair in gratitude and I, misunderstanding his intentions, turned him out for good and all. But have you ever tried to sleep in your soaking wet clothes, with your head two feet under a sheet of corrugated iron on which it is raining hard? I tried, but the rain and the beetles were against me.

Overleaf: 1918: German prisoners of war held at a camp at Longeau, near Amiens, in France.

Sergeant James Duncan, 143rd Siege Battery, Royal Garrison Artillery

My own gun, thirty yards away, is firing a round every two minutes (weighing 300lbs) into the Hindenburg Line. All along the valley and over the crest are guns and still more guns. The bark of the 18-pounders and the creak of the six-inch and 60-pounders, the boom and crash of the heavy artillery, makes one continuous roar that baffles description. To us who are used to it, the only discordant note is the whine or screech of Fritz's returning shell, which by some intuition we can pick out amongst the prevailing thunder. We are, as it were, blazing a trail for the legions in the trenches.

On the road to our left is an endless procession of motor lorries, horse transport, field guns, ambulances etc. etc. The rule of the road is watch yourself because no other one will bother about you. Keep to the right. Ambulances with wounded and guns going into action take precedence of all other traffic. A Boche shell gets a hit on the road. You dodge the splinters of flying wheels and axles. There is a short pause as dead horses and battered limbers are cleared off the track. There is no place or not time to dodge the next shell. If your name is on it, well, then, your luck's out. Wounded men are roughly bandaged and put into passing motor lorries going down the line. The dead are left by the side of the road covered in blankets. A few days later a burial party will come along and put them under the troubled soil. The gap closes up, the stream flows on.

Haig had no intention of slowing the tempo of the offensive and so allowing the Germans time either to regroup or to pause for breath. Logistically, keeping up with the pace of the advance was often harder than advancing itself, although infantry divisions were becoming exhausted and casualties extremely high once men were fighting in the open, leaving the world of trenches behind them. The fortitude of the soldiers was not only commendable, it was astonishing. The men could now see tangible results for their supreme efforts, something that in the past was rarely the case.

Captain George Nichols, C Battery, 82nd Brigade, Royal Field Artillery

We had come over forty miles since 8 August in a series of three- to eight-mile leaps; for the third time the battalions had been brought up to something like strength, and they were full of fight. In the mud and slime of the Somme and Flanders in 1916 and 1917, when each advance was on a narrow front and ceased after a one-day effort, I always marvelled at the patient, fatalistic heroism of the infantry. A man went 'over the top' understanding that, however brilliant the attack, the exultant glory of continuous chase of a fleeing, broken enemy would not be his; and that, should he escape wounds or death, it would not be long before he went 'over the top' again, and yet again. But this open fighting changed all that. It showed results for his grit and endurance to the humblest 'infanteer'. And remember, it was the civilian soldier – unversed in war, save actual war –

who accepted and pushed home the glorious opportunities of achievement that these wondrous days offered.

26 September: Received preliminary orders that Day and I will take a section each and join the artillery brigades to make roads and bridges for them in the advance. Two sections remain in reserve under Cooper. Attack before dawn on the 28th. Went up to the brigade to arrange details and went to bed on return. Roused after an hour's sleep to go out with a section to repair two forward bridges near the front line before daybreak. Got about twenty men and miscellaneous material on to two pontoon wagons and started out in drizzling rain. I sat in the front of the first wagon, and as we lumbered off into the dark I fell into a sort of reverie. I thought lazily of home, and in my mind I went again over the characters of the men, the good ones and the doubtful ones, and detailed them off for different jobs – these and a thousand other thoughts wandered idly through my mind, punctuated by the jolting of the wagon and the barking of the 18-pounders. Then the men began to sing, very quietly and sweetly, and the rise and fall of their voices seemed to add some special significance to the night. We made good progress over the bad roads, stopping occasionally to check our way or adjust a girth. Now they were singing 'Annie Laurie', and I heard Garner say 'Damn' under his breath. I asked him what was the matter with them tonight, and he said, 'Dunno, sir, but I wish they wouldn't sing like that.' The rain had developed into a heavy Scotch mist which swallowed up the lead driver and the mounted corporal. I shivered under my coat, and felt unutterably lonely and sad.

At last the wagons stopped and we went forward on foot towards the work. We bridged three trenches and then came to the main job, a fifteen-foot span across a swollen creek, and not more than 400 yards from the German lines. For about an hour the work went quietly and well and we got an arch across the stream in the form of an old French steel shelter. Suddenly there was a short, fierce whine, a crash, and a livid burst of flame right in the party – three more followed almost instantaneously and then for a second an awful silence. Some one said 'Christ!' and began to cry gently. Five men were killed, three of them practically missing, and three badly wounded. By a miracle the work was practically undamaged. We took

Second Lieutenant George Atkinson, 2nd Army, Royal Engineers

the casualties to the wagons and returned to the job – how the men worked there again I shall never know, but they did, and the bridge was across an hour before dawn. The suddenness of the shock has knocked my nerves to pieces and even as I write my hand trembles. Looking back now I can see something unnatural in the whole of that ride in the pontoons – little details were too impressive, and there was an almost inhuman beauty in the way they sang that song. I am sure that some of those men had a vague premonition of what was coming.

1 October: We are without definite news, but apparently the whole show has been a great success, and the army is only waiting until we can get the roads through. I can never forget the great change which seemed to spread like wildfire over the spirit of the army on the evening of the 28th–29th. We were in the midst of the worst of the mud area, miles of transport wagons were bogged along our single road, it was raining hard, and few of us had eaten anything for twenty-four hours. Nobody was looking forward to the dawn. But from somewhere behind us a rumour came through that Bulgaria had asked for peace. There was no cheering, no demonstration of any sort, but the news seemed to put new spirit into the tired troops. The weary mud-caked horses were lashed and spurred again, men put their aching shoulders to the wheels, and once more the limbers lumbered forward. All night long the wagons toiled painfully up those fateful ridges where scores of thousands of our finest infantry had died, and in the drizzling dawn they saw their reward at last – behind them lay the dull, dead plain, with its memories of misery and mud – before them, they looked down upon a new, unbroken country, and the spire of Tenbrielen church, untouched of shot or shell, beckoned like a winning post against the eastern sky.

Sergeant James Duncan, 143rd Siege Battery, Royal Garrison Artillery

In the spring the Hun sowed the wind and lo, in the autumn he reapeth the whirlwind. The seed was sown by the sweat of tears, the harvest is gathered by the sweat of blood …

A few days ago, in our advance we stopped beside an advanced dressing station. There was a slightly wounded German officer there who could speak English. I pointed to the row of stretchers, each with its burden of battered humanity (German and British) and asked him, 'Well, Fritz,

Villages hitherto untouched by war burn as the Germans are pushed back and the trenches are left behind.

do you think it's worth it all?' He shrugged his shoulders and said 'This is war, nothing but war.' I asked him what victory he thought would be commensurate with the sacrifices made both by him and us. He answered, 'The victory of a lasting peace made by a people strong enough to discipline humanity and lead them along the path of a higher culture.' A typical answer by a typical, well-educated German. I told him that I thought the shaping of the destinies of the future generations would be in the hands of a different people to what he had in his mind. He shrugged his shoulders and gave a weary smile. This same smile is symptomatic of the German frame of mind at present.

I have seen prisoners coming in from the battles of the Somme, the battles of Mons, Messines and down the Menin Road. They had a dour defiant look in their faces that said, 'You've got me but there's plenty left to carry on and we will smash you yet.' Now you will find them an abject lot. The weariness of the mind along with the weariness of the body stamps them with the hallmark of the beaten enemy.

16 October: Reports state that we have taken Courtrai, and streams of refugees coming back along the roads indicate that it may be true. Unfortunately, they are all of the very lowest classes, and as they only speak

Second Lieutenant George Atkinson, 2nd Army, Royal Engineers

Flemish we were unable to get any information out of them. It is a heartbreaking sight to see them trudging through the rain – old men, women, and the tiniest of children. Sometimes they wheel a barrow containing a few of their goods, but most of them are without anything except the miserable rags they stand in.

17 October: Had the company out all day doing road drainage. The tedium of the work was relieved by a ghastly incident, showing how low these poor refugees have sunk. A party of them were trudging listlessly along the road when the leaders noticed a dead horse lying in the ditch. In a few seconds the men and women had taken their knives and were fighting like animals on the distended carcass, chattering and shrieking like a crowd of hungry jackals. As they worked they threw the chunks of bleeding meat into the road, where the children fought for them and stowed them in the barrows. In a few minutes the horse was stripped to his bones, the noise subsided, and the ghouls trudged on their way.

One man who had made it right through the war, and remarkably without a scratch, was Sergeant Major Arthur Cook. He had arrived in France two days before the Battle of Mons and taken part in the Retreat, serving with the Somerset Light Infantry. In November 1918 he was still with his battalion, having accumulated both the DCM and MM along the way. Ten days before the Armistice his battalion went in action once more.

Sergeant Major Arthur Cook, 1st Somerset Light Infantry

1 November: The attack began at 5.15 a.m., under cover of the fiercest barrage I had ever experienced, from 2,000 cannons and hundreds of machine guns carrying out indirect fire. It was pitch dark when we started, the only light coming from bursting shells; the din was indescribable, speech was hopeless. Whistles and signals were out of the question, we just blindly blundered on, close up to the barrage that was blasting everything in front of us and shrouding us in its cloudy fumes. The flash of the bursting shells showed up the blanched faces of the lads in action for the first time, and the barrage that was intended to terrify and break the morale of the enemy was scaring our young warriors stiff – they were half stunned by the unearthliness of it, but it was sweet music to us 'old uns'.

Dawn broke as the attack progressed and we were able to see what was going on. The earth was vomiting forth clods, bodies, trees, houses, in fact anything that came in the way of the blasted line. There were no deep dugouts, what trenches we passed were shallow and hurriedly dug by a retreating enemy ... The smoke from the bursting shells set up a thick fog screen and caused us to lose our direction slightly. Captain Osborne observed this and got his map out. I saw the danger of this officer walking along with a Burberry on and an open map in front of him, advertising himself as an officer, an obvious target for a sniper. I shouted to him, 'Put that map away, Sir, it's getting light!' He replied, 'Oh, I'll be all right, Sergeant Major', but nevertheless I was worried ...

Our instructions were to mop up the village. This is a dangerous and thankless task, for you are an exposed target from all angles ... Snipers, very difficult to locate and dislodge, began to pick off the men. Shells began to fall in the village, making our task still more unpleasant; the men began to group together, probably feeling there was safety in numbers, but I soon realised that a shell amongst us would have disastrous results for the remnant of my poor old company, now about thirty-strong. I warned them of the danger and ordered them to spread out, but it was too late – death was on its way. The shell burst on the hard cobbles and flew in all directions, the broken cobblestones causing as much damage as the shells. Several were killed and the remainder shared the flying pieces. I was hit in the knee; it felt as though a carthorse had kicked me. I could scarcely believe I was wounded. I had begun to feel that I was immune after dodging it for 4½ years. I had been with the battalion from the beginning of the war, and now had the misfortune to be hit in what proved to be their very last action.

7 November: The Huns have definitely asked for an Armistice and we have had orders to look out for their emissaries coming over with a white flag ... Operations, however, are not to be suspended and there is to be no relaxation in our attacks.

10 November: Up very early, according to plan, and soon the news came through that Fritz had retired from the [river] Sheldt during the night ... It was daylight when we got on the move again and continued our march to the river where we found that the Engineers had already thrown across

Sapper Albert Martin, 122nd Signal Company, 41st Division, Royal Engineers a footbridge and had repaired the demolished road bridge sufficiently to carry light transport … It is remarkable that we have not seen a single scrap of war material except huge shells used for mining the crossroads. Fritz seems to have cleared the country of everything before he retired …

11 November: At 8 a.m. I went on duty. We were anxiously awaiting orders when about 8.30 the 'Sounder' started to tap. Campbell was the divisional operator on duty and as the instrument ticked I read off 'Hostilities will cease …' That was enough. I had to suppress the jubilation in the office in order to give Campbell a chance to get his message off. Before he had finished, the office was crowded with inquirers … The excitement among the troops was not great; indeed except for a little spasmodic jubilation here and there, no difference in the ordinary behaviour of the men is to be observed. It is just taken as a matter of course.

There was not much gun firing this morning and what there was ceased at 11 a.m. except for an isolated gun that kept banging away until 3 p.m. I understand that this was an Australian battery that had got out of touch with headquarters and consequently had not received the 'ceasefire' order. But I have my doubts. I fancy they were having a little bit of 'own back'.

Sergeant Major
Arthur Cook,
1st Somerset
Light Infantry

11 November: [England] Hospital routine went on much the same as usual until the electrifying news came through that the Germans had asked for an Armistice. I don't know whether to be pleased or otherwise over my circumstances, for I had been waiting for a nice Blighty wound for years and now I have got it and landed nicely in England, they have gone and stopped the blinking war! What would I give to be with the battalion now!

Overleaf: A ghostly sight: Vimy Ridge days after the guns fell silent on the Western Front.

I have always been a firm believer in prayer and after what I have been through during my war years, my faith is stronger than ever. As long as I live, I shall remember the many hundreds of pals left behind who were not as lucky as I was. One cannot help reflecting on this day and feeling thankful that the slaughter of human beings is over.

Lieutenant Bernard Adams, 1st Royal Welch Fusiliers

I stood in the open, completely hidden from the enemy, on the reverse slope of the hill … Already I could see smoke curling up from the cookers. There was a faint mist still hanging about over the road there, that the strong light would soon dispel. Close to my feet the meadow was full of buttercups and blue veronica, with occasional daisies starring the grass. And below, above, everywhere, it seemed, was the tremulous song of countless larks, rising, growing, swelling, till the air seemed full to breaking point.

Who could desecrate such a perfect June morning? I felt a mad impulse to run up and across into no-man's-land and cry out that such a day was made for lovers; that we were all enmeshed in a mad nightmare, that needed but a bold man's laugh to free us from its clutches! Surely this most exquisite morning could not be the birth of another day of pain? Yet I felt how vain and hopeless was the longing, as I turned at last and saw the first slant rays of sunlight touch the white sandbags into life.

Died of wounds, 27 February 1917.

Corporal James Parr, 1/16th London Regiment
(Queen's Westminster Rifles)

Someone said to me the other day, 'And after all, what's the use of all this? We lose money, we lose the best years of our lives, we run the risk of losing our lives altogether, at any rate of being incapacitated. And what do we gain? We could live and love and work somewhere in the world whether Germany or England won. What's the use of it all?'

What do we gain? I think we gain the one thing that every man has wanted from his boyhood up – opportunity. Opportunity to show what he is made of. Opportunity to show *himself* what he's made of, to show that he can be a hero, he's always wanted to be from the time when he first made up his mind to be a pirate when he grew up. He may not always know that he wanted it, but to my mind it was the thing missing – the thing that made us at times discontented, moody and unsatisfied. What do we gain? We stand to gain everything and to lose – only our lives.

Killed in action, 1 July 1916.

Acknowledgements

The staff at Bloomsbury have been particularly generous in their support and practical help, especially Bill Swainson, the senior commissioning editor, whose continued encouragement and belief in my books is invaluable. I am also very grateful to Liz Woabank, Oliver Holden-Rea, Ruth Logan, Anya Rosenberg, David Mann, Polly Napper and Imogen Corke for the great team effort of bringing *Tommy's War* to publication. As before, I would also like to express my gratitude to Richard Collins for the insight of his editorial comments. This is the fifth of my books he has worked on and I appreciate his continuing interest and precision.

I am indebted, as always, to my great friend Taff Gillingham for reading through the text and picking up a number of small errors; his knowledge of military affairs is boundless and enormously important to the accuracy of my writing. I am also grateful for his permission to use the image which appears on the front of the jacket. I also greatly appreciate the work of my excellent agent, Jane Turnbull, whose professional help, support and friendship I value more than I can say: thank you, Jane.

My warmest thanks must go to my family: to my indomitable mother, Joan van Emden, who, usually at short notice, gives me the benefit of her ideas, advice and expertise in the English language. My debt to my wife, Anna, is incalculable: she keeps me thinking positively and constructively and even remaining calm when I feel overwhelmed by paperwork. I must also thank our splendid six-year-old, Benjamin, who occasionally spares me from games of cricket to allow me time in my study.

I am grateful to the following people for permission to reproduce photographs, extracts from diaries, letters or memoirs: Bob Smethurst, who has been most kind and generous in letting me use some wonderful material from his extensive collection; Laurence Martin, for extracts from the diary of Sapper Martin; Richard Davies and all the staff at the Liddle Archive, Leeds University, whose unfailing enthusiasm and kindness is much appreciated. Thank you, too, to Richard Dabb at the National Army Museum for his help and generosity. I am also grateful to Tony Lund for alerting me to the diary of Sergeant Bradlaugh Sanderson and Bill Teed for permission to quote from the letters of Lieutenant Colonel William Harrison. Thank you also to Jonathan Capek, Dominic Carter and to Dr and Mrs Smallcombe.

My gratitude for help and advice goes to Stephen Chambers and David Empson, as well as my good friends Vic and Diane Piuk, Sue Cox, Jeremy Banning, Mark Banning and Peter Barton.

Sources

Published memoirs

Adam, Arthur Innes, *A Record founded on his letters*, Bowes & Bowes, 1920

Adams, John Bernard Pye, *Nothing of Importance*, R. M. McBride & Co., 1918

Anonymous, 9th Royal Scots (T. F.), *B Company on Active Service*, privately published, 1916

Ashmead-Bartlett, Seabury, *From the Somme to the Rhine*, John Lane, 1921

Atkinson, George Scott, *A Soldier's Diary*, William Collins Sons & Co., 1925

Barnett, Denis Oliver, *In Happy Memory*, privately published, 1915

Bidder, Harold F., *Three Chevrons*, John Lane, The Bodley Head, 1919

Bloor, William Henry, *War Diary of*, privately published, undated

Bolwell, F. A., *With a Reservist in France*, George Routledge & Sons, 1917

Brownlow, Cecil A. L., *The Breaking of the Storm*, Methuen & Co., 1918

Clayton, Rev. Philip, *Letters from Flanders*, The Centenary Press, 1933

Crouch, Lionel William, *Duty and Service: Letters from the Front*, privately published, 1917

Dolbey, R. V., *A Regimental Surgeon in War and Prison*, John Murray, 1917

Down, Cecil Sommers, *Temporary Heroes*, John Lane, The Bodley Head, 1917

Eberle, Ellison, *My Sapper Adventure*, Pitman Publishing, 1973

Fielding, Rowland, *War Letters to a Wife*, Spellmount Classics, 2001

Fildes, Geoffrey, *Iron Times with the Guards*, John Murray, 1918

Floyd, Thomas Hope, *At Ypres with Best-Dunkley*, John Lane, 1920

Garstin, Denis, *The Shilling Soldiers*, Hodder & Stoughton, 1922

Gillespie, Alexander, *Letter from Flanders*, Smith, Elder & Co., 1916

Goodyear, Frederick, *Letters and Remains, 1887–1917*, McBride, Nast & Co., 1920

Gyde, Arnold, *Contemptible*, William Heinemann, 1916

Hall, James Norman, *Kitchener's Mob: Adventures of an American in the British Army*, The Riverside Press, 1916

Hawkings, Frederick, *From Ypres to Cambrai*, The Elmfield Press, 1974

Heath, Arthur George, *Letters of Arthur George Heath*, B. H. Blackwell, 1917

Herbert, Aubrey, *Mons, Anzac and Kut*, Edward Arnold, 1919

Housman, Lawrence, *War Letters of Fallen Englishmen*, Victor Gollancz, 1930 (incl. letters from Pte. James Parr, Lt Theodore Wilson, Lt Headley Goodyear)

Howell, Philip, *A Memoir by his Wife*, George Allen & Unwin, 1942

Hulse, Sir Edward, *Letters*, privately published, 1916

Hutchinson, Graham Seaton, *Footslogger*, Hutchinson & Co., 1933

Keeling, Frederick, *Keeling: Letters & Recollections*, Macmillan Company, 1916

Longley, Cecil, *Battery Flashes*, John Murray, 1916

Lusk, James, *Letters & Memoirs*, B. H. Blackwell, 1916

Lyon, Thomas, *In Kilt and Khaki*, The Standard Press, 1916

Manwaring, G. B., *If We Return; Letters of a Soldier of Kitchener's Army*, John Lane Company, 1918

Martin, Arthur Anderson, *A Surgeon in Khaki*, Longmans, Green & Co., 1915

Martin, Jack, *Sapper Martin: The Secret Great War Diary of Jack Martin*, Bloomsbury Publishing, 2009

Miall-Smith, George, *Two Brothers*, privately published, undated

Mills, Arthur, *With My Regiment from the Aisne to La Bassée*, William Heinemann, 1916

Nichols, George Herbert Fosdike (Quex), *Pushed and the Return Push*, W. Blackwood, 1919

Poulton, Sir Edward Bagnall, *The Life of Ronald Poulton*, Sidgwick & Jackson, 1919

Roe, Edward, *Diary of an Old Contemptible*, Pen & Sword, 2004

Sanders, Leslie, *A Soldier of England*, privately published, 1920

Shears, Edward Hornby, *Active Service Diary*, privately published, 1919

Southwell, Evelyn and White, Malcolm, *Two Men: A Memoir*, Oxford University Press, 1919

Sparrow, Geoffrey, *On Four Fronts with the Royal Naval Division*, Hodder & Stoughton, 1918

Street, Cecil John Charles, *The Making of a Gunner*, Eveleigh Nash, 1916

Sturges, Robert, *On the Remainder of Our Front*, by Private No. 904, Harrison and Sons, 1917

Trounce, Harold Davis, *Fighting the Boche Underground*, C. Scribner's Sons, 1918

Vernede, Robert, *Letters to His Wife*, William Collins, 1917

Villiers, Algernon Hyde, *Letters and Papers*, The Macmillan Company, 1919

Watson, William Henry Lowe, *Adventures of a Despatch Rider*, W. Blackwood, 1916

Unpublished letters – author's collection
Corporal Thomas Belton
Private Harold Butler
Pioneer George Dewdney
Private Ernest Ford

Archives
Durham Light Infantry Museum: by kind permission of Second Lieutenant Hubert McBain, diary ref: D/DLI 7/426/2.

Imperial War Museum: by kind permission of the Department of Documents, with grateful thanks to Tony Richards: private papers of Lieutenant J. S. Walthew – Documents 3980, Private S. T. Fuller – Documents 2607, Rifleman F. E. Harris – Documents 14979, Private D. Sweeney – Documents 7397, Private F. R. Williams – Documents 13573, Private R. Cude – Documents 129.

The Liddle Archive: by kind permission of the Liddle Collection, Leeds University Library, with thanks to Richard Davies: Kenneth Brewster – GS 0195, Sir Geoffrey Rhodes Bromet – AIR 050, E. G. Routley – GS 1389.

The Royal Green Jackets Museum: by kind permission of the Royal Green Jackets Museum, Winchester: Diary of Lt Col. R. T. Fellowes – Ref: 7A-0617.

Somerset Record Office: by kind permission of the Duty Archivist, Somerset Record Office, Taunton: Diary of Arthur Henry Cook – DD/SLI17/1/40.

Surrey History Centre: by kind permission of Surrey History Centre, Woking, with thanks to Julian Pooley: Diary of Lieutenant Colonel J. R. Longley – ESR/25/Long/ 2, 3 & 5.

Picture Credits
All photographs are taken from the author's private collection unless otherwise stated.

Imperial War Museum, London: by kind permission of the picture library at the Imperial War Museum: p. 11 Q 51489, p. 22 Q 49750 and Q 49751, p. 27 Q 8460, p. 30 Q 51224, p. 33 Q 57101, p. 39 Q 51136, p. 127 HU 66269, pps. 136–7 Q 49750 and Q 49751, p. 176 Q 51621, pps. 178–9, HU 63277B, p. 214 HU 87951, p. 221 HU 112461, p. 221 HU 112462 and p. 247 Q 57911.

The Liddle Archive: by kind permission of the Liddle Collection, Leeds University Library, with thanks to Richard Davies: p. 49 NM McCleod Ref. GS 1029, p. 155 KA Brewster Ref. GS 0195, p. 161 R Rapp Ref. GS 1324, pps. 252–3 RC Perry Ref. GS 1813, p. 254 RC Perry Ref. GS 1813, pps. 268–9 RC Perry Ref. GS 1813, p. 286 JD Todd Ref. GS 1607, p. 287 RC Perry Ref. GS 1813, p. 288 JD Todd Ref. GS 1607, p. 298 M Le Blanc Smith Ref. AIR 295 and p. 300 WB Tisdall Ref. AIR 317.

National Army Museum: by kind permission of the picture library of the National Army Museum, with thanks to Richard Dabb: pps. 16–17 NAM 1995-06-89-1-1, p. 99 NAM 1995-06-89-1-13, p. 148 NAM 1986-06-77-45, p. 239 NAM 1997-12-75-99 and p. 333 NAM 1997-12-75-101.

Pen and Sword Books: by kind permission of Pen and Sword Books, with thanks to Jonathan Wright: p. 30, p. 47, p. 54 and pps. 82–3.

Surrey History Centre: by kind permission of Surrey History Centre, with thanks to Julian Pooley: p. 272 album belonging to Captain Birrie, MC – ESR/25/LOVE/1.

Index

Page numbers in *italics* refer to photographs

A NOTE ON THE AUTHOR

Richard van Emden has interviewed more than 270 veterans of the Great War and has written fifteen books on the subject including *The Trench* and *The Last Fighting Tommy*, both of which were top ten bestsellers. He has also worked on more than a dozen television programmes on the First World War, including *Prisoners of the Kaiser*, *Veterans*, *Britain's Last Tommies*, the award-winning *Roses of No Man's Land*, *Britain's Boy Soldiers*, *A Poem for Harry*, *War Horse: The Real Story* and most recently, *Teenage Tommies* with Fergal Keane. He lives in London.

Tickled to Death to Go

Veterans: The Last Survivors of the Great War

Prisoners of the Kaiser

The Trench

Last Man Standing

All Quiet on the Home Front

Boy Soldiers of the Great War

Britain's Last Tommies

The Last Fighting Tommy (with Harry Patch)

Famous 1914–1918

The Soldier's War

Sapper Martin

Tommy's Ark

The Quick and the Dead

Meeting the Enemy